Rhetoric & Composition
PhD Program

PROGRAM
Pioneering program honoring the rhetorical tradition through scholarly innovation, excellent job placement record, well-endowed library, state-of-the-art New Media Writing Studio, and graduate certificates in new media and women's studies.

TEACHING
1-1 teaching loads, small classes, extensive pedagogy and technology training, and administrative fellowships in writing program administration and new media.

FACULTY
Nationally recognized teacher-scholars in history of rhetoric, modern rhetoric, women's rhetoric, digital rhetoric, composition studies, and writing program administration.

FUNDING
Generous four-year graduate instructorships, competitive stipends, travel support, and several prestigious fellowship opportunities.

EXPERIENCE
Mid-sized liberal arts university setting nestled in the vibrant, culturally-rich Dallas-Fort Worth metroplex.

English
DEPARTMENT

Contact Dr. Mona Narain
m.narain@tcu.edu
eng.tcu.edu

Reviewers from March 2017 through March 2018

A journal is only as good as its reviewers. We acknowledge and celebrate the dedication, good will, and expertise of our generous reviewers:

Ann Amicucci, University of Colorado, Colorado Springs
Rebekka Andersen, University of California, Davis
Lora Arduser, University of Cincinnati
Lisa Arnold, North Dakota State University
Elías Dominguez Barajas, University of Arkansas
Jennifer Bay, Purdue University
Casey Boyle, University of Texas at Austin
Meaghan Brewer, Pace University
Christopher Burnham, New Mexico State University
Chris Carter, University of Cincinnati
Sheila Carter-Tod, Virginia Tech University
Jennifer Cellio, Northern Kentucky University
Jennifer Clary-Lemon, University of Winnipeg
Amy Dayton, University of Alabama
Sidney Dobrin, University of Florida
Cristyn Elder, University of New Mexico
Sergio Figueiredo, Kennesaw State University
Greg Giberson, Oakland University
Amy Goodburn, University of Nebraska-Lincoln
Joe Harris, University of Delaware
Eric Hayot, Penn State University
Jay Jordan, University of Utah
Daniel Keller, Ohio State University at Newark
Joyce Kinkead, Utah State University
Alison Knoblauch, Kansas State University
Christina LaVecchia, University of Cincinnati
Carrie Leverenz, Texas Christian University
Lisa Mastrangelo, Centenary University
Janine Morris, Nova Southeastern University
Malea Powell, Michigan State University
Kia Jane Richmond, Northern Michigan University
Hannah Rule, University of South Carolina
Carol Severino, University of Iowa
Shari Stenberg, University of Nebraska-Lincoln
Donna Strickland, University of Missouri
Connie Kendall Theado, University of Cincinnati
Shevaun Watson, University of Wisconsin-Milwaukee

composition STUDIES

Volume 46, Number 1
Spring 2018

Editor
Laura R. Micciche

Editorial Consultant
Bob Mayberry

Book Review Editor
Bryna Siegel Finer

Editorial Assistants
Kelly Blewett
Christiane Boehr
Ian Golding
Christina M. LaVecchia

Former Editors
Gary Tate
Robert Mayberry
Christina Murphy
Peter Vandenberg
Ann George
Carrie Leverenz
Brad E. Lucas
Jennifer Clary-Lemon

Advisory Board
Sheila Carter-Tod
  Virginia Tech University

Elías Dominguez Barajas
  University of Arkansas

Qwo-Li Driskill
  Oregon State University

Susan Martens
  Missouri Western State University

Aja Y. Martinez
  Syracuse University

Michael McCamley
  University of Delaware

Jessica Nastal-Dema
  Prairie State College

Annette Harris Powell
  Bellarmine University

Melissa Berry Pearson
  Northeastern University

Margaret Price
  The Ohio State University

Jessica Restaino
  Montclair State University

Donnie Sackey
  Wayne State University

Christopher Schroeder
  Northeastern Illinois University

Darci Thoune
  University of Wisconsin-La Crosse

SUBSCRIPTIONS

Composition Studies is published twice each year (May and November). Annual subscription rates: Individuals $25 (Domestic), $30 (International), and $15 (Students). To subsccribe online, please visit http://www.uc.edu/journals/composition-studies/subscriptions.html

BACK ISSUES

Back issues, five years prior to the present, are freely accessible on our website at http://www.uc.edu/journals/composition-studies/issues/archives.html. If you don't see what you're looking for, contact us. Also, recent back issues are now available through Amazon.com. To find issues, use the advanced search feature and search on "Composition Studies" (title) and "Parlor Press" (publisher).

BOOK REVIEWS

Assignments are made from a file of potential book reviewers. If you are interested in writing a review, please contact our Book Review editor at brynasf@iup.edu.

JOURNAL SCOPE

The oldest independent periodical in the field, *Composition Studies* publishes original articles relevant to rhetoric and composition, including those that address teaching college writing; theorizing rhetoric and composing; administering writing programs; and, among other topics, preparing the field's future teacher-scholars. All perspectives and topics of general interest to the profession are welcome. We also publish Course Designs, which contextualize, theorize, and reflect on the content and pedagogy of a course. Contributions to Composing With are invited by the editor, though queries are welcome (send to compstudies@uc.edu). Cfps, announcements, and letters to the editor are most welcome. *Composition Studies* does not consider previously published manuscripts, unrevised conference papers, or unrevised dissertation chapters.

SUBMISSIONS

For submission information and guidelines, see http://www.uc.edu/journals/composition-studies/submissions/overview.html.

Direct all correspondence to:

> Laura Micciche, Editor
> Department of English
> University of Cincinnati
> PO Box 210069
> Cincinnati, OH 45221–0069
> compstudies@uc.edu

Composition Studies is grateful for the support of the University of Cincinnati.

© 2018 by Laura Micciche, Editor
Production and printing is managed by Parlor Press, www.parlorpress.com.
ISSN 1534–9322.
Cover art by Giovanni Weissman and design by Gary Weissman.

http://www.uc.edu/journals/composition-studies.html

composition STUDIES

Volume 46, Number 1
Spring 2018

Contents

Reviewers from March 2017 through March 2018 — 4

From the Editor — 9

Composing With — 11

A State of Ungress: Composing as Rambling — 11
Michael Griffith

Articles — 15

Reviewing Writing, Rethinking Whiteness: A Study of Composition's Practical Life — 15
Edward Hahn

Rethinking SETs: Retuning Student Evaluations of Teaching for Student Agency — 34
Brian Ray, Jacob Babb, and Courtney Adams Wooten

Who Learns from Collaborative Digital Projects? Cultivating Critical Consciousness and Metacognition to Democratize Digital Literacy Learning — 57
Julia Voss

Designing, Building, and Connecting Networks to Support Distributed Collaborative Empirical Writing Research — 81
Beth Brunk-Chavez, Stacey Pigg, Jessie Moore, Paula Rosinski, and Jeffrey T. Grabill

The Burkean Parlor as Boundary Object: A Collaboration between First-Year Writing and the Library — 102
Lynda Walsh, Adrian M. Zytkoskee, Patrick Ragains, Heidi Slater, and Michelle Rachal

Course Designs ... 124

Decolonial Theory and Methodology ... 124
Andrea Riley Mukavetz

Writing and Rhetoric 3326: Legal Writing ... 141
Drew M. Loewe

Book Reviews ... 165

Securing Composition's Disciplinarity: The Possibilities for
Independent Writing Programs and Contingent Labor Activism ... 165

A Minefield of Dreams: Triumphs and Travails of Independent Writing Programs, edited by Justin Everett and Christina Hanganu-Bresch

Labored: The State(ment) and Future of Work in Composition, edited by Randall McClure, Dayna V. Goldstein, and Michael A. Pemberton
Reviewed by Nick Sanders

Mikhail Bakhtin: Rhetoric, Poetics, Dialogics, Rhetoricality, by Don Bialostosky ... 174
Reviewed by Ben Wetherbee

The Framework for Success in Postsecondary Writing: Scholarship and Applications, edited by Nicholas N. Behm, Sherry Rankins-Robertson, and Duane Roen ... 178
Reviewed by Jessi Thomsen

Writing in Online Courses: How the Online Environment Shapes Writing Practices, edited by Phoebe Jackson and Christopher Weaver ... 183
Reviewed by Bob Mayberry

Expanding Literate Landscapes: Persons, Practices, and Sociohistoric Perspectives of Disciplinarity Development, by Kevin Roozen and Joe Erickson ... 187
Reviewed by Leslie Taylor

CALL FOR NEW EDITOR(S) OF **Composition Studies** ... 191

Contributors ... 192

From the Editor

With this issue we say farewell to book review editor Kelly Kinney who, over the past four years, has taken an active role in mentoring advanced graduate students and junior faculty, for which I am especially grateful. Kelly has also ensured that book reviews in *Composition Studies* represent a wide swatch of research in the field, appropriate for a journal that has generalist aims. We welcome our new book review editor, Bryna Siegel Finer, who has worked alongside Kelly in the production of this issue. We're excited to have Bryna aboard, and we wish Kelly well as she focuses her energies on her work as chair of the English department at the University of Wyoming.

This issue begins with novelist Michael Griffith wandering through a historic graveyard and into a book project he hadn't intended. Griffith's peripatetic essay, "A State of Ungress: Composing as Rambling," is followed by five articles that represent practical, theoretical, and programmatic juxtapositions within writing studies. Edward Hahn's "Reviewing Writing, Rethinking Whiteness" explores how class-based reviewing practices reveal and conceal racial bias. Examining another form of bias, Brian Ray, Jacob Babb, and Courtney Adams Wooten, in "Rethinking SETs," suggest revisions to student evaluation forms that are centered more on student learning, less on teacher performance. The last three articles address collaboration in various forms. First, Julia Voss's "Who Learns from Collaborative Digital Projects?" suggests strategies for integrating metacognition into collaborative group work as a means for interrogating cultural privilege and its operations in such settings. Next, Beth Brunk-Chavez, Stacey Pigg, Jessie Moore, Paula Rosinski, and Jeffrey Grabill describe large-scale empirical research through the language of designing, building, and connecting networks. Lastly, Lynda Walsh, Adrian M. Zytkoskee, Patrick Ragains, Heidi Slater, and Michelle Rachal, in "The Burkean Parlor as Boundary Object," detail a collaboration between fyw program members and librarians aimed at improving students' research-writing skills.

Two course designs are included in this issue. Andrea Riley Mukavetz's "Decolonial Theory and Methodology" explores some of the complexities that arise between subject matter and course delivery in an online class focused on decolonial thinking. "Writing and Rhetoric 3326: Legal Writing" by Drew M. Loewe details a course that offers students practical experience writing for legal situations and in commonplace legal genres. This issue is rounded out by five book reviews that showcase a wide range of scholarly interests in the field: independent writing programs and contingent labor; Bakhtin studies; postsecondary writing success; writing in online courses; and disciplinary development alongside sociohistorical factors.

Two notes about the present and future of *Composition Studies*: first, I'm very pleased to announce that Bob Mayberry has re-joined the editorial staff as an Editorial Consultant. Bob served as editor of *Freshman English News* (this journal's original title until 1992) from 1981 to 1985. Now, as Editorial Consultant, Bob will provide extensive feedback toward revision to first-time authors who submit manuscripts that show great promise. I think of Bob's role as "manuscript mentor" for first-time authors; we are already benefitting from his experience and perspective. Second, in preparation for the end of my editorship with the spring 2019 issue, you will find a call for a new editor in this issue (and posted on social media); help us spread the word! In the meantime, I look forward to receiving your work and corresponding with authors and reviewers on developing manuscripts.

L.M.
Cincinnati, Ohio
April 2018

Composing With

A State of Ungress: Composing as Rambling

Michael Griffith

When things are going well, I love my attic writing space: the slanted walls, the low ceiling crazed with cracks, the perpetual semidark, the walls a sickly blue like an aquarium's inside. But when the work is a struggle, as it was this past September, the roof looms low, the gloom condenses, and it starts to feel like a coffin.

That analogy was a bit too apt, since the book I was working on was a novel about an obituary writer (and a crossword puzzle deviser, but that's a subject for another day). In times of frustration or anxiety, I've always tended toward compulsive motion—for me, the best thing about the invention of the cellphone is that when I'm forced to talk on it, I can do so while walking, whether in caged indoor circles or, better, in a streetscape or wood—and without cocooning myself in coils of grimy cord I'll have to awkwardly pirouette out of at call's end, as often happened in my teens. So when, late last summer, the novel's flow slowed and nearly halted, the dodge I hit upon (I mean the *strategy I devised*) was to prime the pump every morning with an hour-long cemetery walk.

Headstone at Spring Grove Cemetery

This seemed to have some short-term benefit, but as the days passed I found myself less inspired by my rambles— I should note my great good fortune in having, just half a mile from home, one of the first and, at almost a thousand acres, largest park cemeteries in the world, Spring Grove, founded in 1845—than distracted by them. Then one morning, walking a road I'd walked a hundred times, I noticed to my left an eccentric Art Nouveau font, an artist's palette–shaped headstone, and I stopped, punched the deceased's name into Google, plunged into a story that involved Ulysses S. Grant and William Tecumseh Sherman and early photography and a ghost-hosted dinner party . . . and headed down a rabbit hole from which I haven't yet emerged.

Within days I was embarked, it became clear, on another book, another kind of book. Or another of the same kind. My last, the novel *Trophy*, which takes place in the instant of its protagonist's death and features his desperate, meandering ploys to extend that moment, is also about rambling—rambling as existential necessity. Digression, I've always thought, gets a bad rap. The word itself implies that there's a proper gress from which one has strayed, that every life is a line. But surely linearity is something we impose only afterward, when it's time to make a narrative, when it's time to comb out our gresses and untangle them into something we can call *progress* or *congress*. We are poor, forked animals who live most of our lives, and thank God, in a state of ungress, regress, circumgress. Many people live lives packed with incident—but whose has a *plot*?

And so I found myself extending those morning walks in Spring Grove. This was a literalization of what I'd been doing in *Trophy*: more amblings, more attempts to find narrative where I stumbled upon it or tangled myself up in it. Soon I was traversing the cemetery every day, learning to read it, seeing what caught my eye (odd stones, epitaphs, decorations, spacing, plantings), jotting down names and locations, and then going home to explore in a different way the anomalies or idiosyncrasies I'd noticed. I've always been a bleeder, a compulsive reviser who starts at sentence one every morning and then slowly, miserably accretes (or secretes) a book . . . but this is different. It's as if the momentum of my walks carries over to the keyboard, and somehow I've accumulated 50,000 words in just four months—a number that seems miraculous, given that the first 50,000 words of my last book took seven years.

Much of the pleasure of the writing has derived from the chance to experience narrative as a product of impetus and accident. What details will be thrown into conversation or juxtaposition as I walk? Sheepishly, I've begun thinking in terms of rhapsodomancy, the ancient mode of divination that involves flipping open a manuscript of poems at random, or its cousin stichomancy, which takes the Bible as its revelatory text. My chosen form, it seems, is graveyardwalkomancy.

The walks provide, too, a chance to think, á la Jorge Luis Borges's "Garden of Forking Paths," about the bewildering multifariousness of available routes, about the old but easy-to-forget truth that there's not one inevitable form for material to take, that the writer's job is to find *a* way through the maze, not *the* way. The result of all this, I hope, will be—of course I'm well aware it may turn out to be a disaster—a book fundamentally about the role of retracing and coincidence and surprise connection, whether in a walk or in rereading any familiar text or landscape. Day to day, neither the scape nor its reader remains the same—there are new conditions of light, new angles of vision or vagaries of mood (Back trouble making you wince and slump? Shoe need tying? Clinging to a hedge in driving rain?); trees grow, flowers bloom, leaves fall and mat underfoot; you may follow a turkey or a fox or a wisp of thought over a hill and into an undiscovered glade. You may read a name on a welding shop signboard, then glimpse it on a stone the next day.

For now I'm calling the project *Windfalls in the Bone Orchard*, and I'm trying just to take my luck where I find it, to follow the dead I meet and the links that arise wherever they lead. These are highly discursive essays, in which a gravestone or glimpsed detail may lead to slate-writing spiritualists and Arthur Conan Doyle and Houdini and the origin of the Magic 8-Ball, or where an unusual egalitarian stone listing a couple by first and middle initials, without stipulating gender, may lead to an essay about a leader of the temperance movement, and from there to the Ohio Woman's Crusade of 1874, Cincinnati brewing history, a political party headquartered in a toolshed, Thomas Edison's short-lived movie studio, a version of cornhole involving discarded toilets and beanbags shaped like turds, the geography of urban vice, the local culinary cult of the fish log.

Am I claiming to do something fresh? Dear God no. Others figured out the link between walking and storytelling millennia ago, at least as far back as Plato's strolls in the groves of the Academy, and wandering was a major part of the Romantic poets' philosophy and practice too, and and and. But for me the work of these last months has felt like an utterly new mode of composition, one that's about the conversion of one vector of motion to another. As a high jumper translates speed to altitude, ramble becomes essay . . . and then it turns out that all along, digression wasn't an avoidance of narrative—duh, Michael, you fool—but a subgenre of it.

Because no matter what the spaghetti-ish map of one's wanderings may look like—the loops and eddies, the backtrackings—they turn out, in retrospect, to describe a path. John Barth once wrote, about postmodernism's alleged disdain for narrative, that it's nothing to fret about: "We live in an ocean of story," he said, and wherever one drops one's bucket, it will come up overflowing. It's been nice to rediscover how right he is, and to find, gratefully, that in whatever route one happens to take there seems already inscribed some plan or order. Lately it's occurred to me that for all these years I may have misunderstood the diviners of old, the readers of teacup lees or goat intestines or randomly chosen passages. The object of their faith needn't be God. In the theology Barth implies, when we take the jump into apparent randomness, it's not fate that delivers us; it's narrative. There's nothing we can't make into a story. There's not anything that isn't already one.

Works Cited

Barth, John. "The Ocean of Story." *The Friday Book: Essays and Other Nonfiction*. Putnam, 1984.

Borges, Jorge Luis. "The Garden of Forking Paths." *Ficciones*, edited by Anthony Kerrigan, Editorial Sur, 1944. Rpt. in *Labyrinths: Selected Stories and Other Writings*, edited and translated by D. A. Yates and James E. Irby, New Directions, 1964, pp. 19-29.

Articles

Reviewing Writing, Rethinking Whiteness: A Study of Composition's Practical Life

Edward Hahn

This article argues that the writing classroom's practical life can profoundly impact students' cultural and political beliefs. Privileged here are the mundane activities and interactions associated with reviewing writing, which encompasses the practice of grade comparison as well as the more common, but commonly simplified, practices of peer, teacher, and performance review. The case study unfolded herein shows how an array of review practices enabled one student to develop a critical perspective on both her implicit bias against non-white writers and her own limitations as a writer. An analysis of the case study suggests the value and validity of conceptualizing practical life as a rhetorical and non-functional totality.

"Education scholars have long distinguished between an 'overt' and a 'hidden' curriculum, but see both of these as promoting socially dominant interests. . . . What I am suggesting, however, is that in addition to these curricula, we need to acknowledge as well a curriculum 'hidden' from or ignored or dismissed by the dominant, one that promotes alternative or oppositional interests."

—Bruce Horner (2000)

Antiracism has long been central to composition's research and teaching agenda. In 1969, Haig A. Bosmajian called for research that analyzes the classroom's "subtle and not so subtle racism" (263) and for teaching that contests "racist terms, phrases, and clichés" (272). Four years later, *College English*'s "Resolution Against Racism" urged educators to "organize and support activities to eliminate racist practices and ideas" (91). Antiracist scholarship has since expanded to include theoretical frameworks for antiracist pedagogies (Anderson; Barlow), critical analyses of race-related discourse (Clary-Lemon; Martinez), and teacher reflections on antiracist pedagogies (Beech; McCrary). These scholars' analytical insights and curricular recommendations have enlarged the field's ability to understand and contest the wide range of beliefs that tacitly support institutional racism. At the same time, composition's antiracist scholarship has tended to privilege the classroom's textual corpus over the classroom's practical life, giving more attention to student essays, course readings, and assignments than to the mundane activities and interactions that might constitute the "hidden" yet "oppositional" curriculum intimated by Bruce Horner (*Terms* 117). One explanation for the slight attention given to practical life in composition's antiracist scholarship is perhaps the common misconception of "the practical" as simple, predictable, and arhetorical, as compared to "the textual," which is deemed complex, contingent, and meaningful.

I conceptualize practical life as a *rhetorical and non-functional totality*. Practical life is *rhetorical* in the sense that beliefs are reflected in and affected by mundane activities and interactions. As Pierre Bourdieu argues, processes of persuasion are constituted by the quotidian rituals and "repeated exercises" of everyday life, not just the "symbolic action" of more obviously rhetorical performances (*Pascalian* 180, 172; see also *Logic* 66-79). It follows that the practical and the textual should not be separated when conceptualizing the classroom's rhetorical dynamics. For example, course readings that critique meritocratic ideology might be undermined by the pedagogical ritual of evaluating students' participation, because the merit-based awarding of participation points to individuals can tacitly persuade students to believe that hard work is, indeed, justly rewarded in our society. While a teacher might stop evaluating participation on the sensible grounds that it reproduces a dominant ideology, a *non-functionalist* researcher would need to analyze the contingent and contradictory effects of the practice *in situ* (Giddens 111-15). As Anthony Giddens explains, the "guiding tenet" of anti-functionalism is "don't look for the functions social practices fulfill, look for the contradictions they embody" (131). The practice of evaluating participation might initially enhance the persuasiveness of meritocratic ideology only to later compel students to demand its abolition. That scenario might be farfetched, but a non-functionalist researcher must remain open to such contradictory and unpredictable consequences. Such consequences are more explicable, if not more predictable, once practical life is conceptualized as a *totality* in which seemingly singular activities and interactions are recognized as dynamic moments of an emergent whole, of which students are aware. If we assume that the student revolt is a discrete, spontaneous event rather than a mediated moment, then we might not consider how that revolt was inspired by, say, the teacher's solicitation of criticism or students' frustrations with their grades. As G. W. F. Hegel argues, "The True is the whole" (11). The Hegelian whole is not the "stable coexistence of elements" but rather the product of change wrought by "inner opposition" (Taylor 274), including the conflicts of consciousness and the consciousness of conflicts, both of which shape the activities and interactions of practical life.

My intention here is to suggest the value and validity of conceptualizing practical life as a rhetorical and non-functional totality. I do so by sharing and analyzing a semi-ethnographic tale about one student's experience in a multicultural basic writing class. The tale shows how the mundane activities and interactions associated with reviewing writing enabled the student to develop a critical perspective on both her implicit bias against non-white writers and her own limitations as a writer. As such, the tale contributes to the thin strand of race-conscious peer-review scholarship that is best represented by Carrie Shively Leverenz's study of one diverse peer-review group, whose sole white member reasserted dominant notions of academic writing despite the teacher's advocacy of alternatives. Like Leverenz's insightful tale, mine shows how practices and beliefs interact both within the writing classroom and across the arc of the semester—that is, spatially and temporally. But unlike Leverenz's tale, mine is suggestive of the oppositional possibilities of practical life.[1]

Context and Method

Every fall semester at the predominantly white public university where I conducted my study, there are approximately one hundred sections of fyw, a handful of which are "basic" rather than "intermediate" or "advanced." The twenty-one-student basic writing class that I observed met in a hot, cramped room containing five circular tables capable of seating five students each. Like most students, I arrived early on the first day. Sitting at the back center table, Carolyn, my tale's focal student, tapped her notebook, rocked on her chair, and surveyed her surroundings.[2] Next to her was another student I initially identified as white. To her right was a table of four Black students and one Hmong student. To the front and left of her was a table of five students speaking a mixture of English and Hmong. Next to them, closer to the door, was a quieter table of students whose parents or they themselves came from China, Vietnam, and Thailand. After calling the class to order, the teacher introduced herself, explained that the course would prepare them for intermediate writing, and passed out the syllabus, which prominently displayed the popular Margaret Mead quote: "Never doubt that a small group of thoughtful, committed citizens can change the world; indeed, it's the only thing that ever has." I then stood up and invited students to participate in my study, explaining that my purpose was to develop a better understanding of the fyw experience. Finally, the teacher asked everyone to individually list three topics of personal interest, which she would use to create assignments and lessons throughout the semester. Students expressed interest in microaggressions, privilege, abortion, depression, college life, and many other topics.

Several of these topics were engaged during the next session, which began with a reading and discussion of Peggy McIntosh's canonical article about white privilege, the goal being to introduce students to critical reading practices. The teacher asked the class to discuss in groups the privileges they do and do not possess. Sitting at the table to the left of Carolyn's group, I listened to stories of being expected to live up to certain stereotypes of blackness. I said that, as a white man, I benefited from the privilege of never being expected to represent white people as a group. The students nodded in agreement but also admitted to sometimes seeing white individuals as representative. We also discussed male privilege and student privilege. One tablemate noted that we, as students, could occupy any building on campus, unlike the city's homeless, who were often forced out of libraries. The teacher then gave a presentation about three efforts to challenge white privilege. The presentation reviewed the 1968 "I Am a Man" campaign, the recent "I Am Not a Man" street performance by artist Dread Scott, and, finally, the popular "I, Too, Am Harvard" Tumblr campaign (#ITooAmHarvard). In the Tumblr images, Harvard students held up small dry-erase boards with brief critical comments, such as "Having an opinion does not make me an 'Angry Black Woman.'" The teacher's goal was to establish a lineage of written protest, which the students would soon join.

Conversations erupted at the tables after the teacher asked everyone to discuss the comments they found to be personally meaningful, but Carolyn's group, right next to mine, settled into silence long before the others. Passing out markers and paper, the teacher instructed everyone to create their own #ITooAmHarvard signs, which the class would take outside and show to passersby. One sign read: "I am not ghetto." Two others read: "I am fabulous" and "Just because I'm Asian doesn't mean I can't speak English." As I received a high-five for my sign ("Abolish Tuition"), I thought about how, true to Margaret Mead, we were a small group of people changing the world by encouraging others to review our writing. I would later learn that a few students who appreciated the activity were nonetheless irked that many passersby ignored their signs. One student thought the activity was inauthentic. When class ended, everyone dispersed.

As a participant-observer, I shaped the classroom's practical life as I took field notes, interviewed students, and analyzed texts. The field notes documented the classroom's daily activities and interactions, including who sat where and who worked with whom. I also noted students' body language, movement, and technology use. My face-to-face interviews with ten focal students were semi-structured and informal. This article focuses on one student, Carolyn.[3] Contrary to similar studies in the field of education (Perry; Lewis; Foster), I consciously avoided researcher-centric questions (e.g., "Have the class's activities affected your beliefs about race?") on the grounds that, because such questions are alien to students' everyday consciousness, they can alienate students. Instead, I began every interview with a familiar topic and in a familiar fashion, borrowing from the conventions I had become accustomed to through my participant-observation. My hope was that unforeseen answers to unasked questions about race, belief, and practice would emerge in student-centric conversations. The following tale is derived, in part, from an interview with Carolyn that began with the simple question, "How's your semester going?" Following her lead, we discussed a recent athletic event, her other classes, and, finally, her own "stubbornness." Stubbornness, I would later learn, connoted certain beliefs and practices that many researchers associate with whiteness. The story of the development of Carolyn's critical consciousness of "stubbornness" dramatizes the oppositional potential of the writing classroom's practical life.

Reviewing Whiteness

As I waited for the teacher to begin on that first day, I noted that Carolyn was one of only three white students. Her racial identity seemed to be as clear-cut as her voice would indicate, with her standard pronunciation distorted by nothing but the tendency to make statements sound like questions. My mental statement would, in fact, turn into a question as Carolyn informed the class of her complex ancestry and citizenship. As her #ITooAmHarvard sign declared, "I'm Columbian, not Mexican. There's a difference." She had immediate family in Columbia, but she was raised by her aunt in a nearby affluent suburb, in an English-speaking household, with "only white friends," as she later told me, and she usually self-identified as white. Carolyn respected her "petite Latina aunt" for rising to the top of the predominantly male and Anglo world of high-rolling realtors, but money and power were not the only objects of her admiration. Carolyn also admired her aunt's willingness to demand that customers respect her twenty-seven year-old assistant, Rosa, whose Spanish-accented English upset more than one local resident seeking a seven-figure home in the city's hottest neighborhood. However, throughout the first half of the semester, Carolyn would not embody her aunt's respect for linguistic and cultural diversity. For example, during a peer-review session, she judged one partner's style and errors to be indicative of a "shitty" paper. The paper's author might not have been dumb, but Carolyn viewed herself as smarter than him and the rest of the class. Ventriloquizing her initially stubborn attitude toward the class, Carolyn shared with me the rhetorical question she had asked herself on the first day: "Am I in the dumb class? It's bad to say that and think that, but like, am I in a dumb class? … I'm like white, but it's like, why am I here?" As these statements-cum-questions suggest, like many white Americans, Carolyn held an implicit bias against non-whiteness, believing that non-white faces and non-dominant styles signify "dumbness." Suffice it to say that her attitude underwent a sea change throughout the semester. To understand how, it helps to be in the water.

I did not sit with Carolyn during the second session as the class discussed McIntosh's white privilege article, but I was at the table next to hers, with my back to the wall, so I could get a sense of what was happening there. My interviews with both other students and the teacher helped me understand what happened at Carolyn's table. Carolyn sat with Samayah (Black American), Aifiya (Somalian), Lisa (white), and Carlo (Native American).[4] After the teacher summarized the article and introduced the activity, Carolyn turned to her group and began talking over everyone else. She proclaimed that non-white people can get turned down for jobs simply because "they were not good enough," not because their hirers were racist. In the ensuing silence, she added, "That's not privilege." Lisa nodded. The teacher, overhearing the start to the group's discussion, sat down and explained how Carolyn's commentary missed the mark. "McIntosh isn't arguing that every time a non-white person doesn't get hired it's because of racism. She's arguing that one of the privileges of whiteness is the fact that you can be sure that your racial identity did not prevent you from getting the job." Trying to get the others to speak before leaving to pass out markers, the teacher asked, "Do you guys feel like that privilege applies to your lives? Or do you feel like you can't enjoy any of those privileges?" Samayah did not respond. Aifiya said that she had never really thought about it before, but that McIntosh was "totally right about 'flesh tone' cosmetic products." And then silence, constructed in no small part by Carolyn's comments.

Building upon the opening week's discussions and activities, the first essay assignment invited students to write about a real example of one of "The Five Faces of Oppression," the second required reading, from Iris Marion Young's *Justice and the Politics of Difference*. Students needed to define one face of oppression, explain how their example fits that face, and then reflect on what could be done to address the oppression. During the following week's peer-review session, each student needed to review two peers' rough drafts, beginning with the student to their right. At her table, Carolyn took Lisa's paper, Lisa took Aifiya's paper, Aifaya took Carlo's paper, and Carlo took Carolyn's paper. The teacher wanted students to help each other "show instead of tell." If the essay made a general statement without any follow up, for instance, then the reviewer should help the author flesh it out with explanations and examples. After a whole-table discussion of how they helped each other, the students needed to trade their essays with someone at a different table. Turning around, Carolyn found herself face-to-face with Harrison, a Black student from the Republic of Cameroon, who gladly offered his paper to her. The two barely had time to read each other's work, but it was enough for Carolyn to make a judgment about his writing and to begin expecting a higher grade than him. As she explained in an interview after the session:

> He didn't have any style, and it wasn't fun to read, and there's like lots of grammar [issues], so like the opposite of my [paper]. ... Yeah, like, if I give [a sample of my writing] to you, you'll read it and you'll have a good time. That, kind of like, I'm not trying to toot my own horn, but like I'm really good with style, and then also grammar.

Harrison's essay, in her opinion, was tedious and error-ridden, unlike her engaging and correct prose.

Two weeks later the teacher returned graded essays at the end of class. Glancing at Harrison's essay before storming out of the room, Carolyn learned that sixteen points separated her B- from his A. She was infuriated, telling me later, "I read his. And before he turned it in, I told him, well I didn't say this is complete shit, but I thought in my head, this is complete shit." She thought his work was representative of the "dumb" writing class. Upset at the perceived unfairness, she pressed the teacher and her academic adviser to move her into the intermediate writing course, which proved to be impossible: "I was like, I gotta get out of this class. I'm not stupid. So I went to my adviser and I was like, please put me in [intermediate writing], and I couldn't because there was not enough space." More bad news was to come. After learning that she scored eight points lower than Harrison on the second essay, Carolyn accepted what she had earlier only suspected: that the teacher was biased against white people. As she told me, "He gets a 97 and mine was like perfect, and it got like an 89. And I was like, what? And then I was just bitching to my friends about it, and I'm like blah blah blah blah, she [the teacher] only favors minorities!" Here, the dominant logic that equates grades with intelligence was overridden by the dominant logic that equates non-whiteness with inadequacy. Indeed, the teacher's unwillingness to grade according to the latter logic confirmed Carolyn's belief that the teacher's grading was unfair and incompetent.

Compositionists have many resources for designing, implementing, and justifying peer review, but how many of us conceptualize the practice of student grade comparison as an integral part of a wider peer-review process. The most comprehensive anthology on peer review does not seriously discuss student grade comparison as significant to the peer-review process (Corbett, LaFrance, and Decker). Neither does Leverenz. Amanda E. Lewis's thorough ethnographic study of race and racism at three schools gives only minimal attention to grade comparison, mentioning it once in passing (115). It should not be surprising that the practice is marginalized or simplified in scholarly discourse on peer review, since teachers and researchers are detached from the practical experience of truly needing a good grade, both objectively, in terms of entering academic programs and achieving graduation, and subjectively, in terms of maintaining self-esteem and impressing others. We are accustomed to giving rather than receiving and comparing grades. Furthermore, the course syllabi, assigned readings, and student essays are fairly incapable of capturing the practice, because the practice is not purely textual. Teachers and scholars who are aware of the practice's importance may nonetheless be at a loss when trying to understand it because they do not have access to the moments in which students compare grades.

Comparing grades requires bodily proximity, if not the actual, physical exchange of papers. It also involves a habitual movement of the eye away from the paragraphs and toward the grade at the top or the bottom of the paper, as well as the cautious or rapid flipping of pages to find the teacher's evaluation. It is part instinct, part conscious action. My interviews and field notes helped me understand the practice, but these data sources were totally dependent on my presence in the classroom. Being there allowed me to witness students milling around after dismissal on days the teacher handed back essays, some comparing grades openly, some comparing secretly. As I have since confirmed in my own classes, grade comparison is a review practice that hides in plain sight, and, as Carolyn's comments suggest, it can exert a strong influence on the "hidden persuasion" of a classroom's "implicit pedagogy" (Bourdieu, *Logic* 69). Here, the practice contributed to Carolyn's belief that the teacher was biased against white people and that her peers were being unjustly privileged, both of which would affect her future involvement in the class.

Unable to enter the intermediate course, Carolyn became a more stubborn participant in the basic course. Silence and eye rolls filled the surplus time created by doing the bare minimum during discussions and activities. She regularly used her phone and worked on homework for other classes, despite the teacher's insistence not to, telling herself, "I don't need the teacher telling me what to do!" After reluctantly agreeing to participate in a focus-group session I organized for this study, she left in the middle of her group's conversation, exclaiming that she had better things to do. She appeared to have given up on the class. However, Carolyn's apparent alienation co-existed with a new kind of engagement. Spurred by Harrison's higher grades as well as her frustrations with the teacher's bias, she reviewed her own writing to find evidence of deficiency and, upon discovering none, decided to aggressively press the teacher, in post-class meetings and office hours, to re-review her writing and justify the grades. Unlike many white students' trusting and deferential disposition toward white critical pedagogues (see Reddy), Carolyn directly challenged the white teacher's authority and competence. After listening to her complaints and re-reviewing her writing, the teacher offered both conciliatory praise of her essays' style and, more importantly, sustained criticism of their content. The first essay covered too many topics and failed to accomplish two key tasks laid out in the prompt. Both essays, the teacher told Carolyn, seemed like exercises in "writing what you think I want you to write" rather than genuine engagements with the course readings and class discussions. After calling her out for trying "to BS me," the teacher gave Carolyn the opportunity to revise. The revisions would need to be substantial if she wanted higher grades. Taken together, the teacher's measured praise, tough criticism, and revision opportunity had a profound impact on how Carolyn proceeded to participate in the class and re-perceive its participants.

After pondering her essays' deficiencies, Carolyn asked Harrison if she could read his first essay again. In an interview with me, he said that he did not mind sharing because he had been touched by Carolyn's look of disappointment after they compared grades on their second essay. He also took pride in his essays and believed that writing was meant to be public. If at first Carolyn sought to re-review her partner's paper simply because it had received a higher grade than hers, she soon realized, with the teacher's criticism of her own work in mind, that his essay actually had the organization and focus that her essay lacked. However, his essay also had signs of struggle. Textual treks up conceptual mountains can take many forms, from winding sentences to a series of brief assertions, from laddering repetitions to surprising sidetracks. Harrison's writing had all of the above, which Carolyn initially read as signs of low intelligence and poor writing—an evaluation no doubt influenced by her sense that she was misplaced in the basic writing course. Already aware of what she believed were his essay's many problems, she now attended to his essay's strengths, namely how it moved from a theoretical discussion of powerlessness (one "face" of oppression), to a concrete analysis of the Michael Brown case (Harrison's chosen issue), and, finally, to a discussion of what could be done about powerlessness (Harrison wanted to challenge racial stereotypes). His essay deftly navigated the assignment's demands, regardless of its so-called errors or lack of "style." Carolyn noticed how his short sentences were not "dumb" but rather, in her words, smartly laid "stepping stones," which carved a unique path through the assigned readings, the class discussions, and the prompt's requirements.

In revising her first essay for a higher grade, Carolyn followed Harrison's lead, narrowing her topic and carving an equally deliberate path. She focused on one diamond company's deceptive marketing practices rather than the whole mining, production, and marketing of diamonds, and she structured her essay so that it moved from a description of blood diamonds, to the diamond company's dishonest marketing practices, and, finally, to ways of challenging those practices. However, she would not fully incorporate a specific concept from Young's chapter, which she had not read. Its twenty-page length proved to be too intimidating. And yet, she would resist the urge to fill that inevitable hole in her essay with a "BS" attempt to use one of Young's terms. Reflecting on the composition of her initial draft, with the hindsight of re-reviewing Harrison's essay and revising her own essay, she admitted to getting "caught up in making it sound good, making it sound awesome, … [and] kind of BS-ing around the whole thing." Her new draft "still has really good style and flow and less grammar errors, but actually answers the question. So like, a good thing, that I'm really glad that I took this class, is like, answering the question. Like you have to have all these things, but you have to answer the question too." She credited Harrison as well as the teacher for helping her see how an essay's content matters just as much as its style, and why it might be better to shovel out the bullshit rather than perfume it with clever turns of phrase and academic verbiage.

The whole process of formal peer review, comparing grades, re-reviewing her essays, confronting the teacher, informally re-reviewing Harrison's essay, reviewing her own essays yet again, and, finally, composing new drafts—a prolonged process motivated by mundane goals like getting a better grade and "actually answer[ing] the question"—had the unforeseeable consequence of changing Carolyn's relationships with and perceptions of the teacher and Harrison. Rather than accepting the teacher's authority on the basis of her whiteness or rejecting it on the basis of her bias against white people, Carolyn grew to respect the teacher as a "critical thinker" whose "degree in writing" enabled her to see aspects of students' writing that they may not see initially but could learn to see through practice. Likewise, rather than stubbornly continuing to see Harrison as a poor writer and beneficiary of the teacher's bias, Carolyn eventually leaned toward him as a model of the very strengths that she lacked. She came to believe that he could, and did, in her words, "out-write and out-think" her, as well as help her grasp the limits of her conception of what constitutes good writing and who might be good at it:

> So I think this class really helped me a lot with like not judging people, you know what I mean? Because like someone can like look really ghetto and talk really ghetto, but they can like out-write you and out-think you in many ways, so it's like. I think like a lot of white people think the same way as I do. Like, if one, if a straight up white girl or straight up white guy was put into that class, they would think the same way as me. That's why they would be so stubborn.

The initially problematic peer-review and grade-comparison practices that set everything in motion had become integral moments of a larger rhetorical process that eventually persuaded Carolyn to recognize and question her implicit bias. At the end of the semester, she was grateful for the opportunities to revise her essays not only because she cared about the grade but also because she saw how she "would still be stubborn" if she had not gone through the whole revision process. Instead of gleefully looking forward to intermediate writing, she now worried that it would not permit such revisions.

About twelve weeks into the semester the teacher asked the students what they wanted to do next. A group of students, led by Anh and Samayah, expressed an interest in poetry. It is important to note that Anh had become known as an outspoken feminist to whom Carolyn (and many other students) often gave the cold shoulder, and Samayah was someone whom Carolyn initially disliked, describing her as "talk[ing] very cultured black." The majority of the class supported the poetry idea, so the teacher asked everyone either to prepare a poem to read during the next session or to email her a poem so that she could share it. Carolyn read original verse about gender stereotypes. Harrison emailed the teacher a multilingual Afrobeat song that explored the fallibility of individuals and the value of community. Samayah recited her own intricate and beautiful poem about a rocky romantic relationship. Anh read original prose that can best be described as a phenomenology of alienation. Although it is impossible to know what was passing through each student's mind as they "reviewed" each other's performances, their body language suggested deep engagement with each other's work. For once, no one was looking at phones, planners, or homework. With all eyes on the performer, it seemed like all minds were on the performed.

Carolyn was awestruck by Anh's and Samayah's readings, which surprised me, considering her earlier attitudes. Samayah's poetry "was like phenomenal and like I could not do that, I could not do even three lines of that. You know what I mean?" I agreed. Stumbling through several attempts to articulate ourselves, Carolyn and I decided that we liked Samayah's poem so much because it used precise language to render comprehensible the contradictory emotions involved in the disintegration of intimate relationships. Her poem also illuminated the limitations of Carolyn's previous conception of intelligence, which, in terms of writing, could no longer be identified solely with style and grammar, but, again, had to be identified with complex content. Since Carolyn's conception of good writing had not included the ability to represent complex emotional situations, she now judged her own writerly authority to be far feebler than she had initially estimated. Into that quiet moment of self-doubt came Anh's thundering prose. "When she read her paper," Carolyn later told me, "It's like wow, that is like really amazing writing and it's so detailed, I could not even do that! It's like, wow! You know what I mean?" The experience of Anh's writing led Carolyn to once again grasp the limitations of her own capabilities and criteria. Unlike her own style-centric writing, Anh's prose was full of rich, "detailed" content. Samayah and Anh were "being smart in their own way," as Carolyn put it, a way that illuminated the intellectual poverty of simply "doing grammar right" and "memorizing stuff," which Carolyn came to associate with whiteness.

As much as the poetry day pushed Carolyn's thinking in new directions, her engagement on that day was made possible by her earlier work with Harrison and the teacher. With their help, which is not to say *only* with their help, Carolyn had developed a more positive disposition toward difference, which then enabled her both to learn from Anh and Samayah on poetry day and to continue questioning her beliefs about "good" writing and writers as the semester drew to a close. Although it would be foolish to argue that nothing beyond the writing classroom's practical life contributed to Carolyn's revised attitude, it would be wrong to deny credit to the classroom's mundane activities and interactions. Doing so would accept the "dominant culture's limited conceptions and valuations of composition as low, limited, preparatory, [and] illegitimate," as opposed to the potentially empowering location suggested by the foregoing tale (Horner, "Rewriting" 451). In the following section, I analyze Carolyn's experience in order to elucidate the value and validity of conceptualizing the writing classroom's practical life as a rhetorical and non-functional totality.

Rethinking Review

If the word "persuasion" typically signifies the inducement of belief change, then the inducing agent is usually assumed to be a text and its author. Indeed, the dominant understanding of rhetoric privileges not only the "speaker-text-audience" triangle but also the capital-S speaker (e.g., Barack Obama) and the capital-S Speech (e.g., "A More Perfect Union"). In college writing classrooms across the country, rhetorical analysis assignments usually require students to analyze texts qua texts, rarely asking them to consider the mundane activities and interactions that might enhance or vitiate the persuasive power of texts as they are experienced *in situ*. Academics themselves are especially prone to identifying discrete texts as the change-agents that induced them to alter their worldviews. The inducement is usually portrayed as happening at a singular point in time: *that* book was the bell that, once rung, could not be un-rung. While texts can indeed produce powerful moments of persuasion, persuasion can also be achieved across weeks or months, produced as much by the social-material practices surrounding the act of reading as by the substance of the text being read. In the foregoing tale, the agent of persuasion was not a singular text or even a string of texts. Carolyn rejected McIntosh's argument about white privilege, and she did not fully read Young's theory of oppression. The assigned readings did not have an immediate impact on her beliefs. Nonetheless, her beliefs changed.

She went from harboring an implicit bias against non-white people to cultivating a conscious critique of her past bias, her sense of herself as a writer, and whiteness in general. The class's critical readings might have fostered a pedagogical environment conducive to such reflection and growth, but her change cannot be understood apart from the mundane activities and interactions associated with reviewing writing, which obviously involves—but cannot be reduced to or understood through—texts themselves. The first peer-review activity intensified Carolyn's belief that she was in the "dumb" class, and thereby reinforced her implicit bias against her peers, but three subsequent review-related interactions cumulatively undermined her earlier attitude: first, the teacher's review of her essays during office hours; second, her informal re-review of Harrison's essays; and third, her review of her classmates' performances. Throughout the semester, Carolyn was also self-reviewing her own writing, realizing her own limitations as she learned more about her peers' strengths. What persuaded her to think differently is better described as an embodied "countertraining" rather than an assigned-reading-induced "consciousness raising" (Bourdieu, *Pascalian* 172). Within that embodied and prolonged rhetorical process, the practices associated with grading—the assignment, and receiving, comparing, and contesting grades—were pivotal.

Although the field of composition does not universally reject the practice of grading, the consensus seems to be that grades are pointless at best and harmful at worst. In the landmark collections *The Theory and Practice of Grading Writing* (Zak and Weaver) and *Alternatives to Grading Writing* (Tchudi), grading is criticized for undermining learning, poisoning relationships, destroying morale, encouraging competition, stifling creativity, fostering resentment, and promoting "conservative values" (Bullock 14). For example, Richard Boyd argues that the upshot of grades is reflected in the word's etymology: the Latin *gradus* implies the assigning of rank and the maintenance of hierarchies, which are inimical to learning (11). Likewise, Peter Elbow argues that grades are "one-dimensional" because they are "defined entirely by the austere minimality of numbers: ... B has no meaning other than 'worse than A and better than C'" (173). Many teachers withhold grades until the final hour, so as not to contaminate the classroom with such hollow ranking. My purpose in what follows is not to challenge the critique of grades but rather to prevent the critique's creeping functionalism from blinding us to grades' contradictory and unpredictable consequences *in situ*. Such functionalism is apparent in Elbow's argument that, since grades are numbers—and numbers have minimal meaning—then grades, in practice, have minimal meaning. In Boyd's case, the meaning commonly associated with the word "grades" is presumed to reflect the actual effect of grades in practice: grades rank students because *gradus* etymologically implies rank. The non-functionalist approach advocated by Giddens would, on the contrary, require us to set aside etymological deductions and determine the local effects of grades through concrete analysis of their instantiation in time and space, keeping ourselves open to their multiple, unforeseeable consequences.

The teacher's grading practices in the foregoing tale were more conventional than alternative or oppositional. There were no grading contracts or negotiated rubrics. The object being graded was the product, not the process. Feedback on the product's quality was both positive and negative, contrary to the notion that teachers should give only positive feedback (Zak). Although the teacher used a "criterion-referenced" rather than a "norm-referenced" grading system, on the grounds that the latter explicitly involves the odious task of ranking essays, such ranking nonetheless prevailed in the classroom's practical life, as many students discerned who did better than whom by comparing grades. Finally, when Carolyn contested her grades, the teacher reasserted traditional authority relations by reiterating her previous feedback and dangling the carrot of higher grades. Though the teacher's grading practices were conventional, they contributed to unconventional ends. Carolyn's lower grades initially persuaded her to question the teacher's fairness and competence, but subsequently motivated her to reconnect with Harrison and to reexamine his essays after class, sparking a process of self-examination that culminated in her humble yet active engagement during the poetry-day performances. Conventional grades and grading practices helped Carolyn develop a critical perspective on both her implicit bias against non-white writers and her own limitations as a writer. Again, I am not rejecting the critique of grades but rather suggesting the value and validity of a non-functionalist approach to understanding grades' rhetorical consequences within the writing classroom.

The preceding discussion suggests that the writing classroom is a totality whose content and consequences are constituted by interaction both between the parts and the whole and among the parts, including the students' emergent consciousness of themselves and the class. For example, the peer review "part" motivated the grade comparison "part," both of which interacted to convince Carolyn that the "whole" class was not just dumb but unfair. Her consciousness of the whole class then informed subsequent "parts," namely her disengagement from activities and her challenging of the teacher, both of which shaped the whole class's emergence. Such conceptual movement between part and whole at both the subjective and objective levels—that is, both within and beyond the individual's experience—is indispensible to understanding practical life's rhetorical dynamics. However, it is important to emphasize that conceptualizations of the whole as a well-oiled machine, a biological system, or a computer program are clearly inadequate. These conceptualizations assume that the whole is nothing but its parts, the seamless integration of its parts, or unaffected by human rationality: none of them grasp the constitutive role of the conflicts of consciousness and the consciousness of conflicts.[5] The "inner oppositions" that serially contributed to Carolyn's growth (Taylor 274), within the mediating whole of the classroom's practical life, included the conflicts between her self-conception as "smart" and her placement in the "dumb" class; her desire to escape the class and her need to do well in the class; her lower grades and Harrison's higher grades; her independent quest for a better grade and her dependence on Harrison's help. Taken separately, none of these oppositions would indicate or constitute growth. One would be hard-pressed to find a silver lining in the initial opposition between the brittle confidence that often accompanies privilege and the harmful prejudices that often accompany basic writing. Similarly, the last two inner oppositions in my list suggest not only grade grubbing, which many deem anti-intellectual, but also exploitation: Carolyn could be accused of "using" Harrison. Each part is troubling on its own. However, when grasped within the emergent totality of the classroom's practical life—when grasped spatially and temporally *in composition*—these inner oppositions must be valued and validated as moments of Carolyn's growth, even if, in true Hegelian fashion, they never become unproblematic. Conceptualizing practical life as an emergent totality can help teachers and researchers understand, if not predict, how the classroom's mundane activities and interactions impact students.

It is common to conflate the predictive and the useful: what *use* is a meteorologist who cannot *predict* the weather? However, usefulness is not exhausted by prediction. Conceptualizing the writing classroom's practical life as a rhetorical and non-functional totality is useful, in the non-predict sense. It can help researchers value and validate the work that is not immediately apparent in the writing classroom's textual corpus. For example, when Aja Y. Martinez analyzes her students' personal writing and discovers colorblind ideology, rather than attribute the latter to "the academic voice" or "the white voice," she might consider the mundane activities and interactions that potentially enhance the persuasiveness of colorblind ideology (593). Researchers like Martinez might also look to the classroom's practical life for evidence that students' beliefs about colorblindness are more complex, and perhaps less ingrained, than their personal writing might suggest, keeping in mind that the "Truth" of the textual corpus lies partly in the "whole" of the classroom's practical life, because the latter's practices indelibly shape the former's meaning. While teachers should continue to approach peer review as a powerful means of enabling students to improve both their essays and their ability to collaborate, teachers might also explicitly value peer review's capacity to help students rethink their perceptions and evaluations of other(ed) students. Since it is foolish to expect the latter to happen automatically, teachers should play an active role in the whole peer-review process by publically and privately valuing texts that might appear to lack value, doing so, in part, by giving such writing higher grades. That is not to say that teachers should arbitrarily give higher grades to writing that appears unconventional. On the contrary, through class presentations and discussions as well as written and spoken feedback, teachers should explain the ideational and stylistic strengths of potentially under-valued writing. Conflict may be inevitable, but if the foregoing tale teaches us anything, it is that struggle and alienation can be productive. Teachers might also create space for poetic performances on the grounds that such "expressivist" activities might foster political reflection, in true non-functionalist fashion. The value of conceptualizing practical life as a rhetorical and non-functional totality lies less in predicting future outcomes and more in illuminating the classroom's full potential.

Conclusion

One underappreciated potential of the first-year writing course is the ability to deter the poisonous pedagogical environments described in *Presumed Incompetent*, the aptly named anthology about non-white teachers' experiences in college classrooms (Gutiérrez y Muhs, et al.). Without her work in the basic writing class, Carolyn might have carried her troubling beliefs and attitudes into future classrooms, where she would encounter international students and non-white professors as well as new critical discourses, all of which might have been censored by her "stubbornness." She might have rejected these learning opportunities in the same way that she initially rejected the basic writing class. She might have even impeded the learning of other students. Fortunately, a different outcome seems likely. My study suggests that Carolyn will be less inclined to distrust the competence of non-white students and teachers and more inclined to challenge what she came to critically identify with whiteness: snap judgments, pretension, and narrow-mindedness. In the future, when she encounters antiracist rhetoric in and beyond the university, I believe that she will be more disposed to listen carefully and reflectively. Whether and how that happens for composition students in general will need to be explored through wider and longer studies.

There is no doubt that students like Carolyn still have much to learn about racism and whiteness. One of her final interview comments is indicative of both how she has grown through the course of the semester and what she might need to learn in future classrooms. Reflecting on her whole experience, she ventured, "I don't think this is a possibility because it would be racist if you put different races in a class on purpose, but I think when you do that, you get more perspective on things." Of course, the simple understanding of racism deployed here leaves much to be desired, but I tend to agree with her opinion on getting "more perspective." Difference is certainly vital to the process of coming to know ourselves and thereby becoming capable of changing ourselves. However, this classroom study should remind us that getting "more perspective" is a possibility but not an inevitability of the diverse classroom, workplace, or neighborhood. Getting "more perspective" takes *work*, and that work might involve the rigorous and ongoing labor of reviewing writing. I believe that future investigations of students' work can benefit from conceptualizing the writing classroom as a rhetorical and non-functional totality and seeing mundane activities and interactions as unpredictable, complex moments of potentially belief-changing experiences.

Notes

1. This study was approved by the university's IRB. Students discussed herein signed consent forms and agreed to let me share their stories. All names are pseudonyms. Statements in quotation marks are taken from interviews unless otherwise noted.

2. As part of the university's TRIO program, Carolyn was automatically enrolled in the basic writing course. The program decided that their students would benefit from a yearlong fyw experience, so they made the two-semester sequence (basic and then intermediate) mandatory. TRIO programs support first-generation, underrepresented, and differently abled students.

3. The other nine students interviewed were Harrison (Cameroonian), Anh (Vietnamese), Samayah (Black American), Aifiya (Somalian), Lisa (white American), Carlo (Native American), Jacob (African American), Dib (Hmong), and Michelle (Black American).

4. I capitalize "Black" when referring to participants who self-identified as Black.

5. Cybernetic, mechanical, and biological wholes are present in the discipline. Sidney I. Dobrin's concept of "writing-qua-writing" is a subject-less (i.e., consciousness-free) totality composed of seemingly infinite parts, motions, and relations, similar to mechanical and cybernetic wholes (Dobrin 144-145, 151). Separately, in *A Counter History of Composition*, Byron Hawk explains "complex vitalism" by invoking biological totalities, such as ant colonies, bee swarms, and cellular automata, none of which involve self-consciousness (Hawk 155, 156, 194). Hawk often contradicts his stated commitment to a human-inclusive vitalism by reducing humans to "part of the machine" (160).

Works Cited

Anderson, Virginia. "Confrontational Teaching and Rhetorical Practice." *CCC*, vol. 48, no. 2, 1997, pp. 197-214.

Barlow, Daniel. "Composing Post-Multiculturalism." *CCC*, vol. 67, no. 3, 2016, pp. 411-36.

Beech, Jennifer. "Redneck and Hillbilly Discourse in the Writing Classroom: Classifying Critical Pedagogies of Whiteness." *College English*, vol. 67, no. 2, 2007, pp. 172-86.

Bosmajian, Haig A. "The Language of White Racism." *College English*, vol. 31, no. 30, 1969, pp. 263-72.

Bourdieu, Pierre. *The Logic of Practice*. Trans. Richard Nice. Stanford UP, 1990.

—. *Pascalian Meditations*. Trans. Richard Nice. Stanford UP, 1997.

Boyd, Richard. "The Origins and Evolution of Grading Student Writing: Pedagogical Imperatives and Cultural Anxieties." Zak and Weaver, pp. 3-16.

Bullock, Richard. "Autonomy and Community in the Evaluation of Writing." *The Politics of Writing Instruction: Postsecondary*, edited by Richard Bullock and John Trimbur, Boynton/Cook, 1991, pp. 189-202.

Clary-Lemon, Jennifer. "The Racialization of Composition Studies: Scholarly Rhetoric of Race Since 1990." *CCC*, vol. 61, no. 2, 2009, pp. 1-17.

Corbett, Steven J., Michelle LaFrance, and Teagan E. Decker, editors. *Peer Pressure, Peer Power: Theory and Practice in Peer Review and Response for the Writing Classroom*. Fountainhead Press, 2014.

Dobrin, Sidney I. *Postcomposition*. SIUP, 2011.

Elbow, Peter. "Changing Grading While Working with Grades." Zak and Weaver, pp. 171-84.

Foster, John D. *White Racial Discourse: Preserving Racial Privilege in a Post-Racial Society*. Lexington Books, 2013.

Giddens, Anthony. *Central Problems in Social Theory*. U of California P, 1979.

Gutiérrez y Muhs, Gabriella, et al., editors. *Presumed Incompetent: The Intersections of Race and Class for Women in Academia*. Utah State UP, 2012.

Hawk, Byron. *A Counter-History of Composition: Toward Methodologies of Complexity*. U of Pittsburgh P, 2007.

Hegel, G.F.W. *The Phenomenology of Spirit*. Trans. A.V. Miller. Oxford UP, 1977.

Horner, Bruce. "Rewriting Composition: Moving Beyond a Discourse of Need." *College English*, vol. 77, no. 5, 2015, pp. 450-79.

—. *Terms of Work for Composition: A Materialist Critique*. SUNY P, 2000.

Leverenz, Carrie S. "Peer Response in the Multicultural Composition Classroom: Dissensus—A Dream (Deferred)." *JAC*, vol. 14, no. 1, 1994, pp. 167-86.

Lewis, Amanda E. *Race in the Schoolyard: Negotiating the Color Line in Classrooms and Communities*. Rutgers UP, 2003.

Martinez, Aja Y. "'The American Way': Resisting the Empire of Force and Color-Blind Racism." *College English*, vol. 71, no. 6, 2009, pp. 584-95.

McCrary, Donald. "Womanist Theology and Its Effects for the Writing Classroom." *CCC*, vol. 52, no. 4, 2001, pp. 521-52.

McIntosh, Peggy. "White Privilege: Unpacking the Invisible Knapsack." *Independent School*, vol. 49, no. 2, 1990, pp. 31-36.

Perry, Pamela. *Shades of White: White Kids and Racial Identities in High School*. Duke UP, 2002.

Reddy, Maureen T. "Smashing the Rules of Racial Standing." *Race in the College Classroom*, edited by Bonnie TuSmith and Maureen T. Reddy, Rutgers UP, 2002, pp. 51-61.
Taylor, Charles. *Hegel*. Cambridge UP, 1975.
Tchudi, Stephen, editor. *Alternatives to Grading Student Writing*. NCTE, 1997.
Young, Iris Marion. *Justice and the Politics of Difference*. Princeton UP, 1990.
Zak, Frances. "Exclusively Positive Responses to Student Writing." *Journal of Basic Writing*, vol. 9, no. 2, 1990, pp. 40-53.
Zak, Frances, and Christopher C. Weaver, editors. *The Theory and Practice of Grading Writing: Problems and Possibilities*. SUNY P, 1998.

Rethinking SETs: Retuning Student Evaluations of Teaching for Student Agency

Brian Ray, Jacob Babb, and Courtney Adams Wooten

Student evaluations of teaching (SETs) are frequently used to assess college teachers. However, education research has shown that there is potential for bias in SETs, especially based on instructor variables. Aside from Amy Dayton's 2015 work on assessment that advises using SETs only in concert with other measures, English studies scholars have not extensively studied SETs in many decades. This project codes 1,074 questions from 55 SET forms at different higher education institutions by institution, question theme, content, subject, and sentence subject as well as thirteen categories based on Herbert Marsh's SEEQ form, which serves as the basis for contemporary SETs. Our analysis reveals that instructors are often placed as grammatical subjects in questions despite their lack of agency over some areas such as participation and student devaluation of alternative teaching practices. Such question formation skews students toward evaluating instructor factors that are, at best, uninformed, and, at worst, biased. We recommend that SET questions align with student learning and/or engagement rather than teacher performance, rewriting questions to put students in subject positions and cue them on best practices as a better reflection of rhetorical theorizations of classroom agency.

Every semester, college teachers express a range of emotions—anticipation, anxiety, even dread—about course evaluations, commonly referred to as SETs. While the validity of SETs often fuels heated debates in venues such as *The Chronicle of Higher Education* and *Inside Higher Ed*, SETs still play a dominant role in hiring and personnel decisions. In fact, they now serve as one of the most widely used methods for assessing college teachers (Basow; Basow, Codos, and Martin; Basow, Phelan, and Capotosto; Stark-Wroblewski, Ahlering, and Brill). Despite a wealth of research on SETs in higher education journals,[1] however, little scholarship on them has appeared in our discipline's publications since the 1960s, with the exception of the edited collection *Assessing the Teaching of Writing* (Dayton).[2] Kevin Roozen and Karen J. Lunsford's 2011 review of empirical research in NCTE journals does not include any scholarship that discusses the assessment of teachers, including the use of SETs. Given the importance of SETs in our work as teachers and administrators, we decided to address this gap by presenting the results of a study in which we gathered and analyzed 55 SET forms used in writing programs, seeking quantitative as well as qualitative data regarding the questions appearing on contemporary SETs and what patterns emerge from them.

Our study began with a broad open-ended goal to learn what kinds of questions appear on course evaluation forms used specifically in fyc programs. The last empirical wide-scale study on the forms themselves led Herbert Marsh to develop the Student Evaluation of Education Quality (SEEQ) in 1987—a set of nine items that served as the foundation for contemporary SETs. The SEEQ measured students' perception of learning, instructor enthusiasm, organization and clarity, group interaction, individual rapport, breadth of coverage, tests and grading, assignments, and difficulty. Because Marsh's work is now 30 years old, we decided to conduct a new study on the structure of SETs to determine their relevance and validity for measuring and assessing teaching effectiveness, specifically in writing courses and programs in the twenty-first century. We see this project as vital for writing studies because pedagogy and teacher training comprises a significant component of the discipline, and because many writing teachers are contingent laborers, meaning their livelihood often depends on how they are evaluated by their students.

Due to the absence of research on SETs in our discipline, we found it necessary to conduct our study empirically. Our main goal was to determine what aspects of teaching effectiveness institutions tend to value most highly and how they measure these traits. Our questions led us to generate a database of 1,108 SET questions from these 55 forms that we then coded for a variety of categories, revealing what kinds of data institutions of higher education are collecting to assess teaching effectiveness. We gathered these forms by written request to WPAs or department chairs at 270 institutions comprised of public universities, private colleges, community and technical colleges, historically black institutions, and tribal colleges in all fifty states (see appendix A). The respondents submitted *either* their institution's generic SET form (45 submissions), or a form specifically adapted for writing courses (10 submissions).

After gathering the forms, we coded the questions using grounded theory, enabling us to build an analytical framework to explain significant emergent patterns (see appendix B for a more detailed description of our methods.) Our first key finding was that after 30 years, course evaluation questions still adhere to Marsh's original model of nine categories. Second, we found that a vast majority of the questions focus on instructors' performance, using a predictable pattern of truth statements (i.e., "The instructor graded me fairly…") that may cause students to hyper-focus on their teacher rather than to evaluate their own learning. Such a spotlight on instructors in SET questions reinforces a misleading perception of instructor and student agency for those filling out and reading SETs. Namely, language emphasizing instructor performance makes teachers responsible for every aspect of a student's success, a tacit assumption that conflicts with contemporary pedagogy. Prevailing research discussed later in this article has found substantial issues with validity and objectivity in conventional SETs, a tendency only exacerbated by the language of the questions themselves. Students often rate their instructors lower for many reasons unrelated to the quality of instruction, especially when their definitions of effective teaching differ. Although SETs should serve as formative measures of teaching effectiveness, we argue that the most effective measures should focus on learning and course activities rather than individuals. For example, instead of asking students if "the instructor encouraged active participation," SETs might ask whether "participation played a major role in the course." Focusing on outcomes and actions helps to minimize opportunities for biased evaluations, in which students rate their instructors rather than their learning.

Rhetorical agency is a contested concept, hinging on definitions of "self" and "subjectivity" as well as understandings of how much an individual can assume power and authority in a world governed by many uncontrollable factors. While Steven Accardi identifies humanist notions of agency reflecting "an ability, power, or authority that can be possessed by a subject or subjects" (2), more recent posthumanist or poststructuralist conceptions of agency locate it in experience. For example, Christian Lundberg and Ioshua Gunn claim that "a similar negative theology of the rhetorical agent would allow rhetoric to be practiced without the agent as the decisive horizon for rhetorical agency," looking at agency as "a systemic effect/affect beyond the individual agent—in collectivities, discursive formations, new technologies, and so on" (98). This echoes work that explicates the agentive nature of objects in addition to people. Building on these ideas, scholars such as Amanda Young argue that we need to pay attention to the relational qualities of rhetorical agency, which "resides not just in language, but in the context of the discourse, in narratives that are constructed by speakers, and in the stances that are created or reflected within the discourse" (Young 228). In the context of the classroom, Accardi points out that rhetorical agency is "an attribute of the classroom" (3); this includes the space itself, desks, chairs, materials students bring in as well as the people inhabiting this space. Such a relational view of agency asks us to consider how SETs themselves function as part of the agentive structure of a classroom and institution even as they reflect the power dynamics at work within them.

An example to explore how these concepts play out in considerations of classroom agency may be useful. Helen Rothschild Ewald and David L. Wallace's "Exploring Agency in Classroom Discourse or, Should David Have Told His Story?" points out the difficulty in both teachers and students exercising agency in classrooms, particularly given the many ways discussion in particular will be interpreted by different participants and the many factors involved in the agentive structure of a classroom. For example, David the teacher tries to tell a story for a certain effect (cooling down a heated discussion) but this act is read differently by various students who are simultaneously acted upon by other material and nonmaterial factors. Individually and collectively, the classroom constructs agency in various ways for different participants, troubling the notion that David or even individual students have agency in this situation. The questions typically found on SET forms often replicate a humanist notion of agency, placing full responsibility for a classroom and learning on the instructor. However, rhetorical views of agency call on us to examine more carefully how SETs can begin to account for the dispersed and relational nature of classroom agency that extends beyond people, including both material and nonmaterial agents.

Despite some variation in grammatical construction, most SETs have opted for language that directs attention toward the instructor as the sole agent. As such, the language shapes the evaluation as a rhetorical situation wherein only the instructor's actions matter. Such positioning elides the role that individual students and classes have in constructing a productive classroom environment, instead placing *all* responsibility on instructors to create such spaces. This positioning also overlooks SETs as being part of the agentive structure of classrooms, a part that can provide students an opportunity to speak back to this structure. Although instructors inhabit a central role in classrooms, students influence classroom environments in ways that SETs are not designed to reflect. We maintain that the language found in SETs can, in fact, miscue students and lead to conflicting information that, in the end, does not effectively measure an instructor's teaching or a student's learning. To continue with the example of group interaction, it is certainly possible that an instructor could encourage student participation during class, but it does not follow that students actually participated, or wanted to participate. Presuming the instructor's role as agent when it comes to participation neglects classroom conditions and ignores the agency of students, other objects, and discursive formations as co-creators of an atmosphere conducive to dynamic interaction. This problematic logic, which privileges a humanist "sage on the stage" figure, extends to other areas assessed by SETs, such as enthusiasm, stimulation or engagement, and respect.

Although we acknowledge the importance of professionalism and accountability among teachers, we found the overrepresentation of instructor-based questions problematic in terms of validity. As we explore in this article, researchers on SETs in other disciplines have already pointed out that certain aspects of teaching, such as enthusiasm and clarity, are subjective and open to conflicting interpretations. For example, students may not define what counts as clear as does their instructor. Moreover, language that consistently focuses attention on instructors may exacerbate issues of bias, a problem well-documented in research on SETs. We discuss the patterns we found and their problems, and conclude by offering an alternative model of best practices for SET design that emphasizes student learning. Specifically, we recommend content-based questions as well as phrasings that may provide more direct information about how students view their own learning and performance. These changes can start to account for a fuller view of agency that is rhetorical, relational and dispersed rather than expressed by one agent. In our view, it is most valuable for SETs to take into account the many factors involved in constructing dispersed agency—students, classrooms, tools, and of course teachers—so that students are asked to consider how all of these contribute to their learning experience in a course. Doing so helps those looking at SETs consider the variety of factors that play into students' learning, and it helps students reflect on the constellation of factors that construct their learning rather than fixating on teachers alone.

A Brief History of SETs

The findings of our study and its implications will mean more if readers first understand the larger history of SETs. We ourselves wanted to develop an historical context for course evaluations in order to help interpret the forms we gathered from writing programs. In particular, our historical investigation led us to conclude that the SET itself is rooted in perceptions of instructor performance, rather than an assessment of a student's broader learning.[3] At their outset, SETs were designed to evaluate individual instructors based on a range of subjective traits that included physical appearance and wit. In 1923, psychologist Max Freyd constructed the first known model of teaching evaluation based on instructor characteristics such as "sense of humor," neatness in dress, "tact," "patience," and other features such as "physique," "popularity," and "alertness" (435). Freyd's model became influential: A 1931 study by Chas Knudsen and Stella Stephens of 57 different rating systems identified common features similar to Freyd's (17-27). Ironically, traits such as "fairness" and "intellectual capacity" appeared on only 10 of these rating systems. Early on, then, SETs not only highlighted teacher personality and appearance but also *were constructed* to measure teachers' subjective traits, not student learning. Although Purdue professor Hermann Remmers developed a more objective form based on ten traits associated with effective teaching in 1928, we still see holdovers from Freyd showing up on SETs such as "sense of humor" and "personal appearance" (534). Students were thus put into a position where they were evaluating factors that neither they nor the instructor had sole control over and that they could do little to affect.

The first SETs developed in higher education did not even pretend to measure objective traits. The core idea of evaluating teachers in this format emerged from a context in which "personal appearance" was seen as indicative of teachers' effectiveness. Although these overtly subjective questions have disappeared from the forms themselves, research reviewed in the next section shows how traits such as humor and appearance still influence SETs. The 1970s and 1980s were a period of active research on SETs and their institutionalization.[4] During these decades, Herbert Marsh published numerous studies on SETs that culminated in the creation of the Student Evaluation of Education Quality (SEEQ) form—the basis of most contemporary SETs.

The SEEQ measured nine items including learning, enthusiasm, organization and clarity, group interaction, individual rapport, breadth of coverage, tests and grading, assignments, and difficulty (Marsh 277). A few other SET forms became common, notably the Student Instructional Report (SIR) developed by the Educational Testing Service (ETS) in 1972; the Individual Development and Educational Assessment (IDEA) developed by Kansas State University in 1975; and the Instructional Assessment System (IAS) developed by the University of Washington and delivered online since 2013. More recently, the last ten or so years have seen a trend in supplementing the evaluation of teachers via SETs with other measures—namely, observations, self-ratings, and teaching portfolios. This is a positive trend in higher education that has helped to mitigate problems with SETs by placing teaching evaluations in a broader, richer context.

During the 1960s, SETs became more common across the U.S. On the cusp of this development, our field engaged in some of its only published conversations about SETs. A series of Conference on College Composition and Communication (CCCC) workshops from 1956 through 1962 revealed simultaneous support for and suspicion of SETs. These CCCC workshops reflect the concern that faculty teaching should be taken into account for promotion and tenure, particularly since composition instructors spend much of their time on teaching. In 1957, the fifty workshop participants reported that 50% of their schools evaluated teaching, with SETs as the most popular assessment instrument (Estrin 111). Yet only 2% of these reported that administrators use the SETs and only 25% submitted them to the chair or WPA; 70% reported that the instructor alone saw the SETs (112). While teachers saw value in the use of SETs, they expressed a strong desire for autonomy in their use. Workshop participants strongly discouraged the use of SETs for anything other than formative purposes. By the 1960s, faculty at the CCCC workshops, representing a variety of institutions, were suspicious of SETs when used to make personnel decisions (Neckar, Weast, and Filtz). SETs were "almost entirely voluntary, and generally considered a private matter between instructor and student" until the 1960s and 1970s (Centra). This may have been, in part, because those factors measured were entirely out of students' control and were viewed as personal commentary on instructors' effectiveness rather than objective measures of teaching effectiveness, reflecting the idea that the teacher alone was in charge of the classroom.

Although contemporary SETs have dropped some of the more overtly subjective categories developed by Freyd and Remmers, our analysis of 55 forms shows that instructors remain the primary subject of questions in a way that strongly echoes these early forms. In fact, our view is that current SET forms differ little from those seen in the 1920s. Although classroom dynamics and our understanding of agency have undergone great shifts, SETs have not reflected these changes. The basic premise of the SET as focused on the instructor may distract students from core aspects of their learning and misdirect them to evaluate factors that have an indirect impact on their success and that they are not completely qualified to evaluate, making SETs an ineffective tool for measuring teaching and learning. The next section goes into more depth on some of the problems with SET validity and bias that stem from this preoccupation with the instructor as agent.

Bias in SETs and Instructor Performance

Our coding of SET questions revealed a high number of items focused on instructors. On one hand, this pattern seems intuitive if we assume that course evaluations should measure teacher performance as perceived by students and view classroom agency as entirely resting in instructors' hands. On the other hand, contemporary research has outlined a number of problems with this view of SETs regarding validity, reliability, and agency as we have discussed. For those less familiar with SET research, this section will orient them to the major critiques arising during the past decade. Foremost, studies on SETs have found weak positive correlations between instructor performance on evaluations and student learning (Basow, Codos, and Martin; Pinto and Mansfield; Stehl, Birgit, and Kadmom; Zabaleta). According to a meta-analysis by Dennis Clayson, no study since 1990 has been able to link student success with instructor evaluations. As such, studies have repeatedly affirmed, "students may rate professors highly even when they do not seem to learn from them" (Basow, Codos, and Martin 361). Likewise, students may learn a great deal but still rate their teachers negatively if instructors manage aspects of the course contrary to existing norms or expectations. A study by Michela Braga, Marco Paccagnella, and Michele Pellizzari found an inverse correlation in which students who rate their instructors negatively in introductory courses perform better in their later coursework.[5]

Many concepts on SET forms like clarity and fairness are subjective, and therefore vulnerable to bias. Teachers may already suspect as much at the experiential level, when a student rates them negatively for declining to accept late work, or when they ask for revisions on papers that conflict with what students may have previously learned about writing. It is not uncommon for students to hold "differing views on the importance of classroom decorum, organization, teacher's subject expertise, and encouragement of students' independence" (Goldstein and Benassi 706).[6] Complicating matters further, studies have also found that students often rate overt aspects of an instructor's performance, neglecting to recognize indirect signs of teaching effectiveness unless an instructor or SET explicitly asks them to do so. Perceptions of teachers are important, but as Mary Beth Pinto and Phyllis Mansfield ask, "Is good teaching simply what the students say it is?" (59). SET questions alone cannot provide reliable or consistent information on teaching quality. Students understandably define abstract qualities of teaching uniquely, and vague questions like "Did the instructor come prepared for class?" leave it open for students to define "preparation" in their own way, which can skew SET results.

When discussing evaluations, academics sometimes refer to a phenomenon called the "halo effect," in which students unconsciously rate instructors on their personality rather than the quality of their teaching. The halo effect may sound like a casual term, but aspects of it bear up under scrutiny. One study by Dennis E. Clayson and Mary Jane Sheffet finds that students' ratings of instructors differ little from impressions formed after a five-minute introduction. As they conclude, "students are universally associating perceived personality with instructional effectiveness" (156). According to Deborah Merritt, student evaluations involve largely "System One" cognitive processes that "are typically hurried, superficial, effortless, and charged with emotions" (Pinto and Mansfield 55). Building on Clayson and Sheffet's study, Pinto and Mansfield state that more than half of student evaluations in their sample consider the instructor's personality foremost in their ratings of overall teaching effectiveness. During follow-up questionnaires, students freely admit to taking out their frustrations on instructors, and letting personal factors impact their judgements. One student writes, "If I really like a professor as a person—but they are a lousy teacher—then I feel bad giving them a low grade. I just can't give 'em a low grade" (59). Authors of these studies conclude that an instructor's personality often complicates any attempt by SET instruments to evaluate teacher effectiveness.

Three general factors are found to repeatedly influence student ratings: "course-related variables, instructor-related variables, and finally student-related variables" (Rantanen 224).[7] The first two represent shifts in agency that students intuit and use to evaluate a course, often by accounting for their own lack of agency or *perceived* lack of agency in a given classroom, since SETs do not allow for considerations of the dispersed nature of classroom agency. A 2006 study by Fadia Nasser and Knut Hagtvet describes instructor-related variables, in particular, as accounting for up to 14% of variance in teacher evaluations, variables that often rely on students' misguided perceptions of instructor agency in a given classroom, department, or institution. While some studies endorse SETs as accurate measures of teaching effectiveness (Centra; Feldman; Marsh), a majority of them find potential for bias caused "by factors such as class size, popularity of the instructor, lenient grading or the amount of workload required" (Stehl, Birgit, and Kadmon 889). The most prominent instructor-related variables include gender and ethnicity. Susan Basow has published a number of studies on the role of gender in SET scores, concluding that the gender of an instructor has significant effects on the SET ratings an instructor receives. A study by Susan Basow, Julie Phelan, and Laura Capotosto uncovered that male students are more likely than female ones to nominate a male as their "best" professor, describing them in terms of their ability to innovate and stimulate critical thought, as well as their general knowledgeability. By contrast, when either gender nominated a female professor as their "best," they focused more on attributes such as approachability, flexibility, passion, open-mindedness, and ability to relate to students. This trend informs a larger observation by Basow across her work: gender stereotypes—that men are rigorous and knowledgeable, and that women are student-centered—influence student expectations of faculty in the classroom.

Women must meet a different set of expectations than men, the latter of whom are consistently valued for traditional aspects of teaching effectiveness including expertise, fairness, and clarity. While women must meet these expectations as well, they must also work to be perceived as compassionate and polite. As Basow, Stephanie Codos, and Julie Martin observe in a follow-up study to Basow, Phelan, and Capotosto's study of gender and SETs, "Women and minorities often must work harder to be perceived as equally competent as White men, and it is far easier for them to 'fall from grace'" (353). A study by Joey Sprague and Kelley Massoni confirms these gendered expectations, adding that male professors are rewarded on ratings for being funny, organized, and well prepared. By contrast, women receive lower scores and can be described as "bitchy" if they fail to demonstrate compassion and flexibility due to high expectations or harsh grading. As the authors conclude, such gendered demands result in women and minorities having to put forth much more time and energy for high ratings than do men.

Race also plays a significant factor in SET scores. A study by Landon Reid found distinct racial bias toward African-American male professors on websites such as Rate My Professor (see Kelly Ritter for more about Rate My Professor.) A study by Anish Bavishi, Michelle Hebl, and Juan M. Madera asked entering college students to rate a hypothetical *curriculum vitae* according to teaching qualifications and expertise. Students consistently rated African-American women as the lowest qualified, while rating White and Asian professors the highest. Basow and Martin[8] have found similar evidence of racial bias in student ratings of teachers. These findings have been upheld in a study by Su Boatright-Horowitz and Sojattra Soeung. The evidence presented in such research has eroded academic trust in the usefulness of SETs as singular measures of teaching effectiveness. This evidence also highlights the influence of instructor agency on SETs; if students identify an instructor as coming from an under- or non-privileged group, they often allow this perception to cloud their SET ratings. It is incumbent on WPAs and department chairs in our discipline to take these findings into consideration when making personnel decisions, but our work should not end there. Each article on SET bias reaches a similar conclusion: Administrators should seriously consider reforming SET practices, including redesign of the forms themselves in order to minimize opportunities for bias.

Of course, gender and ethnicity are the most widely studied variables among many factors that get less attention. A study by Francisco Zabaleta found that graduate student teachers received higher evaluations regardless of gender or grading practices, suggesting students felt a stronger connection to those graduate student teachers. Heather Campbell, Karen Gerdes, and Sue Steiner have discovered that physically attractive faculty receive higher global ratings on course evaluations. Mihran Aroian and Raymond Brown have found evidence that teachers who report academic dishonesty are more likely to receive low evaluations from students. A study by Robert Youmans and Benjamin Jee observes that giving out candy prior to the completion of course evaluations can result in higher scores. Such information implies that any kind of reward—such as perceived grading leniency—can impact SETs in ways that obscure their ability to measure teaching effectiveness in large part because students identify these activities as signs of an instructor using their agency to positively affect the class or even to recognize the relational nature of agency by better accounting for students. All of these internal factors may contribute to an instructor's course evaluation averages.

Given this wealth of information on the relative unreliability of SETs, the question becomes how institutions can begin to think differently about the purpose and structure of such measures. Our argument centers on the phrasing of the questions themselves. By focusing on instructor agency and performance, SETs may prompt students to hyper-focus on their teachers rather than their own learning and the broader classroom context. A large number of the nearly 1,100 questions we collected focus attention directly on the instructors and situate them as solely responsible for several aspects of the course's success. Although an instructor plays an undeniable role in shaping course policies, structuring class sessions, and interacting with students, we found ourselves questioning whether most SETs truly reflect the dispersed agentive structures in our classrooms. In fact, the SET forms we analyzed largely promote the single agent model of instruction typical of lecture-style classes that rely on an outdated notion of humanist agency. This model situates control and agency for learning primarily with the instructor and therefore reinforces the notion that the instructor—not the student—is responsible for student success. Such a stance does justice to neither teachers nor students.

We question what it means when SETs situate the instructor as the subject[9] for some inquiry but not others, especially for aspects of the course where the instructor does not have full control—such as participation, student interest, and subjective notions of clarity. As researchers such as Bruce Jackson, John Marshall Reeve and Ching-Mei Tseng have found, many external factors affect how well students learn and how they perceive different facets of a course. The overt position of instructor as subject may also miscue student expectations, asking them to measure aspects of an instructor's work at odds with more recent scholarly stances in higher education advocating a de-centering of instructor presence and authority. In such cases, an instructor's ratings may be downgraded. As Jean Lutz and Mary Fuller find in their examination of authority in a fyc course and a business writing course, students bring different expectations about the teacher and students' classroom agency with them. Such expectations influence how students respond to SETs.

Agency in SET Questions

Our findings indicate a pattern of hyper-attention on the instructor at the expense of other factors that influence learning. We argue that rethinking SETs as instruments that take into account the relational nature of classroom agency, rather than treating them solely as tools to evaluate instructor performance, could lead to more valid measures of teaching effectiveness and student learning. Despite work done by previous researchers, it is impossible to overlook how much our discipline's conception of effective writing instruction has changed in the past thirty years. Trends that emphasize student agency and decentering instructor's authority raise questions about the validity of SETs, particularly those based on generic forms such as the SEEQ or IDEA that do not account for classrooms modeled on distributed agency. As we noted in the previous section about problems in SETs, students may not immediately appreciate de-centered models of teaching in which an instructor acts more as a facilitator or workshop leader. First-year college students in particular may react negatively to instructors who do not fit with their perceptions of college professors as "sages on a stage." Likewise, open-ended writing prompts may appear to many students to lack organization or clarity. Such reactions reflect common beliefs that students may have about instructor agency—that an effective instructor is authoritative, controlling, and/or objectively unimpassioned about their subject.

Our coding revealed potential issues in the very phrasing of the SET questions, not merely the categories or question types. Our study found that instructors frequently appear as the subjects of SET questions, even though their agency is shared with many other actants.[10] A total of 480 questions feature the instructor as the subject, rather than student (144), course (474), or other variables such as time of day that the forms do not account for (see appendix B for more detail).[11] Instructors appear as the central subject and focus in 43% of the questions, the course does so in 43%, and students in 13%.[12] Many SET forms consist exclusively of truth statements centered on the instructor (i.e., "The instructor fostered a climate of respect," or "The instructor stimulated my critical thinking.") In fact, these kinds of questions account for 417 (38%) of the total questions we coded. We also coded the student-focused questions (144) and found them largely directed toward demographic information (43), their own performance and investment in the course (83), and lastly by evaluation of their skills (13).[13] Demographic questions seek information about students' major, GPA, reasons for taking the course, expected grade, and in some cases gender or ethnicity. Questions about performance and engagement most often ask students about their level of interest in the course, how often they attended, and how much time per week they devoted toward assignments. All but five institutions ask questions about student investment in the course. While this trend is encouraging, we see these kinds of questions as offering a limited conception of student agency or distributed agency in the classroom.

Regarding the instructor-focused questions, teachers might object to this kind of representation of their work, preferring instead to think of their teaching in terms of encouraging relational agency in the classroom or of creating situations in which *students* stimulate critical thought among each other. In flipped classroom models, an instructor may outline a task or problem for students to solve in teams, and therefore might not seem to be overtly stimulating the critical thought that occurs because they are encouraging students to view everyone (and, in some cases, every*thing*) as being involved in classroom agency. Table 1 below provides examples of how SETs frame questions of critical thinking:

Table 1
SET Questions about Critical Thinking

> Did the instructor challenge you to engage the material actively?
> The instructor encouraged students to think independently.
> The instructor encouraged students to analyze opinions and ideas.
> My instructor stimulated my interest in the material.
> The instructor stimulated creativity and problem solving.
> The instructor inspired critical engagement with course topics.
> My instructor challenged me to engage with different viewpoints.

We recognize that the idea of classroom agency is not simple, but we need SET forms that reflect a better balance of the relative control that instructors and students each exert in the classroom, control that is often mediated through objects such as SETs. Often, student agency is dependent upon external factors such as identification with academic culture (Jackson 585) or "students' constructive contribution into the flow of the instruction they receive" (Reeve and Tseng 258). Although teachers can encourage student agency, Jackson and Reeve and Tseng claim that students' intrinsic motivations can be as important as the pedagogical approaches of teachers. Other scholars have reinforced the difficulty both teachers and students have in establishing agency in classrooms. Helen Rothschild Ewald and David L. Wallace claim, "within this body of practices [classroom discourse], agency can be understood as both the ability to interpret events as well as the ability to influence, change, or redirect them within a specific situation" (343). Agency often becomes a matter of perspective. Teachers and students often possess more or less agency than they recognize in a given situation, which heavily influences evaluations of instructors.

Instead of asking whether instructors stimulated critical thought, it seems more reasonable to ask if *students* engaged in critical thinking, regardless of who or what facilitated engagement. In some cases, SET questions can and should focus on the instructor's actions, regarding relatively objective qualities of instruction such as starting and ending class on time, holding regular office hours, and responding to emails within two to three business days that are fully within the instructor's responsibility and often serve as visible marks of their roles in classroom agency. However, we question the extent to which SET forms situate instructors as agents for other aspects of the classroom experience, such as stimulation and engagement, respect, and participation, which are often much more relational. Consider the examples of how SET forms inquire about participation levels, as documented in table 2. As with critical thinking, questions about participation seem to miscue expectations and convey value of the "evaluate-response" mode, in which teachers lead class discussion by posing all of the questions to students and then responding to and evaluating their answers:

Table 2
SET Questions about Participation Levels

> The instructor welcomes questions.
> The instructor encouraged students to participate in class discussion.
> The instructor's encouragement of class participation was excellent.
> My instructor has built an environment in which ideas can be exchanged freely.
> The instructor encouraged students to ask questions during class.
> The instructor encouraged class discussion.
> My instructor conducted class discussion effectively.
> I had an opportunity to ask questions.
> The instructor encouraged questions and/or discussion.

These questions place the instructor at the head of the sentence, and by doing so seem to invoke notions of an authority figure actively in charge of a class. At the least, the phrasing of these questions misaligns with how many writing instructors structure their lessons. The question that comes closest to capturing a dynamic instruction model reads, "The instructor has built an environment in which ideas can be expressed freely." We contend that questions about topics like participation could be rewritten with different subject positions to better reflect the relational agency often at work in classrooms. For instance, they could ask whether "discussion and group work played an important role in this course." This simple but important change removes the instructor as the subject and focuses on the real topic through which many people and even objects interact. There is less risk of miscuing or confusing students regarding who is responsible for participation and less risk of bias and subjectivity.

Toward Redesigning SET Forms

In their study of the potentially negative impacts of SETs on faculty members, Lori R. Kogan, Regina Schoenfeld-Tacher, and Peter W. Hellyer conclude that "designing SETs to offer the best opportunity for constructive feedback is of paramount importance" (630). Other studies have likewise concluded that SET design should aim to gather useful feedback for instructors (Abrami; Algozzine, Beattie, Bray, Flowers, Grets, Howley, Mohanty, and Spooner; Berk; and Frick). Such moves would make SETs more useful instruments for teacher evaluation, although SETs should always be part of a broader context that includes multiple forms of teacher evaluation and reflection. We argue that SETs can also be redesigned to become more useful for students to evaluate their own learning, encouraging a broader view of classroom agency than those typically reflected in the forms. Such changes would align well with our field's emphasis on metacognition, as exemplified in the *Framework for Success in Postsecondary Writing Instruction,* and on the often-relational nature of agency, as seen in posthumanist scholars' work.

Our study has identified the representation of agency as a major point for improvement in SET design. The ratio between instructor-focused and student-focused questions indicates that SET forms place too much emphasis on instructor performance. Similarly, the phrasing of the questions can cue latent biases toward instructors and prompt unfair evaluations, especially in categories where questions assume a model of teaching that conflicts with an instructor's pedagogy. To address these concerns, we propose an alternative way of thinking about SETs, not as rating the instructor *per se* but as instead reflecting on and evaluating learning that happens in the course. Instructors are ultimately held responsible for what students learn, but they may often operate in the background and periphery of the course. Shifting the focus to learning acknowledges that many factors—teachers, students, and objects—play pivotal roles in the learning that occurs in any given course.

This alternative model would be based on a writing program's stated learning goals and outcomes, with some questions that address practical elements of instruction (holding class regularly, communicating with students, returning work in a reasonable timeframe). SETs that emphasize learning and development serve both instructors and students better. Even if students struggle to define their agency, they can at least report on activities they have engaged in such as library orientations, research workshops, peer review sessions, and revision activities. Maintaining a focus on students, more effective questions would ask them about the abilities they have developed such as writing introductions or conclusions, gathering and integrating source material into their writing, developing main ideas, using online databases, and reading texts critically for multiple meanings. The phrasing of these questions should make the outcomes and activities the primary subject in order to avoid misinterpretation. A small number of the institutions we surveyed included these kinds of questions. One SET form asks students to reflect on their understandings of and experience during the completion of each major writing assignment in the course. Such questions direct students to evaluate their own intellectual development, rather than focus on their opinions of an instructor.

Of course, generic forms can be valuable for analyzing trends across programs and departments at the institutional or national level. Despite such utility of generic SETs, we strongly advocate that English and writing programs develop and administer their own locally sensitive forms that can provide more specific data. These forms do not need to replace generic forms, but they should be given equal weight, especially regarding personnel decisions like reappointment, promotion, and tenure. We acknowledge that many institutions do not allow programs to design their own SET questions. We suggest that programs facing such limitations should institute an additional form that enables them to gather the kinds of information focused on student learning that can make SETs more powerful instruments for measuring what students are learning in our writing classes. Only by retuning SETs to focus on student learning can we transform these tools that have so often been used to measure student perceptions of instructors into instruments that encourage students to identify the interconnected aspects of classroom agency through reflection on their own learning.

Notes

1. An article by Centra counts 2,000 different studies on SETs, and the number has certainly grown since then. However, Gump indicates that many of these studies were carried out during the 1970s using problematic methods. In any case, the volume of studies demonstrates a sustained interest.

2. Specifically, Amy Dayton overviews some current scholarship on SETs and concludes with recommendations that WPAs use them for formative rather than summative purposes, avoid "norm referencing," and include them as but one measure alongside teaching portfolios, reflective letters, and observations (41). We have also published recommendations for how WPAs can use existing SETs or craft SETs for their programs (Adams Wooten, Ray, and Babb).

3. Our history is indebted to John Centra, who segments the history of SETs in the U.S. into four stages. During the first stage, 1927-1960, only a handful of universities began developing SETs, partly inspired by student-driven review venues like the Harvard *Crimson*'s publication, titled *Confidential Guide to College Courses* (*Confi* for short).

4. Algozzine, et al. build on Centra's history to offer a fifth stage oriented toward "alignment of student-teacher expectations for quality of teaching," use of "midterm formative evaluations" as opposed to end-of-semester ones, and greater attention to qualitative feedback in the form of "letters of evaluations by students" and "narratives by faculty" (135).

5. They also found that students' evaluations of teachers increased on foggy and warm days and decreased on rainy days, adding more suspicion to the value of SETs in reporting student effectiveness but more support to the idea that nonhuman factors such as weather contribute to the distributed agency of a class.

6. Goldstein and Benassi specifically found that students tend to place more value on personal disclosure and imparting factual knowledge, whereas faculty place more value on "challenging students intellectually" (700) and stimulating independent, critical thought.

7. For a full overview of external variables, see Marsh. Also, Gump provides a review of studies on the leniency hypothesis, the idea that faculty can secure positive evaluations by giving good grades. While there is no consensus that grading leniency *actually* leads to better scores, it is a commonly held assumption by faculty. The assumption, rather than an actual causal link, could contribute to grade inflation at some universities.

8. This study used facial animation and voice software to modify the same three-minute lecture by an engineering professor to emulate gender and racial differences. The lecture was given to 329 predominantly Caucasian college students who actually rated the African-American and female avatar professors higher than the white male, though they did less well on a post-quiz, which indicated they may have paid less attention to the minority avatar and compensated by giving higher ratings. The authors conclude that "student evaluations may not be a good indicator of teaching effectiveness," given that "[s]tudents may rate professors highly even when they do not seem to learn from them" (Basow, Codos, and Martin 361). This study seems to have taken the most effort to account for other external factors.

9. Halliday and Matthiessen define a subject as a nominal or noun group that satisfies one of the three criteria: it is the theme of the sentence, responsible for the truth of the statement, or a doer of action. As Biber, et al. demonstrate, subjects can be an agent (i.e., instructor) but also an instrument (course), a recipient or affected subject (student), or eventive (classroom). Sentences can also contain what Biber, et al. refer to as "dummy subjects," such as the pronoun in "It was not as cold on the previous night" (125). In the case of SETs, the researchers found instructors meeting not just one but all three of Halliday's criteria in a large number of questions (Halliday and Matthiessen 77-81).

10. To determine the potential significance of this trend, we cross-coded each question for its sentence subject, using Halliday and Matthiessen and Biber's definitions of a subject as responsible for theme, truthfulness, or agency, as well as whether the expressed subject was an agent/doer, instrument, recipient, or dummy. A subject does not always have to appear at the beginning of a sentence, and in fact can appear in a variety of forms. We therefore built a robust and flexible definition of a subject in order to guide our analysis.

11. We were unable to categorize ten of the questions by subject (instructor, student, course).

12. A t-test confirmed a statistically significant difference between these proportions, $p < .0001$.

13. Three questions defied categorization.

Appendix A: Request Letter

March 28, 2016

Dear Writing Program Administrator or Chair,

We are writing to request a blank copy of your institution's and/or composition program's course evaluation surveys, as part of an ongoing study regarding the role of course evaluations in first-year composition programs. This study began in 2014 with a survey we distributed through the CWPA listserv and direct emails to writing program administrators. An article analyzing the survey results has been accepted for publication in *WPA: Writing Program Administration*. It will appear within the next year.

The blank course evaluation forms will be coded and analyzed using corpus software for trends in language and question type. Similar studies have appeared on scoring rubrics and other administrative documents in journals such as *Written Communication*, *WPA*, *CCC*, *RTE*, and *College English*. No identifying information will be shared, and we will only summarize general trends.

The investigators plan to present an analysis of this data at upcoming conferences, and in an article submitted for peer review. No part of any institution's course evaluation forms will be reproduced without permission.

Appendix B: Methods and Data

Our initial coding revealed some need to modify Marsh's original nine categories to better reflect our data. Once we solidified our categories, we began to generate frequency counts in order to identify statistically significant trends. We conducted tests of statistical significance to determine if any of these categories were overrepresented in our sample and found that questions about the instructor's organization and clarity and overall perception of learning appear more frequently than any of the other 12 types, $p = .0001$. Table 3 shows p-values for every category of question compared to the average of 54 questions per category.

Table 3
Ratios and Probability Values for Question Categories

Question Category	Question Type	P Value
Organization and Clarity	127 (11%)	P <.05
Respect	27 (2%)	P <.05
Perception of Overall Learning	202 (18%)	P <.05
Instructor Enthusiasm	31 (3%)	P <.05
Breadth of Coverage (Writing & Reading)	131 (12%)	P <.05
Group Interaction/Participation	36 (3%)	P <.05
Assignments/Test	61 (6%)	P >.05
Feedback	46 (4%)	P >.05
Individual Rapport/Availability	41 (4%)	P >.05
Grading/Expectations	40 (4%)	P >.05
Stimulation/Engagement	61 (6%)	P >.05
Syllabus/Objectives/Expectations	61 (6%)	P >.05
Student Demographics	43 (4%)	P >.05
Student Investment	83 (7%)	P <.05
Other (i.e., learning materials, technology)	100 (9%)	P <.05

We then coded and computed z-tests for each question category, comparing the instructor-themed questions against student- or course-themed questions, whichever was highest. In many categories, instructors dominate as agent at statistically significant levels (p<.0001). Table 4 summarizes our analysis:

Table 4
Summary of Analysis of Question Focus

Question Type	Instructor (N=480)	Student (N=144)	Course (N=474)	Unclear (N=10)	P Value (Student vs. Instructor/Course)
Organization and Clarity	112	0	14	2	P <.05
Instructor Enthusiasm	31	0	0	0	P <.05
Respect	27	0	0	0	P <.05

Breadth of Coverage	11	12	107	1	P <.05
Syllabus/ Objectives/ Expectations	26	0	35	0	P <.05
Group Interaction/ Participation	25	0	11	0	P <.05
Stimulation/ Engagement	32	1	27	1	P <.05
Individual Rapport/ Availability	40	0	1	0	P <.05
Assignments/Tests	6	2	53	0	P <.05
Feedback	46	0	0	0	P <.05
Perception of Overall Learning	73	0	126	3	P <.05
Grading/ Expectations	23	0	16	0	P <.05
Other (Student-focused questions)	28	129	84	3	P <.05

Works Cited

Abrami, Philip C. "How Should We Use Student Ratings to Evaluate Teaching?" *Research in Higher Education*, vol. 30, no. 2, 1989, pp. 221-27.

Accardi, Steven. "Agency." *Keywords in Composition Studies*, edited by Paul Heilker and Peter Vandenberg, Utah State UP, 2015, pp. 1-5.

Adams Wooten, Courtney, Brian Ray, and Jacob Babb. "WPAs Reading SETs: Confronting Authority and Contingency." *WPA: Writing Program Administration*, vol. 40, no. 1, 2016, pp. 50-66.

Addison, William E., John Best, and John D. Warrington. "Students' Perceptions of Course Difficulty and Their Ratings of the Instructor." *College Student Journal*, vol. 40, no. 2, 2006, pp. 409-16.

Algozzine, Bob, John Beattie, Marty Bray, Claudia Flowers, John Grets, Lisa Howley, Ganesh Mohanty, and Fred Spooner. "Student Evaluations of College Teaching: A Practice in Search of Principles." *College Teaching*, vol. 52, no. 4, 2004, pp. 134-41.

Aroian, Mihran, and Raymond Brown. "The Whistleblower Effect." *Academe*, Sept.-Oct. 2015, pp. 16-20.

Basow, Susan. "Student Evaluations of College Professors: When Gender Matters." *Journal of Educational Psychology*, vol. 87, no. 4, 1995, pp. 656-65.

Basow, Susan, Julie Phelan, and Laura Capotosto. "Gender Patterns in College Students' Choices of their Best and Worst Professors." *Psychology of Women Quarterly*, vol. 30, no. 1, 2006, pp. 25-35.

Basow, Susan, Stephanie Codos, and Julie Martin. "The Effects of Professors' Race and Gender on Student Evaluations and Performance." *College Student Journal*, vol. 47, no. 2, 2013, pp. 352-63.

Bavishi, Anish, Michelle Hebl, and Juan M. Madera. "The Effect of Professor Ethnicity and Gender on Student Evaluations: Judged Before Met." *Journal of Diversity in Higher Education*, vol. 3, no. 4, 2010, pp. 245-56.

Berk, Ronald A. "Survey of 12 Strategies to Measure Teaching Effectiveness." *International Journal of Teaching and Learning in Higher Education*, vol. 17, no. 1, 2005, pp. 48-62.

Biber, Douglas, Stig Johansson, Geoffrey Leech, Susan Conrad, and Edward Finegan. *Longman Grammar of Spoken and Written English*. Longman, 1999.

Boatright-Horowitz, Su, and Sojattra Soeung. "Teaching White Privilege to White Students Can Mean Saying Good-bye to Positive Student Evaluations." *American Psychologist*, vol. 64, no.6, 2009, pp. 574-75.

Braga, Michela, Marco Paccagnella, and Michele Pellizzari. "Evaluating Students' Evaluations of Professors." *Economics of Education Review*, vol. 41, 2014, pp. 71-88.

Campbell, Heather, Karen Gerdes, and Sue Steiner. "What's Looks Got to Do With It?' Instructor Appearance and Student Evaluations of Teaching." *Journal of Policy Analysis and Management*, vol. 24, no. 3, 2005, pp. 611-20.

Centra, John. "Will Teachers Receive Higher Student Evaluations by Giving Higher Grades and Less Course Work?" *Research in Higher Education*, vol. 44, no. 5, 2003, pp. 495-518.

Clayson, Dennis E. "Student Evaluations of Teaching: Are they Related to What Students Learn? A Meta-Analysis and Review of the Literature." *Journal of Marketing Education*, vol. 31, no. 1, 2009, pp. 16–30.

Clayson, Dennis E., and Mary Jane Sheffet. "Personality and the Student Evaluation of Teaching." *Journal of Marketing Education*, vol. 28, no. 2, 2006, pp. 149-60.

Council of Writing Program Administrators, National Council of Teachers of English, and National Writing Project. *Framework for Success in Postsecondary Writing*. CWPA, NCTE, and NWP, 2011, wpacouncil.org/files/framework-for-success-postsecondary-writing.pdf.

d'Apollonia, Sylvia, and Philip C. Abrami. "Navigating Student Ratings of Instruction." *American Psychologist*, vol. 52, no. 11, 1997, pp. 1198-1208.

Dayton, Amy, editor. *Assessing the Teaching of Writing: Twenty-First Century Trends and Technologies*. Utah State UP, 2015.

Estrin, Herman. "Measuring the Quality of the Teaching of English." *CCC*, vol. 9, no. 2, 1958, pp. 111-13.

"The Evaluation of Teaching." *CCC*, vol. 13, no. 3, 1962, pp. 79-80.

Ewald, Helen Rothschild, and David L. Wallace. "Exploring Agency in Classroom Discourse or, Should David Have Told his Story?" *CCC*, vol. 45, no. 3, 1994, pp. 342-68.

Feldman, Kenneth A. "Course Characteristics and College Students' Ratings of Their Teachers: What We Know and What We Don't." *Research in Higher Education*, vol. 9, no. 3, 1978, pp. 199-242.

Freyd, Max. "A Graphic Rating Scale for Teachers." *Journal of Educational Research*, vol. 8, no. 5, 1923, pp. 433-39.

Frick, Theodore W., Rajat Chadha, Carol Watson, and Emilija Zlatkovska. "Improving Course Evaluations to Improve Instruction and Complex Learning in Higher Education." *Educational Technology Research and Development*, vol. 58, 2010, pp. 115-36.

Goldstein, Gary, and Victor Benassi. "Students' and Instructors' Beliefs about Excellent Lecturers and Discussion Leaders." *Research in Higher Education*, vol. 47, no. 6, 2006, pp. 685-707.

Gump, Steven. "Student Evaluations of Teaching Effectiveness and the Leniency Hypothesis: A Literature Review." *Educational Research Quarterly*, vol. 30, no. 3, 2007, pp. 56-69.

Halliday, M. A. K., and Christian Matthiessen. *Halliday's Introduction to Functional Grammar* 4th ed., Routledge, 2014.

Jackson, Bruce. "Education Reform as if Student Agency Mattered: Academic Microcultures and Student Identity." *Phi Delta Kappan*, vol. 84, no. 8, 2003, pp. 579-85.

Knudsen, Chas, and Stella Stephens. "An Analysis of Fifty-Seven Devices for Rating Teachers." *Peabody Journal of Education*, vol. 9, no. 1, 1931, pp. 15-24.

Kogan, Lori R., Regina Schoenfeld-Tacher, and Peter W. Hellyer. "Student Evaluations of Teaching: Perceptions of Faculty Based on Gender, Position, and Rank." *Teaching in Higher Education*, vol. 15, no. 6, 2010, pp. 623-36.

Kuzmanovic, Marija, Gordana Savic, Milena Popovic, and Milan Martic. "A New Approach to Evaluation of University Teaching Considering Heterogeneity of Students' Preferences." *Higher Education: The International Journal of Higher Education and Educational Planning*, vol. 66, 2013, pp. 153-71.

Lundberg, Christian, and Ioshua Gunn. "'Ouija Board, Are There Any Communications?' Agency, Ontotheology, and the Death of the Humanist Subject, or Continuing the ARS Conversation." *Rhetoric Society Quarterly*, vol. 35, no. 4, 2005, pp. 83-105.

Lutz, Jean, and Mary Fuller. "Exploring Authority: A Case Study of a Composition and a Professional Writing Classroom." *Technical Communication Quarterly*, vol. 16, no. 2, 2007, pp. 201-32.

Marsh, Herbert. "Students' Evaluations of University Teaching: Research Findings, Methodological Issues, and Directions for Future Research." *International Journal of Education Research*, vol. 11, no. 3, 1987, pp. 253-388.

McPherson, Michael, Todd Jewell, and Myungsup Kim. "What Determines Student Evaluation Scores? A Random Effects Analysis of Undergraduate Economics Classes." *Eastern Economic Journal*, vol. 36, no. 1, 2009, pp. 37-51.

"Measuring the Quality of Teaching." *CCC*, vol. 8, no. 3, 1957, pp. 155-57.

Merritt, Deborah J. "Bias, the Brain, and Student Evaluations of Teaching." *St. John's Law Review*, vol. 82, no. 1, 2008, pp. 235-87.

Nasser, Fadia, and Knut Hagtvet. "Multilevel Analysis of the Effects of Student and Instructor/Course Characteristics on Student Ratings." *Research in Higher Education*, vol. 47, no. 5, 2006, pp. 559-90.

Neckar, Dan, Kathryin Weast, and Cecily Filtz. "Taking a Look into the History of Student Evaluation of Instructors." U of Wisconsin Stevens Point, *The Pointer Online*, Jan 13, 2016. thepointeruwsp.com/2012/05/10/taking-a-look-into-the-history-of-student-evaluation-of-instructors/.

Pinto, Mary Beth, and Phylis M. Mansfield. "Thought Processes College Students Use When Evaluating Faculty: A Quantitative Study." *American Journal of Business Education*, vol. 3, no. 3, March 2010, pp. 55-62.

Rantanen, Pekka. "The Number of Feedbacks Needed for Reliable Evaluation. A Multilevel Analysis of the Reliability, Stability, and Generalisability of Students' Evaluation of Teaching." *Assessment & Evaluation in Higher Education*, vol. 38, no. 2, 2013, pp. 224-39.

Reeve, John, and Ching-Mei Tseng. "Agency as a Fourth Aspect of Students' Engagement During Learning Activities." *Contemporary Educational Psychology*, vol. 36, no. 4, 2011, pp. 257-67.

Reid, Landon. "The Role of Perceived Race and Gender in The Evaluation of College Teaching on Ratemyprofessor.com." *Journal of Diversity in Higher Education*, vol. 3, no. 3, 2010, pp. 137-52.

Remmers, Herman. "The Relationship Between Students' Marks and Student Attitudes Towards Instructors." *School and Society*, vol. 28, 1928, pp. 759-60.

Ritter, Kelly. "E-Valuating Learning: *Rate My Professors* and Public Rhetorics of Pedagogy." *Rhetoric Review*, vol. 27, no. 3, 2008, pp. 259-80.

Roozen, Kevin, and Karen Lunsford. "'One Story of Many to Be Told': Following Empirical Studies of College and Adult Writing Through 100 Years of NCTE Journals." *Research of Teaching in English*, vol. 46, no. 2, 2011, pp. 193-209.

Sprague, Joey, and Kelley Massoni. "Student Evaluations and Gendered Expectations: What We Can't Count Can Hurt Us." *Sex Roles*, vol. 53, 2005, pp. 779-93.

Stark-Wroblewski, Kimberly, Robert F. Ahlering, and Flannery M. Brill. "Toward a More Comprehensive Approach to Evaluating Teaching Effectiveness: Supplementing Student Evaluations of Teaching with Pre-Post Learning Measures." *Assessment and Evaluation in Higher Education*, vol. 32, no. 4, 2007, pp. 403-15.

Stehl, Sebastian, Spinath Birgit, and Martina Kadmon. "Measuring Teaching Effectiveness: Correspondence Between Students' Evaluations of Teaching and Different Measures of Student Learning." *Research in Higher Education*, vol. 53, no. 8. 2012, pp. 888-904.

Youmans, Robert J., and Benjamin Jee. "Fudging the Numbers: Distributing Chocolate Influences Student Evaluations of an Undergraduate Course." *Teaching of Psychology*, vol. 34, no. 4, 2007, pp. 245-47.

Young, Amanda. "Disciplinary Rhetorics, Rhetorical Agency, and the Construction of Voice." *Rhetoric in Detail: Discourse Analyses of Rhetorical Talk and Text*, edited by Barbara Johnstone and Christopher Eisenhart, John Benjamins, 2008, pp. 227-46.

Zabaleta, Francisco. "The Use and Misuse of Student Evaluations of Teaching." *Teaching in Higher Education*, vol. 12, no. 1, 2007, pp. 55-76.

Who Learns from Collaborative Digital Projects? Cultivating Critical Consciousness and Metacognition to Democratize Digital Literacy Learning

Julia Voss

Collaborative group work is common in writing classrooms, especially ones assigning digital projects. While a wealth of scholarship theorizes collaboration and advocates for specific collaborative pedagogies, writing studies has yet to address the ways in which privilege tied to race, gender, class, and other identity characteristics replicates itself within student groups by shaping the responsibilities individual group members assume, thereby affecting students' opportunities for learning. Such concerns about equity are especially pressing where civically and professionally valuable twenty-first century digital literacies are concerned. This article uses theories of cultural capital and the participation gap to (1) analyze role uptake in case studies of diverse student groups and (2) suggest ways to expand writing studies' current use of metacognition to address such inequities.

"[S]tudents in a collaborative project may want to divide work so that each does what he or she is most comfortable—or interested—in doing. Although dividing the project this way may be efficient, it can also diminish the range of students' learning. If teachers do not pay careful attention to groups' work habits and dynamic, for example, they may find that a technology-savvy group member on a team has done all the technological work and the other group members have learned very little about new software, editing, or multimodal composing."

—Anne-Marie Pedersen and Carolyn Skinner (2007)

Group projects in print and digital forms offer considerable benefits in the writing classroom, allowing students to tackle larger projects, learn from their peers, and prepare for the professional environments typical of white-collar workplaces. The American Association of Colleges and Universities (AACU) endorses collaboration, noting its benefits to students' "intellectual and practical skills" while "deepening personal and social responsibility" (Kuh 6). Recent writing studies scholarship on collaboration has examined best practices for group composing with digital tools both conceptually (Cummings and Barton) and in terms of specific technologies and pedagogies (Kennedy and Howard; Kittle and Hicks), while other researchers have re-opened the theoretical discussion of collaboration to focus on discursive and intellectual conflict in student groups (Duffy; Restaino). Connecting the digital focus of many recent discussions of collaboration to these considerations of tension in collaborative relationships, I use Pierre Bourdieu's concept of cultural capital to understand how members of diverse digital composing groups assume and perform project responsibilities and offer a critical metacognitive pedagogy to address the inequities that can plague it.

This project focuses on equity of uptake in digital student group projects, a concern highlighted by the composition and location of the class I study here:

- The course was a community-based course, placing students in a historically Black neighborhood and asking them to study local Black churches as sponsors of literacy.
- The makeup of the class was unusually diverse for the predominantly white Research I institution where it was offered, with a majority of non-White and female members, constituting a mixture of undergraduates, graduate students, and non-matriculated community members.
- The course used designated roles (group leader, technology expert, group secretary, community liaison) to manage project work.

The course's Black community context and content drew students' attention to race, while the process of working through the project highlighted additional gender, class, and age factors that shaped how groups distributed responsibilities in ways that writing studies research on collaboration does not fully address.

The students from the case studies discussed below varied considerably in their backgrounds and preparedness for the roles that structured the collaborative digital composing task, with levels of digital literacy ranging from nearly nonexistent (barely using email) to experience in creating multimodal texts. Their varied backgrounds introduced multiple types of capital into the groups, accumulated through different configurations of age, race, gender, educational status, and digital literacy expertise. As the case studies illustrate, some of these capital sources positioned traditionally empowered individuals—White, young, male, or well-educated group members—as "natural" fits for leadership and technical expert roles. Often these sources of capital aligned to reproduce what Bourdieu calls *doxa*, the natural social order that is largely invisible and therefore beyond question due to its pervasive, tacit nature (*Outline*). However, shifts in the project throughout the composing task allowed some members to renegotiate their responsibilities, allowing them to develop additional digital literacy skills and to exert more control over the project as time went on. Drawing attention to the way capital shapes the group composing process creates opportunities to offset the tendency to structure technology-intensive group work on the basis of *doxa*, offering a means to challenge the conservative propensities of collaboration that John Trimbur notes.[1] Making visible how cultural capital structures opportunity in student composing groups and using reflective (re)allocation of members' responsibilities modifies and/or extends current practices to democratize access to digital literacy learning opportunities in collaborative student projects.

Cultural Capital and Access to Digital Literacies

Many teachers can attest to the fact that students contribute unequally to collaborative projects, especially ones involving digital composing. As indicated by Pedersen and Skinner's epigraph and the following case studies, this has to do with both real disparities in skills and resources and with students' perceived suitability for various project roles, what Bourdieu calls objective and embodied forms of capital ("Forms"). And where Bourdieu focuses on how the French educational system perpetuates class-based achievement gaps by relying on students' inherited cultural capital, my cases draw attention to how—in American higher educational contexts that integrate technology into collaborative work—race and gender also structure opportunity. Dennis Shirley's and David Swartz's analyses of Bourdieu's concept of "misrecognition" show how cultural capital can restrict educational opportunities while seeming to democratize them, explaining how specific pedagogies (such as high-stakes testing, lecturing, and oral exams) empower bourgeois students while subtly disadvantaging working class students. Although collaborative pedagogy represents one of writing studies' challenges to such hegemonic, gate-keeping pedagogies, it still risks re-introducing privilege in other ways because of the tendency to replicate in student groups the inequities found in society as a whole. As a result, some students' inherited symbolic capital allows their assets and experience to be recognized and rewarded while others' are ignored (see Carrington and Luke).

Where digital literacy learning opportunities in collaborative projects are concerned, unequal opportunities mirror what Henry Jenkins and other scholars in communication and sociology call the digital participation gap. Researchers like David R. Brake, Jen Schradie ("Digital"), and Eszter Hargittai and Gina Walejko find that young, White, male, wealthy, and educated individuals much more frequently create content for blogs, social media sites, discussion fora, and other online venues—a divide Hargittai also frames in terms of cultural capital. And this participation gap persists as digital technologies shift toward mobile devices and the mobile Internet, continuing to hold true for racial and economic minorities likely to be "mobile-only" users. Philip M. Napoli and Jonathan A. Obar and Katy E. Pearce and Ronald E. Rice have found that, as with desktop computers and digital content creation more generally, non-White, female, poor, less educated, and older users tend to engage in more passive activities (such as browsing) rather than production and agentive practices like composing written or multimedia content, participating in discussion fora, or developing games and apps.[2] Use disparities are further complicated by capital-influenced perceptions of technological ability. Where gender is concerned, Hargittai and Aaron Shaw argue that despite increasing technology use across demographic groups, women tend to underestimate their technical expertise compared to men which, they suggest, makes women less likely to compose online digital texts.

As a result of such differences in uptake and self-perception according to race, class, age, gender, and education level, Schradie ("Trend") and Pearce and Rice argue that such privileged early adopters benefit not only first but also *more* from digital literacy: "[T]hose with the most resources (status, cognition, education, income, access) adopt first, have and gain more skills, and use more and different activities more effectively. They thus obtain earlier and more benefits, thereby increasing, rather than reducing, knowledge gaps in society" (722). This is particularly important because it limits access to what S. Craig Watkins identifies as the power digital, multimodal literacies confer through "critical thinking, inquiry, discovery, and real-world problem solving. Tools literacy is foundational; design [multimodal] literacy is transformational" (9). Watkins' ideas echo those of the National Council of Teachers of English (NCTE), which argues for writing teachers' duty to help students "Develop proficiency and fluency with the tools of technology" and "Build intentional cross-cultural connections and relationships with others so to pose and solve problems collaboratively and strengthen independent thought" (NCTE "Definition"). The nature of these tasks encourages, even mandates, group work by virtue of the number and variety of skills involved (NCTE "Position Statement"). Writing studies' commitment to promoting collaborative digital composing also reflects the skills twenty-first century employers seek. Studies commissioned by the AACU have repeatedly identified both "staying current on changing technologies" (digital literacies) and the "ability to work effectively with others in teams" (collaboration) among the qualifications employers value most in future workers (Hart Research Associates 2004, 2010, and 2015 reports).

Equity and Metacognitive Writing Development in Student Groups

While group-based pedagogies are widespread in writing classrooms, many of our theories of collaboration are based on studies of professional, not student, writers.[3] The focus this research places on (1) the relationship between cultural capital and responsibility allocation and (2) the potential for changing group structure throughout the composing task also applies to student collaboration but must be modified to account for differences of context. Students are brought together on an ad-hoc basis: they do not know each other or invest in the group's task in the way that members of self-sponsored professional writing groups do, which Candace Spigelman argues can prevent co-construction of knowledge (a central benefit of collaboration) by foregrounding questions of individual credit. Furthermore, Margaret Tebo-Messina notes that unlike academic coauthors with designated areas of expertise or coworkers with specific job titles, students are "peers," implying equal access to all aspects of a collaborative task. However, especially in digital composing groups, this equality often proves illusory. The lens of gender illustrates how this can play out in collaborative projects. Meg Morgan and Joseph Janangelo describe how gender bias can prevent women's expertise and leadership from being recognized, despite the work they do (Morgan), especially when gender stereotypes create the expectation that female group members will nurture or cover for slacking partners (Janangelo). Studying mixed-gender groups working on writing-intensive website projects, Joanna Wolfe and Kara Poe Alexander find that group members tend to value the technical work the group did (building the website) over the written content that populates it, and that the "computer experts" who took over this technical work were overwhelmingly male and in some cases prevented female partners from working on the group's website. Although writing studies lacks parallel research on differential role uptake according to students' racial and economic background—a gap this project addresses—existing research on the relationships between race, class, and technology (see Banks; Berry, Hawisher, and Selfe; Critel; Medina and Pimentel; Monroe; Nakamura and Chow-White; Scenters-Zapico) suggests the need to investigate the links between race, class, and learning opportunities in digital collaborative projects.

Existing research on structuring group projects to promote equity of opportunity shows how cultural capital, when left unaddressed, can lead students to divide a digital group composing task along lines of existing expertise, defeating the assignment's purpose as a learning exercise. To combat this, technical communication scholars like Wolfe and Alexander describe various methods of project-structuring that make individual responsibilities explicit and (for Wolfe) connect these responsibilities to students' individual learning goals. The approach they advocate closely parallels the roles according to which my case study groups operated and the metacognition[4] students engaged in to consider the demands of the project and assume the responsibilities for which they were best qualified. Scholarship on transfer suggests a partial means for deepening and democratizing the learning opportunities embedded in such group structuring pedagogies. However, such research rarely discusses group (as opposed to individual) composing and tends to focus on transfer from the past (rather than transfer into the future). Based on their research on the composing practices students transfer from high school to college, Angela Rounsaville, Rachel Goldberg, and Anis Bawarshi recommend metacognitive exercises which discourage students from engaging in "low-road" transfer that simplistically imposes prior experience to new tasks and discourages students from learning new writing skills. Mary Jo Reiff and Bawarshi introduce the idea of focusing on students' "novice" status when drawing on their prior knowledge as a means to discourage low-road transfer, emphasizing that even experienced student writers still have much to learn. In their work on teaching for transfer, Liane Robertson, Kara Taczak, and Kathleen Blake Yancey go further to advocate reflective activities that emphasize what students *do not* already know (as well as what they do), priming students to "remix" prior and new knowledge about composing.

However, asking students to reflect on prior experience and manage their group's collaboration is not enough to fully offset opportunity inequity and limited learning. The case studies highlight how issues of race, class, and age affected the responsibilities different group members assumed. Despite the fact that the task's structure placed students into peer groups that helped them learn new digital composing skills, the roles individual members assumed often replicated race, class, and age hierarchies based on their prior experience, allowing cultural capital to interfere with the course's learning goals. And although turning points throughout the collaborative composing task offered opportunities to redistribute responsibilities, the metacognition used to guide groups' project management was not explicitly tied to their background, future-oriented learning objectives, or rising levels of skill and confidence as the project progressed, resulting in missed opportunities to democratize digital literacy learning.

Detailing the Case Studies

The case studies draw on IRB-approved research conducted in an advanced writing course taught in 2011 at a large, public research institution located in a mid-sized Midwestern city which I joined as a participant-observer. (See appendix for details about the research protocol.) The instructors—Lisa, an endowed university professor, and two experienced community organizers, Sylvia and Donna—brought together undergraduates, graduate students, and community members who collected and analyzed the literacy narratives of members of local Black churches. Sylvia and Donna, both Black women, identified as community members, and Lisa and I, both White women, identified as teacher-researchers affiliated with the university. Instead of meeting on the main university campus, the class met at a community center located in the same historically Black neighborhood as the churches. Course readings focused on literacy and race, specifically the role Black churches play as literacy sponsors in African American communities. The class was two-thirds female, very diverse in terms of race and relationship to the university, and included a broad age span ranging from traditionally and non-traditionally aged undergraduates to graduate students, working professionals, and senior citizens (see table 1).

Table 1
Racial Identification and University Affiliation of Class Members (real numbers)

Race	
African	1
Black/African American	10
Asian	1
White/Caucasian	3
Relationship to University	
Community Member	4
Graduate Student	2
Undergraduate Student	9

The instructors placed students in groups of four to six, each responsible for completing a two-part collaborative digital composing task:

- conducting audio or video literacy interviews with congregation members and uploading the edited files[5] to an online database
- creating a final project using written, visual, audio, and video content to (1) analyze the role of literacy in the Black church they studied and (2) report on what group members learned during the project[6]

Projects were presented at an end-of-term community sharing night attended by students, interviewees, and other guests.

Scaffolding Group Digital Composing

Because the entire course was designed around this extended group project, the instructors built explicit consideration of group dynamics and project management into the second class meeting, during which they placed students into groups and introduced the course project. Sylvia led the class in a discussion of group work followed by a reflective skills inventory—as Tebo-

Messina, Alexander, and Wolfe advocate—asking students to consider "what it meant to work in a group, and the roles of different participants in the group, and how what you do affects everybody else in the group and affects the outcome of the project." Similar to the standard roles of project manager, subject expert or researcher, and primary writer that Wolfe recommends, instructors designated project-specific responsibilities (see table 2).

Table 2
Group Member Roles

Group leader	Monitors group's progress on literacy interview collection and final report composing process; delegates interviewing and digital composing tasks to individual group members
Technology expert	Serves as in-group technical advisor and trouble-shooter, takes lead in producing final project
Group secretary	Manages paperwork used to document literacy interviews (permission forms, interview metadata forms, notes on content, etc.)
Community liaison	Connects other group members to parishioners at their home church to arrange interviews

The instructors' approach to scaffolding group work reflects the alternating style of group project work Wolfe describes as "layering" face-to-face collaboration with distributed individual work (9-10). Although members chose individual responsibilities, regardless of what role they assumed, each member helped conduct interviews and present their group's final project at the Community Sharing Night. So while the group's digital composing task was not completely compartmentalized, the roles members assumed encouraged them to contribute in specific ways. As Alexander advocates, students were invited to take up roles that aligned with their typical ways of contributing to group projects and their existing abilities, making for an efficient—though problematic—division of labor.

Access to Group Member Roles and Digital Composing Responsibilities

The four roles were not equally available to all group members. The community liaison role was restricted to non-matriculated members of partner churches who joined the class to connect group mates with other parishioners to interview, while the group leader and technology expert roles were more subtly shaped by age, experience, gender, and race. Nia, a Black psychology major in her thirties and mother of two who worked full-time as a retail manager, emphasized her age and gender as factors influencing both her assumption of the group leader role and her leadership style:

> I was the sole woman in my group. And I just also happened to be the oldest, and you have three boys [her three traditionally aged undergraduate groupmates], and you kind of just need to tell them what to do. They were very good at doing what they were told . . . they said "Nia, just tell us what to do." I said "That works for me. I can handle that." So that's how the team worked.

In addition to age capital, the *doxa* of race closely correlated with educational and professional experience to position some group members as natural fits for the leader role. Charlie—a White high school teacher in his thirties with a master's degree in education who was pursuing his doctorate—explained that he assumed the role of group leader in part because he was the only graduate student, even though the group also contained another adult member (a non-traditionally aged Black female undergraduate). He also emphasized his relevant experience: in recent years Charlie had organized projects in which his students interviewed residents of the neighborhood around their school, the same historically Black neighborhood where the group's partner churches were located. Charlie's experience was especially significant, his group mate Jacob noted, because no one else in the group had ever done an interview-based project before. The maturity and expertise that Nia, Charlie, and Jacob describe provided logical reasons for older, more experienced, better-educated group members to take on leadership roles. But the ways in which these pragmatic concerns aligned age and experience with gender and race foreclosed group leadership to other members, undermining the project's potential to provide *new* learning opportunities. Furthermore, the tendency of these identity characteristics to cluster with other kinds of privilege raises troubling issues of equity.

While age, education, and professional experience shaped which group members assumed leadership roles, race, expertise, age, and student status influenced which group members assumed the technology expert role. Melissa, a White undergraduate in her thirties working full time as a registered nurse while pursuing a bachelor's degree in nursing, described how she ended up as her group's technology expert following Sylvia's reflective skills inventory: "I knew the most about the technology, which was still very little. So I just kind of stepped up and offered to do it." In other groups, relative expertise intersected with other identity characteristics—such as age and full-time student status—to recommend certain members for the technology expert role. Jacob, a White traditionally aged undergraduate double-majoring in Development

Studies and African American and African Studies, explained that he assumed the technology expert role both because of his relative proficiency and because he had the time to learn new technical skills:

> Because in my group, most of the students were either . . . they just did not know how to use technology. Or they were older and busier, or they were grad students. So I had a little bit more lead-time than they did . . . It was like, "Well, I don't really know the technology." So those people went towards one thing. And I was like "Well, I'm not perfect at technology, but I know it better than you."

Although students did not explicitly discuss the relationship between race and technical expertise, it's significant that the technology experts in two of the three groups identified as White (the third was the class's single Asian student), and that Jacob and Melissa were two of only three White students in the class (the third was Charlie, the leader of Jacob's group). The relative expertise Jacob and Melissa describe tallies with long-standing digital divides that fall along race and class lines, underscored by their groups' acceptance of Jacob and Melissa as technology experts. In addition to the racial capital Jacob and Melissa drew on, economic capital also supported their technology expert roles: both were Apple users. Based on the instructors' own technical expertise and the hardware available to them, they chose Apple video-editing software for the class (QuickTime Pro and iMovie). They quickly trained students to use these applications and provided a pop-up classroom lab supplied with MacBook Pro laptops borrowed from Lisa's department. As a result, students noted that proficiency with and unrestricted access to Apple computers were major material issues that affected their digital composing work. Students who were unfamiliar with the Apple interface (as well as with video editing and multimodal composing) struggled to use the provided machines during class meetings. Students who owned their own Apple computers were therefore at a class advantage, given that Apple laptops in 2011 ranged in price from $1000-$2500, compared to an average cost of around $500 for a PC laptop.[7] This material issue points to the ways in which class, as well as race, provided a *doxa* that positioned White and wealthier group members as natural fits for the technology expert role. While ownership of an Apple computer does not correlate perfectly with wealth (both Jacob and Melissa described the hard work required to purchase and maintain their machines), Apple ownership nonetheless served as capital that contributed to certain group members' recognition as technology experts.

Collaboration as a Mechanism for Digital Literacy Learning

To the credit, however, of the project's layered collaborative structure, designated technology experts like Jacob and Melissa did at times help their group mates learn digital literacy skills associated with video recording and editing. As Jentery Sayers asserts in his argument for designating technological expertise in the classroom, group members could and did go to these technology experts for one-on-one, point-of-need instruction. Jacob described how groupmates came to him to learn how to edit video files:

> We all kind of came to this [class] with "We want to learn how to do this. I want to figure it out." It was never like "Jacob, will you edit my videos?" It was like "Jacob, would you show me how to edit these videos?" . . . And I was like, "Yeah, sure, we'll teach you how to do it." That's the one thing about the class that was really trying to give you knowledge, rather than give you the presentation, give you the completed product.

So although Jacob remained the group's go-to technology expert, other members used his expertise to learn technical skills that could enable them to compose digital texts independently. This dynamic suggests one way in which the task's layered structure facilitated the transfer of digital literacy skills between group members, especially since individual group members had to produce some video content independently for the midterm and final projects.

When I interviewed Nia the following term, she was enrolled in an advanced digital media course in which students worked individually to create podcasts, digital stories, and documentaries. When I asked Nia how her experience with the Black church literacy project affected her current work, she focused on multimodal storytelling techniques that combined technical and rhetorical skills, despite the fact that she had served as her group's leader rather than its technology expert:

> I've always loved PowerPoints [the platform her group used for the final project]. So I thought I knew a whole lot about PowerPoints. Until this class. You know, putting videos in, and music and sound. I finally figured out how to put the music with the video . . . I enjoyed the video, I enjoyed the editing portion, trying to figure out where to put the content, creating a story.

Nia and another classmate, Denise, both approached the course project as an opportunity to develop digital composing skills that they continued to cultivate both inside and outside the classroom. Not only did both women enroll in the same advanced digital composing course the next term, but they both used course projects to begin work on digital family history projects (now complete) that used the media collecting, editing, and composing skills developed during the courses to create self-sponsored projects.[8] Denise, a Black woman in her forties with a doctorate in communication who was working outside academia and served as her group's community liaison, explained how she planned to use the media production skills she learned to preserve her deceased mother's letters as part of her family history project: "And I'm even thinking now how will this be useful to me in the future, by saying OK, I can read my mom's letters. OK, buy a Flip [video] camera . . . And just read those letters and then download the letters, my reading of them, to my computer.'"

Project Turning Points as Opportunities for Redistributing Responsibilities to Expand Digital Literacy Learning

The "agenda" with which Nia and Denise approached the course project—using the Black church literacy project to learn skills they could apply to self-sponsored digital composing tasks—provides a model for scaffolding a more equitable collaborative digital pedagogy. Because of the family history projects they had in mind, Nia and Denise took on multimodal storytelling and media production responsibilities while working on the final project that went beyond the roles they assumed at the beginning of the course. Their experience suggests ways to expand the use of metacognition in collaborative writing pedagogy, moving beyond focusing primarily on prior experience to include students' plans for the future in order to encourage role uptake that facilitates self-directed transfer. This can be done by highlighting turning points in the project as opportunities to reallocate responsibilities, informed by group members' personal, intellectual, and professional goals and by calling students' attention to established relationships between technical expertise and race, gender, and age capital.

A detailed examination of how case study groups navigated the final project illustrates the utility of such a critical, sustained metacognitive approach to collaborative digital composing, structured around the project's roles and its changing demands. While the four roles suited the first phase of the project well, the nature of the composing task shifted as groups finished gathering literacy interviews, completed their individual midterm assignments, and began working on their final projects, which asked groups to create a large, complex digital text (see table 3).

Table 3
Components of Final Project

	Written components	**Multimodal components**
Introduction	Short introduction summarizing the work the group did throughout the term (150 words)	Short carefully edited video clips of each group member describing 1 aspect of the group's work
Focusing questions	2-3 focusing questions for the project with a short written paper explaining how these questions grow out of 3+ course readings (700 words)	[none]
Church history	Brief history of the church the group worked with and short bios of the parishioners they interviewed (400 words)	1 short carefully edited clip from each interview (10 clips total) and 3-4 clips/photographs depicting the church and its history
Answers to focusing questions	A concise written argument that identifies the group's key observations about how this Black church has influenced the literacy of its members, answering the team's focusing questions (1000 words)	6-8 interview clips that provide evidence for argument's claims
Learning reflection	Group abstract and short descriptions of what each group member learned through collecting literacy interviews (150-word group abstract + 500 words per person)	Video learning reflection from each group member that does not duplicate material in their written piece

The demands of this project were considerable: groups used new formats—media-enriched slideshows or html documents[9]—to generate multimodal texts showcasing their research on the Black church as a literacy sponsor and reflecting on what they learned throughout the project. The project included a set of written documents (totaling 4000+ words) and over an hour of carefully selected, arranged, and edited video. The project was mostly group-authored but included individual components.

The scope of the final project prompted groups to change their structure. As Denise explained:

> One person could not do that whole thing alone . . . And so then they started to pool their resources and realized that they were stronger, I think, and more complete together than any of them had been separately. I think that was part of it, that whole notion of the assignment being so large that they couldn't comprehend how they could do it individually.

Jacob's group illustrates how such a turning point in the project can function as a prompt to restructure group work. The early framing stages of the final project were so interdependent that the group members collaborated on them face-to-face, departing from their designated roles: "[Y]ou have to discuss with somebody else, because all the parts of the project are so interrelated, that if I'm doing one part, it affects how somebody else would do another part. So while dividing up labor, the work, you have to really work together at the same time." Furthermore, because some responsibilities tapered off as the focus shifted from conducting literacy interviews to analyzing and reporting on them, the final project provided an opportunity for group members to redefine their roles, although not all groups recognized this or took advantage of it. Group members whose responsibilities related more to conducting literacy interviews could shift to helping design the visual/conceptual framework for the final project and drafting text for the final written report. As Rebecca Schoenike Nowacek and Kenna del Sol argue, although distinct roles can help groups begin work on composing tasks, shifting these roles as the task changes over time lets the group adapt to the task as it develops, illustrating the kind of flexible layered approach to team projects Wolfe advocates and which successful groups like Jacob's employed.

Contrasted with the instructors' explicit discussion of role assumption at the beginning of the term, these mid-point structural changes happened organically within individual groups rather than as a guided, class-wide process. By this point group members knew each other, understood the project's demands, and had new skills acquired during the first half of the course. They were therefore positioned differently to choose which final project responsibilities to take on than they had been at the beginning of the term. However, in the absence of an explicit discernment process about final project roles as learning opportunities, much of the responsibility and opportunity for constructing the final project fell without deliberation to single group members, often technology experts like Jacob and Melissa. These technically skilled group members collected video and written content from their group mates to put together their groups' written documents and multimedia texts.

Jacob emphasized that putting together his group's final project was a simple act of compilation, because the group's vision for the final project was so cohesive following their face-to-face collaborative design of the project's governing ideas and aesthetic:

> I assembled it, as the technology person, put it all together . . . I was able to just go through different parts of what people had already written, and I was able to quickly summarize what their idea was and just take that and put that into the presentation. Even though I did put the PowerPoint together, it was work I was taking from what they've done.

Melissa's group, however, suffered from conflict during the interview-conducting phase, which resulted in an unclear vision for their project. As a result, her work on the final project involved more than simply combining group members' individually composed texts:

> We each did a portion of the group papers. Then I got kind of stuck in the role of team leader towards the end, so I kind of put it all back together and combined everybody's stuff, and made that final PowerPoint that they showed at the event at the Sharing Night. I had the other girls [members of this all-female group] give me their input and look at it once over at the end, but I kind of put it together.

As Melissa notes, being responsible for combining group members' written and video texts gave her considerable control over her group's final project. This was also true in Jacob's case, although he exercised less of this power because his group already enjoyed such strong consensus. While Melissa's phrasing suggests that she resented bearing the burden of this work, her group mate Denise observed that Melissa did not always trust her group members to fulfill their responsibilities fully or on time, describing Melissa's attitude as "'I have my own schedule, and I have so many things to do that I need to keep on track with my other stuff. And I'm not going to let this group pull me off of my grade in this class, much less throw me off the other things I have to do.'" Similarly, Nia—despite serving as her group's leader rather than its designated technology expert—took responsibility for her group's final project because she wanted to control its quality. Having learned a lot throughout the course about digital composing and multimedia storytelling, Nia edited heavily her groupmates' written and video content to ensure that the project was worthy of parishioners represented in it:

> I did it all. Not that I didn't think they could do it, but I wanted the final presentation to be a tribute to the church. And I didn't trust

anyone else to do that, to really understand how much these people [the interviewees] sacrificed . . .

   Because I think when you have too many people in the pot, it looks somewhat disconnected, or disjointed. And that's not what I wanted. I wanted to make sure that we said the mission, we completed the mission that we wanted to, and that it looked like a cohesive assignment.

Digital literacy functioned as valuable capital within these groups: only members who had sufficient technical expertise could build the final project, giving these group members a unique degree of control over the group's grade and the public presentation they gave at the Community Sharing Night. Especially when the group collaborated less on the final project (as in Melissa's and Nia's cases), the work these technical experts did resulted in them developing their own digital composing expertise at the expense of others' opportunity to learn these skills, despite the fact that this happened organically rather than deliberately.

Using Critical Consciousness and Metacognition to Promote Democratic Digital Literacy Acquisition in Collaborative Projects

These shifts in groups' working structures illustrate concerns about equity of learning opportunity in digital collaborative projects. Some group members exerted more control over the composing task than others, setting and enforcing deadlines and altering others' work to fit the final project. And access to these roles, even as they shifted over time, was significantly shaped by the various kinds of capital—age, experience, time, and personal investment—which were the products of the racial, economic, and gender capital available to different group members. One change that would extend the kind of digital literacy learning experienced by students like Nia, Melissa, and Jacob would be to encourage all group members to advocate for their own learning and to take up roles strategically at points *throughout* the project. To promote such counter-*doxa* investment in digital group projects, I call for additional metacognition and reflection at both the outset and at project turning points to emphasize the unequal distribution of digital literacies in society. This approach expands and reconceptualizes the kind of skill inventory that Sylvia led and Alexander and Wolfe describe.

   Framing opportunities to learn digital literacy skills and assume leadership roles in terms of accumulating valuable cultural capital that students can use to forward their own causes, careers, and projects emphasizes agency in metacognitive exercises like those Sylvia used to structure the project described here. This approach provides a political and social context for the preparation for future writing tasks that Yancey, Robertson, and Taczak argue is necessary for transformative learning processes. Scaffolding collaborative group composing tasks with metacognitive exercises that ask students to consider not just their previous experience and inclinations toward group work, but also their future aspirations would encourage more students to identify and act on the investments and connections that characterized the group members profiled here:

Nia: My sister and I have been thinking of doing some sort of video for my mother's 75th birthday next year . . . I want to incorporate pictures of her as a child and interviews with her grandchildren, her siblings, and other family members. And I don't want it be a video of just interviews. So I know I'm going to incorporate music and maybe other videos. I want to make it this grandiose project.

Melissa: I think if I would want to get my Master's [in nursing] it would probably help me a lot, the technology aspect of it.

Jacob: Lisa and I were talking recently, and I'm working on getting an internship first here in town so then I can from there branch out and look for internships abroad. And the one I'm getting here is with a refugee service in here. And we were talking, "You know if you don't get that internship, you should really look into taking graduate credit here [at the university]."

These students adopted a future orientation that motivated them to engage deeply in the course's digital composing task, combining leadership and technical expertise responsibilities during the final phase of the project. Because they approached the project with self-designated learning goals, these students fared better when it came to taking on major responsibilities in the group and dramatically increasing their digital composing abilities. Asking all students to follow this example of explicitly setting such individual learning goals should augment existing uses of skill inventorying and role selection in the structuring of collaborative digital projects to help them function as opportunities for all students to learn personally, professionally, and civically valuable skills.

Assumption of roles at all points of a digital collaborative project also needs to be contextualized by attention to the inequities created by cultural capital. Although transfer scholars typically frame metacognition in individual terms, students should also be called to consider how *doxa* aligns skills and roles with stereotypes about digital literacy. Metacognition throughout the project should include explicit discussion of the participation gap context in which role uptake decisions are made. The case studies here problematize low-road transfer in ways that go beyond limited individual learning, adding participation gap concerns for members of marginalized groups based on access to learning opportunities in collaborative digital projects. Casting students' prior experience as both expert and novice challenges the idea that only students with pre-existing digital composing and leadership expertise should volunteer for responsibilities, democratizing access to valuable learning experiences. In addition, adapting Yancey, Robertson, and Taczak's "critical incidents" pedagogy of focusing on turning points that challenge or expose the limits of prior knowledge suggests a way to further question the digital literacy *doxa* promoted by the privilege-compounding alignment of prior experience with current project responsibilities. Framing the structuring of group digital composing tasks in terms not just of individual experience and goals but also the wider social context of the participation gap provides an intervention point to promote uptake by individual group members and discourage the replication of existing hierarchies of digital literacy expertise and authority predicated on racial, economic, gender, and age capital. As Elizabeth Wardle argues, using pedagogy to challenge such *doxa* represents one of the most powerful impacts writing instruction can have on students' intellectual, personal, civic, and professional lives. Such critical metacognition recasts the work of project-structuring from mere bureaucracy to a potentially counter-cultural act.

This call to critical socio-technical consciousness can help students be more aware of how cultural capital structures collaborative digital work, shifting how students think of their existing skills and experiences and how they select project responsibilities. And to resist the deficit rhetoric that participation gap research often suggests, this scholarship should be presented alongside research that highlights the long-standing traditions of multimodal and digital composing by people of color (see Baca; Banks; Haas; Medina), women (see Blair, Gajjala, and Tulley; DeLuca), and other groups typically seen as digital divide have-nots. Examining these traditions can help students transfer skills from material and digital cultures they already participate in (but whose salience they may not recognize) by highlighting composing traditions with which students who are placed into participation gap demographic groups can identify.

Acknowledgments

Thank you to the students and teachers of the community-based course this article examines: I deeply appreciate you welcoming me into your class and being so generous with your time and insights. I'm also extremely grateful for the many readers whose feedback shaped this project during its lengthy incubation: Beverly Moss, Cynthia Selfe, Harvey Graff, and Annie Mendenhall at Ohio State; my Santa Clara colleagues in the Writer's Brown Bag workshop and the English Department Shut Up And Write group; my colleagues in the Writing Group of Doom; and two anonymous *Composition Studies* reviewers.

Notes

1. Although Trimbur is primarily concerned with the intellectual conservatism collaboration risks by emphasizing consensus, the tendency to structure groups according to existing social hierarchies on the basis of the "natural" roles suggested by *doxa* poses another threat to collaborative work and learning.

2. Although mobile devices did not factor into this 2011 course (for example, students used instructor-provided Flip video cameras to record interviews, not the cameras on their mobile phones), the repetition of the participation gap in mobile device use illustrates that the capital-based equity issues this piece focuses on persist even as mobile devices increase Internet and digital technology access across racial, economic, gender, and age groups.

3. For example, Lisa Ede and Andrea Lunsford's influential concepts of dialogic and hierarchical collaboration were developed based on workplace coauthorship, and the shifts Kami Day and Michelle Eodice identify between full and partial collaboration were observed in the work of faculty coauthors.

4. The case study instructors, Wolfe and Alexander, do not identify this reflective process explicitly as metacognition. However, the experience inventory they describe (included in the "Team Preparation Worksheet" [Wolfe] and "Project Roles Sheet" [Alexander] that students complete when drawing up their group charter) parallels the techniques of metacognition about prior writing experience found in transfer-oriented writing pedagogies, a link I'm arguing for and expanding on here.

5. Editing digital literacy interviews entailed "cleaning up" the recordings and excising anything interviewees wanted to retract.

6. Students' course grades were based on the final project (group grade), midterm (graded individually), and an individual assessment by the group leader.

7. This platform price disparity persists: 2017 prices for Apple laptops range from $1000-$2800 (see "Laptop Mag"; Loyola "Which Mac"; Piltch), while buyers' guides recommend reliable budget PC laptops or tablet/laptop hybrids in the $300-$650 range (see Murray).

8. For an in-depth discussion of Denise's family history project, see Julia Voss and Lillie R. Jenkins' "Essence of Mom 2.0: Media, Memory, and Community across an Extended African-American Family," forthcoming in Cruz Medina and Octavio Pimentel's *Racial Shorthand: Coded Discrimination Contested in Social Media*.

9. While such multimodal texts have become increasingly common in writing curricula over the past five years, few students in this 2011 course had ever produced such a document. My focus here is on how groups navigated novel digital composing tasks rather than on the specifics of the technologies involved. On this conceptual basis, I offer recommendations for democratizing learning opportunities in digital collaborative projects, rather than discussing how best to teach specific digital composing skills, which change as rapidly as technology changes.

Appendix

The research described here was conducted in 2011-2012 as part of a larger study (including two other sites, a first-year writing class and scholars composing multimodal pieces for a digital edited collection) examining how individuals access material and rhetorical resources to compose digital texts. Specifically, the study investigated how resources gained through contexts influenced by cultural capital (such as family, peer, affinity group, and professional spheres) shape the emergent organizational dynamics in collaborative digital projects and how different methods of labor distribution promote and/or discourage individual members' digital literacy learning. I gathered data using participant observation in the classroom during the term, an online questionnaire administered after the course ended, and a follow-up interview in which I asked students to elaborate on their questionnaire responses. Scripts are available online for questionnaire (https://goo.gl/DpyJLX) and follow-up interview (https://goo.gl/VdMdAK). The quotations incorporated here draw on interviews, but the analysis is informed by all three phases of data collection.

Works Cited

Alexander, Kara Poe. "Collaborative Composing: Practices and Strategies for Implementing Team Projects into Writing Classrooms." *Collaborative Learning and Writing: Essays on Using Small Groups in Teaching English and Composition*, edited by Kathleen M. Hunzer, Mcfarland, 2012, pp. 181-200.

Baca, Damián. *Mestiz@ Scripts, Digital Migrations, and the Territories of Writing*. Palgrave Macmillan, 2008.

Banks, Adam. *Race, Rhetoric, and Technology: Searching for Higher Ground*. NCTE, 2006.

Berry, Patrick W., Gail E. Hawisher, and Cynthia L. Selfe. *Transnational Literate Lives in Digital Times*. Computers and Composition Digital P/Utah State UP, 2012, ccdigitalpress.org/transnational/.

Blair, Kristine, Radhika Gajjala, and Christine Tulley. *Webbing Cyberfeminist Practice: Communities, Pedagogies, and Social Action*. Hampton P, 2008.

Bourdieu, Pierre. "The Forms of Capital." *Handbook of Theory and Research in the Sociology of Education*, edited by John G. Richardson. Greenwood P, 1986, pp. 241-58.

—. *Outline of a Theory of Practice*. Trans. Richard Rice. Cambridge UP, 1977.

Brake, David R. "Are We All Online Content Creators Now? Web 2.0 and Digital Divides." *Journal of Computer-Mediated Communication*, vol. 19 no. 3, April 2014, pp. 591-609.

Carrington, Vicki, and Allan Luke. "Literacy and Bourdieu's Sociological Theory: A Reframing." *Language and Education*, vol. 11, no. 2, 1997, pp. 96-112.

CCCC. "CCCC Position Statement on Teaching, Learning, and Assessing Writing in Digital Environments." *CCCC*, Feb. 2004, www.ncte.org/cccc/resources/positions/digitalenvironments.

Critel, Genevieve. "Remixing the Digital Divide: Minority Women's Digital Literacy Practices in Academic Spaces." *Stories That Speak to Us: Exhibits from the Digital Archive of Literacy Narratives*, edited by H. Lewis Ulman, Scott Lloyd DeWitt, and Cynthia L. Selfe, Computers and Composition Digital P/Utah State UP, 2013, http://ccdigitalpress.org/stories/chapters/critel/.

Cummings, Richard E., and Matt Barton, editors. *Wiki Writing: Collaborative Learning in the College Classroom*. Michigan UP, 2008.

Day, Kami, and Michele Eodice. *(First Person)²: A Study of Co-Authoring in the Academy*. Utah State UP, 2001.

DeLuca, Katherine M. "'Can We Block these Political Thingys? I Just want to get f*cking recipes?' Women's Ethos and Politics on Pinterest." *Kairos*, vol. 19, no. 3, Summer 2015, http://kairos.technorhetoric.net/19.3/topoi/deluca/index.html.

Duffy, William. "Collaboration (in) Theory: Reworking the Social Turn's Conversational Imperative." *College English*, vol. 76, no. 5, May 2014, pp. 416-35.

Ede, Lisa, and Andrea Lunsford. *Singular Texts/Plural Authors: Perspectives on Collaborative Writing*. SIUP, 1990.

Haas, Angela M. "Wampum as Hypertext: An American Indian Intellectual Tradition of Multimedia Theory and Practice." *Studies in American Indian Literatures*, vol. 19, no. 4, Winter 2007, pp. 77-100.

Hargittai, Eszter. "The Digital Reproduction of Inequality." *Social Stratification*, edited by David Grusky, Westview P, 2008, pp. 936-44.

Hargittai, Eszter, and Aaron Shaw. "Mind the Skills Gap: The Role of Internet Know-How and Gender in Differentiated Contributions to Wikipedia." *Information, Communication & Society*, vol. 18, no.4, April 2015, pp. 424-42.

Hargittai, Eszter, and Gina Walejko. "The Participation Divide: Content Creation and Sharing in the Digital Age." *Information, Communication & Society*, vol. 11, no. 2, March 2008, pp. 239-56.

Hart Research Associates. *Falling Short? College Learning and Career Success Selected Findings from Online Surveys of Employers and College Students Conducted on Behalf of the Association of American Colleges & Universities*, 20 Jan. 2015, www.aacu.org/sites/default/files/files/LEAP/2015employerstudentsurvey.pdf.

—. *Raising The Bar: Employers' Views On College Learning In The Wake Of The Economic Downturn. A Survey Among Employers Conducted On Behalf Of: The Association Of American Colleges And Universities*, 20 Jan. 2010, www.aacu.org/sites/default/files/files/LEAP/2009_EmployerSurvey.pdf.

—. *Summary of Existing Research on Attitudes Toward Liberal Education Outcomes for the Association of American Colleges and Universities*. Aug. 2004, www.aacu.org/sites/default/files/files/LEAP/HartExistingResearchReport.pdf.

Janangelo, Joseph. "Intricate Inscriptions: Negotiating Conflict between Collaborative Writers." *Journal of Teaching Writing*, vol. 15, no. 1, 1996, pp. 91-105.

Jenkins, Henry, with Katie Clinton, Ravi Purushotma, Alice J. Robison, and Margaret Weigel. *Confronting the Challenges of Participatory Culture: Media Educa-*

tion for the 21st Century. MacArthur Foundation/MIT P, 2009, mitpress.mit.edu/sites/default/files/titles/free_download/9780262513623_Confronting_the_Challenges.pdf.

Kennedy, Krista, and Rebecca Moore Howard. "Collaborative Writing." *A Guide to Composition Pedagogies*, 2nd ed, edited by Gary Tate, et al., Oxford UP, 2013, pp. 37-54.

Kittle, Peter, and Troy Hicks. "Transforming the Group Paper with Collaborative Online Writing." *Pedagogy*, vol. 9, no. 3, Fall 2009, pp. 525-38.

Kuh, George. "High-Impact Educational Practices: What They Are, Who Has Access to Them, and Why They Matter." *Association of American Colleges & Universities*, 30 Sep. 2008, secure.aacu.org/store/detail.aspx?id=E-HIGHIMP.

Laptop Mag Editorial Staff. "Apple: Best and Worst Laptop Brands." *Laptop Mag*, 10 Apr. 2017, https://www.laptopmag.com/articles/apple-brand-rating.

Loyola, Roman. "Buying guide: Macs (2011)." *Macworld*, 21 Nov. 2011, www.macworld.com/article/1163603/mac_buying_guide_2011.html.

—. "Which Mac Should You Buy?" *Macworld*, 29 Nov. 2016, https://www.macworld.com/article/2018990/macs/buying-guide-2012-macs.html.

Medina, Cruz. "Tweeting Collaborative Identity: Race, ICTs, and Tweeting Latinidad." *Communicating Race, Ethnicity, and Identity in Technical Communication*, edited by Miriam F. Williams and Octavio Pimentel, Baywood, 2014, pp. 63-86.

Medina, Cruz, and Octavio Pimentel, editors. *Racial Shorthand: Coded Discrimination Contested in Social Media*, Computers and Composition Digital P/Utah State UP, forthcoming.

Monroe, Barbara. *Crossing the Digital Divide: Race, Writing, and Technology in the Classroom,* Teachers College P, 2004.

Morgan, Meg. "Women as Emergent Leaders in Student Collaborative Writing Groups." *JAC* vol. 14, no.1, January 1994, pp. 203-19.

Murray, Matthew. "The Best Cheap Laptops of 2017." *Laptop Mag*, 28 Sep. 2017, https://www.pcmag.com/article2/0,2817,2371334,00.asp.

Nakamura, Lisa, and Peter Chow-White, editors. *Race After the Internet*. Routledge, 2011.

Napoli, Philip M., and Jonathan A. Obar. "The Emerging Mobile Internet Underclass: A Critique of Mobile Internet Access." *The Information Society*, vol. 30, no. 5, 2014, pp. 323-34.

NCTE. "Position Statement on Multimodal Literacies." *NCTE*, Nov. 2005, www.ncte.org/positions/statements/21stcentdefinition.

—. "The NCTE Definition of 21st Century Literacies." *NCTE*, Feb. 2013, www.ncte.org/positions/statements/21stcentdefinition.

Nowacek, Rebecca Schoenike, and Kenna del Sol. "Making Space for Collaboration: Physical Context and Role Taking in Two Singing and Songwriting Groups." *Writing Groups Inside and Outside the Classroom*, edited by Beverly J. Moss, Nels P. Highberg, and Melissa Nichols, Lawrence Erlbaum, 2004, pp. 169-86.

Pearce, Katy E., and Ronald E. Rice. "Digital Divide from Access to Activities: Comparing Mobile and Personal Computer Internet Users." *Journal of Communication*, vol. 63, no. 4, August 2013, pp. 721-44.

Pedersen, Anne-Marie, and Carolyn Skinner. "Collaborating on Multimodal Projects." *Multimodal Composition: Resources for Teachers*, edited by Cynthia L. Selfe, Hampton P, 2007, pp. 39-47.

Piltch, Avram. "Average Price of Laptop Now Just $8 More Than iPad." *Laptop Mag.* 26 Apr. 2012, www.laptopmag.com/articles/the-average-pc-laptop-cost-507-in-march.

Reiff, Mary Jo, and Anis Bawarshi. "Tracing Discursive Resources: How Students Use Prior Genre Knowledge to Negotiate New Writing Contexts in First-Year Composition." *Written Communication*, vol. 28, no. 3, July 2011, pp. 312-37.

Restaino, Jessica. "Writing Together: An Arendtian Framework for Collaboration." *Composition Forum*, vol. 30, Fall 2014, compositionforum.com/issue/30/writing-together.php.

Robertson, Liane, Kara Taczak, and Kathleen Blake Yancey. "Notes toward a Theory of Prior Knowledge and Its Role in College Composers' Transfer of Knowledge and Practice." *Composition Forum*, vol. 26, Fall 2012, compositionforum.com/issue/26/prior-knowledge-transfer.php.

Rounsaville, Angela, Goldberg, Rachel, and Anis Bawarshi. "From Incomes to Outcomes: FYW Students' Prior Genre Knowledge, Meta-Cognition, and the Question of Transfer." *WPA*, vol. 32, no. 1, 2008, pp. 97-112.

Sayers, Jentery. "Tinker-Centric Pedagogy in Literature and Language Classrooms." *Collaborative Approaches to the Digital in English Studies*, edited by Laura McGrath, Computers and Composition Digital P/Utah State UP, 2011, ccdigitalpress.org/cad/Ch10_Sayers.pdf.

Scenters-Zapico, John. *Generaciones' Narratives: The Pursuit and Practice of Traditional and Electronic Literacies on the U.S.-Mexico Borderlands*. Computers and Composition Digital P/Utah State UP, 2010, ccdigitalpress.org/generaciones/.

Schradie, Jen. "The Digital Production Gap: The Digital Divide and Web 2.0 Collide." *Poetics*, vol. 39, no. 2, April 2011, pp. 145-68.

—. "The Trend of Class, Race, and Ethnicity in Social Media Inequality: Who Still Cannot Afford to Blog?" *Information, Communication & Society*, vol. 15, no. 4, 2012, pp. 555-71.

Shirley, Dennis. "A Critical Review and Appropriation of Pierre Bourdieu's Analysis of Social and Cultural Reproduction." *Journal of Education*, vol. 168, no. 2, 1986, pp. 96-112.

Spigelman, Candace. *Across Property Lines: Textual Ownership in Writing Groups*. SIUP, 2000.

Swartz, David. "Pierre Bourdieu: The Cultural Transmission of Social Inequality." *Harvard Educational Review*, vol. 47, no. 4, Dec. 1977, 545-55.

Tebo-Messina, Margaret. *Collaborative Learning in the College Writing Workshop: Two Case Studies of Peer Group Development*. 1987. SUNY Albany, PhD dissertation.

Trimbur, John. "Consensus and Difference in Collaborative Learning." *College English*, vol. 51, no. 6, 1989, pp. 602-16.

Voss, Julia, and Lillie R. Jenkins. "Essence of Mom 2.0: Media, Memory, and Community across an Extended African-American Family." *Racial Shorthand: Coded*

Discrimination Contested in Social Media, editors Cruz Medina and Octavio Pimentel, Computers and Composition Digital P/Utah State UP, forthcoming.

Wardle, Elizabeth. "Creative Repurposing for Expansive Learning: Considering 'Problem-Exploring' and 'Answer-Getting' Dispositions in Individuals and Fields." *Composition Forum,* vol. 26, Fall 2012, compositionforum.com/issue/26/creative-repurposing.php.

Watkins, S. Craig. "Digital Divide: Navigating the Digital Edge." *International Journal of Learning and Media*, vol. 3, no. 2, 2011, pp. 1-12.

Wolfe, Joanna. *Team Writing: A Guide to Working in Groups*. Bedford/St. Martin's, 2009.

Wolfe, Joanna, and Kara Poe Alexander. "The Computer Expert in Mixed-Gendered Collaborative Writing Groups." *Journal of Business and Technical Communication*, vol. 19, no. 2, 2005, pp. 135-70.

Yancey, Kathleen Blake, Liane Robertson, and Kara Taczak. *Writing across Contexts: Transfer, Composition, and Sites of Writing*. Utah State UP, 2014.

Designing, Building, and Connecting Networks to Support Distributed Collaborative Empirical Writing Research

Beth Brunk-Chavez, Stacey Pigg, Jessie Moore, Paula Rosinski, and Jeffrey T. Grabill

To speak to diverse audiences about how people learn to write and how writing works inside and outside the academy, we must conduct research across geographical, institutional, and cultural contexts as well as research that enables comparison when appropriate. Large-scale empirical research is useful for both of these moves; however, we must consider how writing studies prepares us to conduct such research. Reflecting on our experience, we understand that the important research negotiations that enabled our research to scale can be described through the language of designing, building, and connecting networks. By designing networks, we refer to the moments of imagining and planning the possible shape of a network. By building networks, we refer to making or designing the conditions or support structures needed to achieve a particular network design. Finally, by connecting networks, we refer to realizing the linkages that establish new communicative objects that can move forward and perform some kind of work.

"As when a body undermines its own immune system, when college composition as a whole treats the data-gathering, data-validating, and data-aggregating part of itself as alien, then the whole may be doomed. Even now, the profession's immune system—its ability to deflect outside criticism with solid and ever-strengthening data—is on shaky pins. It lacks a "systematically produced knowledge" (Carr & Kemmis, 1986, p. 8) to defend its central practices from outside attack, lacks a coherent body of testable knowledge connected to class size, computer pedagogy, group work, part-time teaching, interdisciplinary instruction, 1st year sequenced syllabi, and the list can go on."

—Richard Haswell (2005)

More than a decade later, Richard Haswell's call for "solid and ever-strengthening data" continues to highlight the need for writing studies to produce research that can speak persuasively to diverse audiences. Joanne Addison and Sharon James McGee similarly call for "an expanded view of how best to accomplish our varied missions as we help students negotiate literacy demands in the academy and beyond" (169). To achieve these goals, writing studies must conduct research that seeks to understand how writing is learned and practiced across geographical, institutional, and cultural contexts both inside and outside the academy as well as research that enables comparison when appropriate. Large-scale empirical research is useful for both of these moves.

Similar to the Stanford Study of Writing, "a national comparative study of student errors" (Lunsford and Lunsford); the Citation Project, "a multi-institutional research [project concerning] plagiarism, information literacy, and the teaching of source-based writing" ("What Is the Citation?"); and the Meaningful Writing Project, "a cross-institutional study in which college seniors reflect on their meaningful writing experiences" ("What Is the Meaningful?"), the Revisualizing Composition (RC) research group developed a multi-phase, multi-institution and multi-year research project that analyzed what college students write, why they write, where they write, what technologies they use, and how they value their writing. The project, which we believe to be beneficial for enabling new research questions, pedagogical innovations, and informed policies, focuses on practical, personal, interpersonal, community, workplace, and classroom writing experiences and attempts to provide the field with the most comprehensive snapshot possible of the writing lives of students inside and outside the classroom at the moment the project was conducted. As we designed and conducted the RC project, we considered:

- How can we research students' writing when we understand it to be persistent and embedded within various and far-reaching experiences, inside and outside the classroom?
- How do we balance a new sense of writing's breadth with the field's historical need for contextual depth to account for the highly situated nature of literate practice and development?
- What models of collaboration and infrastructure can best support inquiries that are both large-scale and sufficiently local?

The task of aggregating this comprehensive snapshot of writing exceeded our capacities as individual researchers situated within individual institutions of higher education. Thus, the RC project team needed to develop and employ explicit collaborative structures and processes to enable large data set research across multiple, diverse, and geographically distant institutions.

To do this, we looked to a robust literature that encourages writing studies to abandon the myth of the individual author or genius (Sullivan) and embrace and better theorize collaborative writing in personal practices and institutional value systems (Ede and Lunsford; McNenny and Roen; Yancey and Spooner).

In 1992, Duane H. Roen and Robert K. Mittan extend what had been a longstanding interest in collaborative writing in the field (Ede and Lunsford; Trimbur) toward a more overt focus on collaborative research. Roen and Mittan argue for understanding collaborative writing and research as intertwined with collaborators representing diverse roles and thus participating as various kinds of audiences when interpreting data and drafts. Advancing Roen and Mittan's ideas, Paul Benjamin Lowry, Aaron Curtis, and Michelle Rene Lowry's useful taxonomy and nomenclature of collaborative writing identifies collaborative writing activities, document control modes, roles, software products, strategies, and work modes as relevant variables of collaborative writing processes. Work in technical communication such as that by Marie Paretti, Lisa McNair, and Lissa Holloway-Attaway encourages us to implement pedagogies that reflect an increasing globalization "enabled by a dynamic network of communication technologies" (328). They contend that students will eventually work in "flexible communities of practice" that "call all workers to continually adapt to and communicate with new colleagues, negotiate new organizational structures, and learn new skills" (328) and that it is incumbent upon instructors to help students navigate this collaborative, shifting, distributed environment. As Mary P. Sheridan and Lee Nickoson suggest in their recent introduction to *Writing Studies Research in Practice*, collaborative research is increasingly normalized and persistent across research journals and books in writing studies as scholars find value in collaborative writing and research as "a feminist practice," as "an ethical move," and as "the engine that drives the research project in the first place" (8).

However, while such scholarship from across writing studies points to the importance of preparing for and conducting collaborations, writing studies research has not sufficiently addressed the rhetorical practices that are foundational to the myriad moments of collaborative empirical writing research. How are we to go about actually planning, designing, and implementing collaborative studies? We seek to fill this gap by envisioning collaborative large-scale empirical research processes as iterative cycles of networking and putting writing studies' collaborations in conversation with burgeoning studies of multi-institutional research collaborations in the sciences (e.g., Corley, Boardman, and Bozeman; Chompalov, Genuth, and Shrum; Katz and Martin; and Cummings and Kiesler).

By networking, we mean strategic acts that design, build, and connect people and materials to produce objects taken up in later research stages. Understanding collaborative research processes through networked lenses enables writing studies to name and describe meaningful research process moments often overlooked in discussions about how to create reliable and valid empirical findings. In moments such as developing sustainable team relationships, building communication platforms, and coming to agreement about interpretations, research teams undertake negotiations that affect whether findings will have relevance in ongoing public and disciplinary conversations. To illustrate what we mean by this vocabulary, we draw on descriptions of the RC project. While we do not claim to be the first writing studies team to engage in similar research processes (and we would further gesture to platforms such as the REx, or Research Exchange Index, designed to facilitate such processes), we are not aware of writing studies scholarship that provides a vocabulary for identifying and naming the rhetorical moments, practices, and arrangements that are central to carrying out large-scale, distributed collaborative research. Furthermore, our example points to particular network shapes or arrangements of teams, data sets, interpretations, and contributions well-suited to teaching and practicing multi-institutional collaborative research.

Networked Research Processes

In *Keywords for Writing Studies* Jason Swarts explains how the term "network" offers generative conceptual grounding for writing studies. Drawing on social theorist Manuel Castells, Swarts introduces the idea of a network as a "set of interconnected nodes" (Castells qtd. in Swarts 120), which may be either "conventional" as in the case of computer servers or "heterogeneous" in assembling different kinds of "components" (120). Particularly useful for writing studies, Swarts suggests, has been to use the term "network" to name interconnected nodes that establish settings, objects, or infrastructures where connections stimulate "a 'feedback loop' spurring the continued innovation, development, distribution, and integration of information generating, processing, and networking technologies into the world around us" (120-1). In short, networks can be "thing-like" or "place-like" objects or settings established through the interconnection of different kinds of components (Swarts 120).

Collaborative research processes continually build upon and produce what Swarts refers to as these "thing-like" or "place-like" networks of interconnection that require networking practices to establish and sustain them. For example, consider the language Lisa Ede and Andrea Lunsford use to describe activities that sustained the work practices of well-known collaborative teams such as the iText working group or Carnegie Mellon's Community Literacy Center. In such cases, Ede and Lunsford suggest

> a group of humanities researchers has come together to identify an issue or problem of shared interest or concern, drawn up plans for addressing the issue from different perspectives and areas of expertise, and begun the hard work of carrying out those plans (362).

Through the lenses that we have just described, we might imagine the initial act of "com[ing] together" as a networking practice designed to forge a new interconnected space: the "issue or problem of shared interest of concern." After this stage of interconnecting, it would then be necessary to aggregate ideas and interpretations to "draw up plans" that bring together "different perspectives and areas of expertise." Though Ede and Lunsford do not detail what "carrying out those plans" looks like in practice, we can imagine that these implementations would require further spaces of interconnection forged through bringing together multiple potentially disparate texts and objects. Establishing aggregated interconnections is central to making products or objects—the deliverables—that characterize collaborative research at every stage.

Beyond the commonplace stages of empirical research (design and plan, collect data, analyze data, report results), thinking of research as a networking process draws our attention to the ongoing rhetorical negotiations that bring together disparate objects and viewpoints. Conceiving of research as ongoing rhetorical negotiations, rather than a linear attempt of steps that continually seek to objectively represent nature aligns well with a critical research stance (Sullivan and Porter). However, while a critical lens suggests that research is (or should be) messier than a set of identifiable linear stages, there is also usefulness to identifying, naming, and articulating research stages. Clearly describing moments of practice enables us to divide a complex process into manageable practices that can be explained, examined, and taught. Here we suggest that new divisions and articulations of research practice can make explicit what is largely tacit in the practice of collaborative research while emphasizing important rhetorical negotiations that take place along the way.

Reflecting on our experience with RC, we understand that the negotiations that enabled our research to scale can be described through the language of designing, building, and connecting networks. To be more specific, by designing networks we refer to the moments of imagining and planning the possible shape of a network. By building networks, we refer to making or designing the conditions or support structures needed to exist in order to achieve a particular network design. Finally, by connecting networks, we refer to realizing the linkages that establish new objects that can move forward and perform some kind of work.

Figure 1 illustrates four moments and four corresponding objects aggregated during collaborative research processes in which the cycles of designing, building, and connecting networks are particularly important. Collaborative researchers in writing studies can design, build, and connect networks during planning to create particular kinds of teams during data collection to create particular kinds of data sets, during data analysis to create particular kinds of interpretations, and during the dissemination of results in order to create particular kinds of contributions. These objects, in turn, participate in future research and interpretation stages in which their arrangement—their network shape—influences the possibilities for action. Designing, building, and connecting networks is particularly challenging in collaborative research that attempts to account for large-scale writing practices and populations. We now address how these processes affect each moment of research design we have identified, drawing on RC to offer illustrative details.

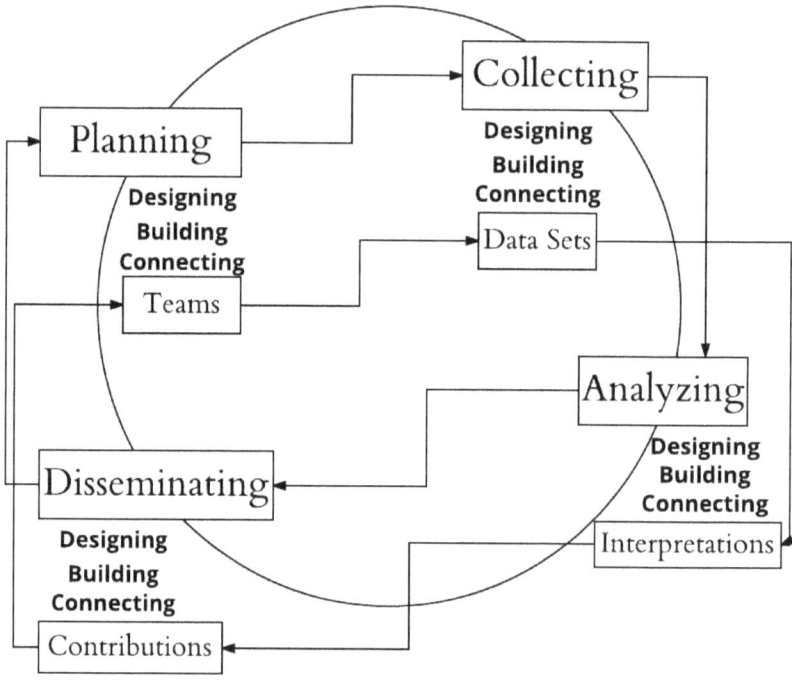

Figure 1. Moments and objects within collaborative research process.

Planning: The Rhetorical Work of Assembling Teams

Planning stages of research typically include forming research questions and conducting literature reviews. For distributed collaborative research, planning additionally includes designing, building, and connecting teams. Designing teams focuses on how the particular arrangement or network shape of a collaborative team significantly impacts the kind of collaboration that can take place, what kinds of technologies will be needed to facilitate that arrangement, and what kinds of authorship will be likely in the future. Building teams focuses on assembling the technologies and practices that enable ongoing multidirectional communication that corresponds to and facilitates the team design. Finally, connecting teams involves the communication between the collaborators that establishes shared goals and directions and defines everyone's roles. Building on Roen and Mittan's observation that the unique expertise assembled by different collaborators directly affects the potential for team knowledge generation, we now use the example of our project to discuss the rhetorical work of assembling teams.

Designing a Team's Network Shape

The collaborative research project discussed here began in 2008 when researchers at the Writing in Digital Environments (WIDE) Research Center at Michigan State University (MSU) realized the need for writing studies to provide "better (and supported) accounts of college student writing that will allow us to respond to claims being made in the popular media and in our field's scholarship" (Project Update 2/5/2010). There was renewed public interest about the cultural and social meanings of new forms of networked writing, but little data was available to adequately address those questions. WIDE researchers began discussing how to design an organizational model, or network shape that would help us understand what kinds of writing are prevalent and valuable to college students.

The hub-and-cluster, or hub-and-spoke, network shape that the RC network chose for its organizational structure is commonly utilized in disciplines such as economics and computing sciences that manage large amounts of data and information. Business clusters, for example, share large datasets to understand customer behavior as well as transportation and knowledge management costs to operate more efficiently. In this research model the hub acts as a centralized location, or core, for organizing interactions and materials, while the clusters or spokes engage in data collection and analysis depending upon expertise, availability, and location. Pooling knowledge or expertise, bridging space, saving time, increasing innovation, and taking advantage of economies of scale are a few of the benefits of this organizational research model (Boja).

RC adopted the hub-and-cluster organizational research model as a way to answer research questions that require both local and broadly informed data. We were especially interested in pooling data from our individual institutions, which were diverse in terms of institution type, geographic location, and student demographics, as well as utilizing a model that would allow each of us to capitalize on our scholarly and institutional expertise.

Our colleagues at MSU acted as the hub in our model (see fig. 2). Located at a Research I institution, they possessed the resources to design the online survey and data-collection database, provide statistical support for data analysis, and maintain organizational memory through a data repository that created the possibility for sustaining a large project over time. As will be shown in detail, the hub-and-cluster model both enabled and influenced our approaches to selecting and inviting research partners, establishing research questions, designing research instruments, selecting research participants, collecting and analyzing data, writing up the results, disseminating our data and conclusion, and determining the next steps. In general, the hub-and-cluster model allowed individual researchers to remain semi-autonomous and to shape the research to the needs and contexts of their institutions, which ranged from very high research activity universities to community colleges.

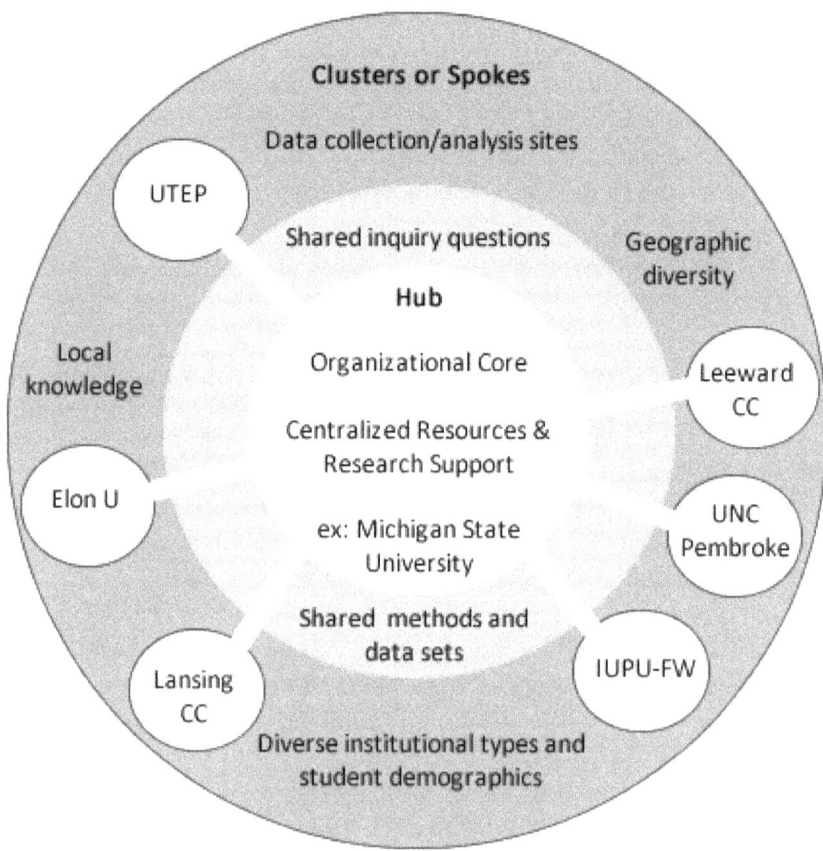

Figure 2. Hub-and-Cluster Model for Revisualizing Composition.

Building a Team's Foundation

During the planning stage, the hub's role was to begin the conversation, provide the infrastructure for communication, establish the baseline goals, draft the survey instrument, and provide the initial documentation required to conduct research on individual campuses. The clusters' roles were to finalize the research goals and survey, work with local IRB offices, and consider which and how survey participants would be recruited.

As Andrea Lunsford and Karen Lunsford note, the effects of an "expanded and non-collaborative IRB system [can be] chilling" (787). Therefore, one of the hub's goals was to mitigate or manage elements of research that typically become barriers to multi-institutional collaboration. In order to streamline the process of obtaining institutional approval, we designed the project as a "one IRB study." As the hub of this project, WIDE submitted to MSU's IRB office a protocol detailing a survey to be administered through the hub. Participating researchers from each institution were entered into MSU's system as "guest researchers" and received training through the national Collaborative Institutional Training Initiative, or CITI, program. Once the protocol, instruments, and researchers had been approved at MSU, researchers from each institution were able to inform their local review boards about the research and its prior approval at the hub institution. To assist with the local authorization agreements, WIDE researchers created documents for each of the cluster researchers to share with their local IRBs, and each participating institution was willing to accept MSU as the IRB of record.

Connecting a Team's Members

A year after the RC project's inception, emails were sent to potential research collaborators explaining the goals of the project and gauging interest in participation. Collaborators were identified based on three criteria: research interests, institutional type and location, and collaborative experience and effectiveness. During the initial conference call, we explored the study in general, including the theories and research that were foundational to the project and the procedures and timeframes we hoped to follow. We discussed roles and responsibilities of the researchers given that this research project would be unusual to those of us trained in the humanities. We also began a conversation about the role of WIDE as the hub that would set and monitor goals and deadlines, the need for researchers to develop a shared sense of the team, and processes the team would follow to meet goals and deadlines. Team members understood that at the very least, they were asked to assist in data collection. The level of participation in interpreting and disseminating the data was negotiable depending on interest, motivation, and flexibility. The hub-and-cluster model allowed for varying levels of participation without slowing down or significantly altering the project. Attention to these connecting activities from the beginning countered the correlation Jonathon Cummings and Sara Kiesler found from their study of 491 research collaborations in the sciences in which increasing the number of participating institutions predicts fewer outcomes for the collaborations.

Collecting and Analyzing: The Rhetorical Work of Assembling Datasets and Interpretations

Discussions of best practices for data analysis and interpretation (such as Peter Smagorinsky's discussion of collaborative coding practices [401]) frequently invoke the importance of drawing upon multiple kinds of expertise while developing interpretations. In our discussion of the expansive negotiations of collaborative data collection and analysis, designing data sets highlights the importance of working with a collaborative team to imagine the potential shape or arrangement of a data sample. Building data sets focuses on building the technologies and practices that enable access to data and its eventual archiving. Connecting data sets refers to assembling that data into a sample for analysis. We continue by considering the unique work of analyzing collaborative data. Designing interpretations refers to imagining the arrangement or network shape of interpretation processes (i.e., deciding how to discuss and negotiate). Building interpretations focuses once more on building the technologies and practices that enable exchange of readings, direct manipulation of data, and the ability to come to shared understandings about meanings. Finally, connecting interpretations refers to the acts that bring those interpretations together. This section will discuss two phases of data collection: surveys and case studies.

Designing a Data Set

To create a baseline understanding of college students' writing practices and values, the RC group determined that the first phase of our research would consist of a large-scale survey study of college students across the country. The hub-and-cluster model of collaboration was instrumental to the survey research because it created a way to address sampling issues more systematically than, for example, distributing a survey through disciplinary listservs. Because the clusters/collaborators in the research network had access to diverse student populations, we were able to form a sampling strategy that allowed us to survey a diverse demographic population and achieve a defensible sample of the undergraduate student population in the United States.

The findings from the survey raised questions about rhetorical context and value that were difficult to explain with the available data and therefore created an exigence for continued research. Furthermore, while our survey provided the clusters with ways to address local, situated contexts, case study research enabled us to look more closely at the writing lives of students and how their writing practices were made meaningful locally.

Several institutions were not able to continue with the case study research, which left the hub and two clusters to continue with this phase. This flexibility in commitment to long-term research is another advantage of the hub-and-cluster collaborative model. Because we had a centralized organizational hub, the data collection continued even when several researchers could not.

Building a Data Set

The hub-and-cluster model allowed for some autonomy at the cluster level when it came to the procedures used for building data sets via recruiting student survey participants. That autonomy was important because the local cultures of each institution and the kinds of writing courses was diverse. Thus, we concluded that the clusters would identify their research sample; four of the institutions chose to recruit participants directly from first-year writing courses or a writing-intensive first-year seminar, and three institutions asked writing instructors to send the survey link to their writing classes of any kind. All participants were directed to the hub's centralized online platform that hosted the survey and aggregated the results.

As we began phase two, the case study research, we discussed the kinds of data needed to answer our research questions and again depended on the hub to build the data set. Now supported by an undergraduate student researcher, the hub modified the IRB and developed a new recruitment strategy that the cluster teams adapted to the context of their institution and student population. To triangulate data, we identified three data collection instruments: the original survey, short-message-service (SMS) prompts and responses at regular intervals, and daily online diaries. Because the software and collection process was complex enough that none of the individual researchers could develop it independently, the hub's programmer created, tested, and then provided the mechanisms that would collect it and constructed a database to aggregate the data.

Connecting a Data Set

To illustrate how the research clusters supported by a hub enabled us to draw on and manage a large and fairly diverse population, we turn to the demographics of our participants. Of the 1,366 students who completed the survey (representing a completion rate of 65%): 394 were from the University of Texas at El Paso (UTEP), 388 were from MSU, 191 were from the University of North Carolina at Pembroke, 158 students were from Elon University, 100 were from Lansing Community College, 81 students were from Indiana University-Purdue University, and 54 were from Leeward Community College. Our participants were primarily (90%) in the 18-23 age range. In terms of racial diversity, 43% of the sample was non-white, with 28% Hispanic, 8% Asian, 5% Black, and 2% Native American.

For the case study phase, the clusters recruited students in ways that best aligned with their local context. For example, at both MSU and UTEP, fliers for the study were posted in locations likely to attract the attention of undergraduate writers. Once students expressed interest via email, the local researcher contacted them with more information about the study. In contrast, at Elon University, researchers asked writing instructors to distribute prepared email invitations to classes, knowing that students at their institution are more likely to participate in a research project if invited by a faculty member.

Because we did not have even participation across the students who took part in the SMS and diary data collection, our team needed to be systematic in how we created a small sample of case studies to analyze (Pigg, et al.). After the SMS and diary data was collected, a participant profile was created for each student, and depending on site-specific contexts, the undergraduate researcher and a local cluster researcher examined the thoroughness of student responses to determine which students would be appropriate for interviews. Once the interviewees were identified and recruited, the student researcher collaborated with the clusters to create interview questions specific to each student's SMS data that would be asked along with the "standard" questions determined by the research network. While this sample included only a fraction of the survey participants, the kind of data collected required a robust centralized system that was best managed by a hub with the resources and expertise to do so.

Designing Interpretations

As the survey data became available, the RC group considered how to approach both individual and collaborative analysis. During the planning stages, our research group agreed to make the data available to any member for individual or institutional research. However, we had also agreed to conduct collaborative analyses that we intended to publish as an entry to scholarly and public conversations about contemporary writing practices. As mentioned above, the hub-and-cluster model enabled us to sustain the work of interpretation when the network was reduced to the hub and two four-year institutions. Ultimately, the RC team agreed to publish a white paper authored by everyone participating in the first phase of research; a journal article co-authored by many, but not all of those in the original research network; a second journal article co-authored by the researchers involved in the second phase of research; and several conference presentations.

Building Interpretations

Because the survey gave us the opportunity to use statistical analysis to answer the research questions and because the data was centralized at MSU, it was expedient for us to work with a statistical consultant from MSU's Center for Statistical Training and Consulting to make sense of the large amount of data generated. The consultant, Paul Curran, who is listed as a co-author on the publications, first created a Statistical Package for the Social Sciences database so we could run descriptive statistics for frequencies that helped us understand what students are writing most often and the types of writing they most highly value. Curran also aided in more sophisticated statistical analysis (some seventy tables) that correlated student responses to the kinds of writing they did most frequently with both gender and institution type as well as how the frequency of their writing correlates to the kinds of writing they most value. A memo outlining "a useful process for wading through the data" was provided for those of us not fully adept at reading and analyzing this type of research. Additionally, Curran was available for frequent consultations at the hub, via email for researchers at the clusters as well as included on phone conferences during which the researchers discussed the data. Because this consulting work occurred in a centralized location and was shared across multi-institutional participants, the team developed evolving collaborative understandings of the data as we participated in conference calls to discuss the statistical analyses.

For the case study research, the hub again provided assistance with the survey and diary data. The interviews, however, were handled by the clusters. Each cluster team performed and recorded the interviews and then uploaded the audio and de-identified transcribed interviews to our password-protected shared Dropbox account. Each researcher then read all interviews, commented on them, and made observations that were summarized in multiple research memos to the RC group and then discussed during conference calls and face-to-face meetings at national conferences. The researchers took turns working individually, in pairs, and then in different pairs to sort through and analyze the data.

Connecting Interpretations

Once the RC group understood how to read the survey data, the research team was asked to "sort, group, and start forming" plausible claims from our statistical analyses that could be translated into "storylines." By storylines, we meant findings that would be meaningful both to academics across disciplines and levels as well as to the public. At this point, we continued to be interested both in storylines that could be published collaboratively as well as findings that individual members of the research group would deem relevant because of their research, teaching, or administrative interests. During a conference call, the network drafted five "initial findings" that responded to our research questions and that we would write up and circulate broadly. The team then composed the self-published white paper discussed in more detail below. Different clusters of researchers continued to analyze the survey data by looking beyond the initial findings and focusing in more depth on specific issues. For example, one cluster of researchers focused on students' flexible understanding and use of composing technologies (see Moore, et al.).

Again, the hub-and-cluster model worked well for the case study research because of the complexity of the data collection as well as the complexity of data itself. The model facilitated an intense and sustained collaborative writing process where a large amount of complex data required the expertise and commitment of the cluster researchers to produce valuable scholarship for the field. As with the surveys, individual researchers within the collaborative also had access to data that could be analyzed in various ways, depending upon research interests or institutional needs.

Dissemination: The Rhetorical Work of Assembling Contributions

With a collaborative project, conversations about the dissemination of data need to be continuous to make sure that the research network is working toward the same goals and agrees to how the data will be presented. In this section, we discuss how the RC project encountered challenges and surprises in disseminating the research results. By designing contributions, we refer to imagining the shape of our contributions by designing a strategy that accounts for multiple team members' goals for the public and disciplinary influence we envisioned the project would take. By building contributions, we refer to assembling the technologies and practices that would enable us to both create and circulate research reports that corresponded to the arrangements that we designed (writing teams, targeted venues). Finally, by connecting contributions, we refer to realizing these contributions through connecting our words to develop storylines and address the needs and interests of diverse audiences.

Designing Contributions

We knew that publishing in peer-reviewed scholarly journals was important not only to share our findings with members of the discipline but also to legitimize the research in the academy, and, to be honest, contribute to the members' research profiles that would be measured at their institutions. In our case, while results contribute to ongoing scholarly conversations at the intersections of literacy, technology, and students' everyday writing practice, the dynamics of scholarly publication meant that these results would only be available in scholarly peer-reviewed venues at least four years after the RC group was convened. The fast-paced change of new writing technologies means that exclusively publishing in these venues risks diminishing the validity of the results before they can emerge from the submission-peer review-revision-acceptance-publication cycle. This is particularly a problem for large collaborative studies because collecting complex data sets as well as coordinating analysis and distributed authorship across geographies and institutions demands a significant time commitment to coordinate schedules, to accommodate inevitable conflicts, and so on. We again drew on the collaborative model described throughout this article when making decisions about how to disseminate the results of our research including when and where we would send our work, who would take the lead authorship roles, and the ordering of the researchers' names in the publications.

Building Contributions

In addition to developing scholarly publications, researchers also made use of local, regional, and national media channels to circulate the results. At the University of North Carolina at Pembroke, a university press release featuring an interview with researcher Dundee Lackey focused on the need to adjust writing pedagogies to account for emerging genres. Researcher Jeffrey T. Grabill recorded a short "Academic Minute" audio segment for *Inside Higher Ed* that focused on a provocative question raised by the study's findings ("Is Texting Writing?"); the podcast was republished on the National Writing Project's website "Digital Is." Both of these examples directed an interdisciplinary academic audience to the online white paper, thus meeting one of our larger goals of producing research that could inform the larger public conversation on writing and computer networks.

Although this dissemination strategy did allow us to confront the challenge of quickly publishing findings related to the rapid pace of changing technologies to a wide audience, it also presented challenges. While we understood academic peer-reviewed journals to be distinct channels of dissemination from the public and social circulation described above, after publishing the white paper, we learned that several scholarly journals have strict guidelines concerning the submission of articles for peer review when the scholarship has been previously published, even in part, in online forums. Our approach to publication is consistent with knowledge-sharing practices in other disciplines, particularly the sciences. However, we have learned that scholars in the humanities looking to make their work quickly and broadly available by drawing on the speed and reach of online social technologies must weigh the advantages and disadvantages of this strategy as it may conflict with their ability to continue with future academic publication related to the same study.

As tenure and promotion guidelines weigh the rigor of scholarly peer review over the speed and applicability of public dissemination, these decisions may be particularly tricky for untenured scholars who simultaneously are looking to build national reputations and establish a record of peer-reviewed scholarship. Therefore, when we finished data analysis from the case study research, the network elected not to release preliminary results quickly and publicly. Instead, we prepared our findings exclusively for scholarly peer review. The RC network sees opportunities for more questions and debates around these publication issues as the field continues to research rapidly changing writing technologies and to make its research relevant to a variety of stakeholders within and outside of academia.

Connecting Contributions

During the first phase, the writing process emerged directly from the survey analysis, and different members of the research team took responsibility for drafting sections of the report. The information was chunked in useable sections, pull-outs were strategically placed, and multiple data visualizations were created. Once again, the research hub supported the group by providing web development support from full-time staff and document design from undergraduate students. The research hub also supported the online publication of the document that was available via HTML and PDF.

After the white paper was published, each research cluster was encouraged to contextualize and share it with local, regional, and national stakeholders and media. First, the report was circulated through informal social media channels such as Twitter and Facebook, where both the hub and cluster researchers provided links to the white paper through their own networks.

As might be expected, publishing the results of survey research as a white paper and then pushing it through formal and informal online communication networks resulted in more timely and widespread readership than if we had moved through the traditional academic process for this phase of our research. Between 2010 and 2015—before we were able to submit, revise, and publish our survey and case study findings—the white paper had been cited in a wide range of venues including textbooks, graduate and undergraduate projects, syllabi, blogs, and even high school newsletters. This dissemination strategy was successful in that the research achieved a broad reach quickly. Our experiences of responding to email queries about the project, and discussing it with colleagues both within and outside of rhetoric and composition, further suggested to us that the news of the project had circulated broadly. In contrast, given competing demands on team members' time, the complexity of peer-review cycles, and limited annual page space in academic journals, a slice of the RC project that uses the same initial data set (Moore, et al.) was not published until 2016.

Suggestions for and Challenges of Multi-Institutional, Distributed, Collaborative Research

Writing studies needs more large-scale replicable, aggregate, and data-supported research capable of informing our disciplinary and local approaches to the teaching of writing as well as speaking clearly to public audiences about the meaning and value of writing in people's lives--particularly the learning needs of developing writers. We also need more explicitly shared questions and concerns because it is in sharing those that we will facilitate the necessary conversations that knit us together. Both our need to speak more clearly to public and policy audiences with evidence that is recognizable and our need for explicit, shared concerns require infrastructure. Given our disciplinary history as largely an outgrowth of English studies, a discipline that privileges the individual scholar, we have an insufficient understanding of how to build research infrastructure. This article is an attempt to improve that understanding.

In a networked research process, each stage is affected but not completely limited by the central object or articulation. In this case, the hub-and-cluster model enabled the RC network to access a diverse set of participants, which further expanded our ability to account for where and how meaningful writing happens and to confront the tension between rich, situated portraits of writing lives, which we value, and equally rich, though generalized, portraits of writing in the world. In turn, assembling our interpretations through meaningful dialogue among this group shaped our interpretations, which then shaped the storylines that were relevant to public and disciplinary venues, and so on. Our rhetorical negotiations at the beginning created the foundation for the project to eventually build out or scale.

We believe the particular network shape of the RC team may be useful for other writing researchers. In particular, a hub-and-cluster collaboration model may work well for writing research in the following circumstances:

- When the data required to answer research questions is significantly large, necessarily diverse, and impossible for singular researchers to collect, analyze, and write-up individually;
- When a research center or other organizational hub is able to support the work of the research clusters with infrastructures such as creating documentation (e.g., IRB and recruitment protocols), gaining access to statistical and technological support, providing re-

search assistance and webspace for online publication, and keeping a project archive;
- When flexibility is necessary across research collaborators because of diverse institutional cultures or commitments;
- When researchers' institutions can benefit from the data collected or research findings for making local pedagogical or curricular decisions; and,
- When researchers are willing to draw on local and individual social networks for informal dissemination of research results as well as willing to commit to what may be a long process of analyzing the data and submitting multiple scholarly projects.

Understandably, however, building and sustaining a hub-and-cluster research model is a large and complex undertaking. Some challenges to the hub-and-cluster model include:

- Funding to support the hub. If a research center or other organizational structure is not already in place, it can be difficult to gain support needed for large-scale data collection and analysis.
- Maintaining ongoing communication among researchers. Because researchers are necessarily distributed across time and space, it is crucial to create easily accessible mechanisms for researchers to share developing understandings.
- Providing the participants with access to materials in a timely manner. If and when databases are housed at one institution, it can be difficult to ensure that each researcher is able to work with the data when he or she needs it and is able to ask questions about the data presentation or statistical analyses.
- Sustaining the research and continuing to build the database. A clear advantage to the hub-and-cluster research model is the ability to draw together diverse researchers. However, that diversity can also work against the project over time. Institutions place different demands on their faculty researchers. Those without the pressure to research and publish frequently may not have the time or need to continue collecting and working with the data. In this case, new cluster members can be recruited at the cost of the time spent attending to the other activities of the research network.
- Negotiating power dynamics. While our collaboration was, and continues to be, a successful one, researchers designing and implementing hub-and-cluster networks for collaborative research will always need to attend carefully to the power and access dynamics that

are associated with models of organization that can easily become more hierarchical than decentered.

We believe that the RC project, and projects similar to it, are a necessary next step for the field of writing studies which both enjoys and suffers from a tension between the need to conduct research that attends to local literacy contexts—institutional or otherwise—and the need to produce findings that extend beyond institutional contexts and that help us respond to questions that circulate within broader cultural, social, and political contexts. We therefore call for continued discussion that addresses how researchers can build, design, and connect networks that can help us plan, collect, analyze, and disseminate writing research to diverse audiences.

Works Cited

Addison, Joanne, and Sharon James McGee. "Writing in High School/Writing in College: Research Trends and Future Directions." *CCC* vol. 62, no. 1, 2010, pp. 147-79, ncte.org/library/NCTEFiles/Resources/Journals/CCC/0621-sep2010/CCC0621Writing.pdf.

Bigelow, Scott. "White paper heralds a new age of writing." *University of North Carolina at Pembroke University NewsWire*. October 5, 2010.

Boja, Catalin. "Clusters Models, Factors and Characteristics." *International Journal of Economic Practices and Theories*, vol. 1, no. 1, 2011, pp. 34-48, ijept.org/index.php/ijept%20/article/view/8/7.

Chompalov, Ivan, Joel Genuth, and Wesley Shrum. "The Organization of Scientific Collaborations." *Research Policy*, vol. 31, no. 5, 2002, pp. 749-67, doi.org/10.1016/S0048-7333(01)00145-7.

Corley, Elizabeth A., P. Craig Boardman, and Barry Bozeman. "Design and the Management of Multi-Institutional Research Collaborations: Theoretical Implications from Two Case Studies." *Research Policy*, vol. 35, no. 7, 2006, pp. 975-93, doi.org/10.1016/j.respol.2006.05.003.

Cummings, Jonathon N., and Sara Kiesler. "Coordination Costs and Project Outcomes in Multi-University Collaborations." *Research Policy*, vol. 36, no.10, 2007, pp. 1620-34, doi.org/10.1016/j.respol.2007.09.001.

Ede, Lisa, and Andrea Lunsford. "Collaboration and Concepts of Authorship." *PMLA*, vol. 116, no. 2, 2001, pp. 354-69, jstor.org.lib.utep.edu/stable/463522.

Grabill, Jeffrey T. "Is Texting Writing?" Academic Minute, *Inside Higher Ed,* insidehighered.com/audio/academic_pulse/is_texting_writing.

Grabill, Jeffrey T., William Hart-Davidson, Stacey Pigg. "New Data!" Message to VizComp Research Group. 26 July 2010. E-mail.

Haswell, Richard. "NCTE/CCCC's Recent War on Scholarship." *Written Communication*, vol. 22, no. 2, 2005, pp. 198-223, doi: 10.1177/0741088305275367.

Katz, J. Sylvan, and Ben R. Martin. "What is Research Collaboration?" *Research Policy*, vol. 26, no. 1, 1997, pp. 1-18. doi.org/10.1016/S0048-7333(96)00917-1.

Lowry, Paul Benjamin, Aaron Curtis, and Michelle Rene Lowry. "Building a Taxonomy and Nomenclature of Collaborative Writing to Improve Interdisciplinary Research and Practice." *Journal of Business Communication*, vol. 41, no. 1, 2004, pp. 66-99, doi: 10.1177/0021943603259363.

Lunsford, Andrea, and Karen Lunsford. "Mistakes Are a Fact of Life." *CCC*, vol. 59, no. 4, 2008, pp. 781-806, ncte.org/library/NCTEFiles/Resources/Journals/CCC/0594-june08/CO0594Mistakes.pdf.

McNenny, Geraldine, and Duane H. Roen. "The Case for Collaborative Scholarship in Rhetoric and Composition." *Rhetoric Review*, vol. 10, no. 2, 1992, pp. 291-310, doi: 10.1080/07350199209388973.

Moore, Jessie L., et al. "Revisualizing Composition: How First-Year Writers Use Composing Technologies." *Computers and Composition*, vol. 39, 2016, pp. 1-13, doi: 10.1016/j.compcom.2015.11.001.

Oh, Erin Wilkey. "Is Texting Writing?" *Digital Is*. September 12, 2011, http://thecurrent.educatorinnovator.org/resource/2470.

Paretti, Marie, Lisa McNair, and Lissa Holloway-Attaway. "Teaching Technical Communication in an Era of Distributed Work: A Case Study of Collaboration Between U.S. and Swedish Students." *Technical Communication Quarterly*, vol. 16, no. 3, 2007, pp. 327-52, doi: 10.1080/10572250701291087.

Pigg, Stacey, et al. "Ubiquitous Writing, Technologies, and the Social Practice of Literacies of Coordination." *Written Communication*, vol. 31, no. 1, 2014, pp. 91-117, doi: 10.1177/0741088313514023.

Revisualizing Composition Study Group. "The Writing Lives of College Students: A WIDE Survey and Whitepaper," wide.msu.edu/special/writinglives.

"REx: The Research Exchange Index." *The Research Exchange Index*, researchexchange.colostate.edu.

Roen, Duane H., and Robert K. Mittan. "Collaborative Scholarship in Composition: Some Issues." *Methods and Methodologies in Composition Research*, edited by Gesa Kirsch and Patricia A Sullivan, SIUP, 1992, pp. 287-312.

Sheridan, Mary P., and Lee Nickoson, editors. *Writing Studies Research in Practice: Methods and Methodologies,* SIUP, 2012.

Smagorinsky, Peter. "The Method Section as Conceptual Epicenter in Constructing Social Science Research Reports." *Written Communication*, vol. 25, no. 3, 2008, pp. 389-411, doi: 10.1177/0741088308317815.

Sullivan, Patricia A. "Revising the Myth of the Independent Scholar." *Writing With: New Directions in Collaborative Teaching, Learning, and Research,* edited by Sally Barr Reagan, Thomas Fox, and David Bleich, SUNY P, 1994, pp. 11-29.

Sullivan, Patricia, and James E. Porter. *Opening Spaces: Writing Technologies and Critical Research Practices*, Ablex, 1997.

Swarts, Jason. "Networks." *Keyword in Writing Studies*, edited by Paul Heilker and Peter Van Den Burg, UP of Colorado, 2015, pp. 120-24.

Trimbur, John. "Consensus and Difference in Collaborative Learning." *College English*, vol. 51, no. 6, 1989, pp. 602-16, doi: 10.2307/377955.

"What Is the Citation Project?" *The Citation Project: Preventing Plagiarism, Teaching Writing,* citationproject.net.

"What Is the Meaningful Writing Project?" *The Meaningful Writing Project,* meaningfulwritinproject.net.

Yancey, Kathleen Blake, and Michael Spooner. "A Single Good Mind: Collaboration, Cooperation, and the Writing Self." *CCC*, vol. 49, no. 1, 1998, pp. 45-62, ncte.org/library/NCTEFiles/Resources/Journals/CCC/0491-feb98/CO0491Single.PDF.

The Burkean Parlor as Boundary Object: A Collaboration between First-Year Writing and the Library

Lynda Walsh, Adrian M. Zytkoskee, Patrick Ragains, Heidi Slater, and Michelle Rachal

This article details a collaboration between the fyw program and the library at the University of Nevada, Reno. The departments share a goal of helping students develop better research-writing skills; however, institutional and disciplinary boundaries presented well-known challenges. To surmount these challenges, the cross-disciplinary team settled on the Burkean Parlor as a boundary object, which is a shared metaphor that scaffolds effective work among diverse communities. Once the metaphor was mobilized, the team realized it could also scaffold work across the boundaries between expert and novice writers and between facts and arguments in research writing. Accordingly, the team designed a curricular intervention around the Burkean Parlor metaphor and taught it collaboratively to a group of 900 second-semester first-year students while a roughly equally sized group served as a control. Students submitted pre- and post-surveys of their attitudes toward library research, and their final research papers were collected and rated on several criteria relating to rhetorical purpose and source use. The team found that the intervention group's research papers presented significantly better articulations of rhetorical purpose, and students reported increased confidence in their abilities to access and use library sources in research writing.

"I should try to enact and live out in my classroom the Burkean metaphor of intellectual life as an unending conversation. This is what we academics do: carry on an unending conversation not just with colleagues but with the dead and unborn."

—Peter Elbow (2000)

Introduction

Composition studies has gotten quite comfortable in the Burkean Parlor (Burke 110-11). The "conversation" metaphor dominates our fyw textbooks and pedagogy (cf. Davis and Shadle; Goodburn and Camp; Graff and Birkenstein; Purdy and Walker). The Burkean Parlor provides a handy script for teaching the research process to our students, if a dozen YouTube videos are any indication. Also, it serves as the theme of roughly an article a year in this journal, not to mention other composition studies journals. Such a pervasive trope demands critique, and lately it has started getting just that.

Aja Martinez and Jennifer Trainor, among others, have called attention to the agonism inherent in the Burkean Parlor (BP): Trainor with respect to literacy development in the composition classroom and Martinez with respect to racial bias in scholarly discourse. Both scholars demonstrate convincingly that agonism can produce chilling effects on student collaboration and access to knowledge.

This critical work about BP is crucial. However, if we focus exclusively on the dynamics the BP creates *within* composition studies, we miss the ways in which the conversation metaphor also circulates *outside* our field among related communities of practice. Based on our experience with a cross-disciplinary collaboration, we argue that the BP metaphor can serve as an effective boundary object. Boundary objects proliferate rather than focus or restrict meaning; so doing, they enable collaboration among disparate communities.

In this article, we detail a collaboration that used the BP metaphor as a boundary object. In a research and literacy project conducted with library personnel, we found that the conversation metaphor bridged differences not only between discourses of composition and library science but also between "school/non-school" discourses for students (Trainor) and between academic and administrative cultures. Here we describe the curriculum that we developed, provide examples of student work, and show assessment results that demonstrate some of the boundary-crossing effects of the BP trope.

The Institutional Situation

In the spring of 2013, Maggie Ressel, the Director of Access Services at the University of Nevada, Reno (UNR), approached Lynda Walsh, the Director of Core Writing, to discuss ways to bolster information literacy and the role of the library in fyw. Serendipitously, fyw personnel, in preparation for periodic assessment of English 102, a second-semester argumentation and research writing course, had just identified documentation and use of research sources as areas needing improvement—a common concern in the wake of findings from the Citation Project (Howard and Jamieson). Thus, in fall 2014, our two departments enthusiastically embarked on a joint curriculum intervention and assessment. Readers familiar with literature on cross-disciplinary collaborations of this nature can immediately anticipate some of the challenges we faced.

As Chris Thaiss and Tara Porter note, the rise of WAC and WID programs over the last 20 years and an increase in independent writing programs and centers have brought many new stakeholders to the fyw table. Library and information service professionals are among these stakeholders, and a concurrent push toward information literacy has only strengthened the exigence for collaboration between composition programs and librarians (D'Angelo and Maid). Accordingly, reports of such collaborations have proliferated over the last decade in journals such as *Libraries and the Academy* and *Research Strategies*, while several edited volumes provide both concrete ideas and philosophical support for these endeavors (e.g., Deyrup and Bloom; McClure and Purdy; Ragains; Sheridan).

However, the boundaries mitigating such collaborations are not trivial. For instance, experts in both disciplines understand "research" and "writing" in different ways. Collaborations that neglect this difference have resulted in the framing of research toward library skills and away from writing as well as in conflicting outcomes for student research papers (Barratt, et al.).

Political boundaries underscore these disciplinary differences. Ironically for members of a profession that has for years fought its perception as a service field, compositionists sometimes treat librarians the same way—as technicians who supply a valuable service to faculty but not as equal partners in writing instruction (D'Angelo and Maid; Ivy; Manuel, Beck, and Molloy).

Our fledgling project could have run aground on these boundary markers. But we were committed to finding an interdisciplinary approach to teaching research writing that went beyond "one-shot" treatments and did not (a) segregate the research process from the writing process, (b) subjugate the interests of one discipline to the other, and (c) require us to sign off on exactly the same definitions of "research" and "writing" (Artman, Frisicaro-Pawlowski, and Monge; Paretti, McNair, Belanger, and George). We needed a scaffold for collaboration that enabled us to achieve our programmatic goals—to improve research writing and show that improvement through institutional assessment—while allowing our differing kinds of expertise the breathing room each deserved and needed. In other words, we needed a boundary object.

Boundary Objects

A boundary object is a problem, metaphor, or other *topos* (strategic rhetorical stance) that two politically divergent communities use to scaffold successful collaboration. First defined by science studies scholars in the late 1980s, boundary objects work precisely because they make space for divergent values while facilitating joint action (Star and Griesemer). An example of a boundary object is the *topos* of "uncertainty," which allows politicians and scientists to work together on an issue like climate change because, although each discourse community may mean something different by "uncertainty," both are eager to reduce it (Gieryn; Shackley and Wynne).

In our collaboration, we did not have to look far to find our boundary object—the conversation metaphor. We have already mentioned its ubiquity in composition studies. But librarians have their own version of the trope. In fact, "scholarship as conversation" is one of the six frames of the Association of College and Research Libraries' *Framework for Information Literacy in Higher Education*:

> Instead of seeking discrete answers to complex problems, experts understand that a given issue may be characterized by several competing perspectives as part of an ongoing conversation in which information users and creators come together and negotiate meaning. . . . While novice learners and experts at all levels can take part in the conversation, established power and authority structures may influence their ability to participate and can privilege certain voices and information. (10)

Given this common ground, it is no surprise that fyw and library collaborations that emphasize the composition process have turned to the BP as a boundary object. A particularly compelling project along these lines was carried out by Jeanne R. Davidson, a librarian, and Carol Ann Crateau, a writing instructor from Oregon State University. They designed and co-taught a collaborative curriculum based upon the BP metaphor. After teaching this curriculum, Davidson and Crateau believed that their students had come to "understand conversation as a means of communication, so introducing research as a 'written' conversation provides a context for the process of searching for and evaluating information" (253). In a related project at the same university, Paula S. McMillen and Eric Hill also concluded with the observation that the BP metaphor "restores contextual considerations, embodies the iterative recursive nature of the research process, offers a scaffolded skill-building approach, helps students construct meaning, and easily translates the key concepts in both composition and information literacy" (20).

Our collaborative team was excited by the potential of the Oregon State models. When looking at the models, fyw personnel were most concerned with the coherent assembly and effective framing of source material to support a persuasive rhetorical purpose. Meanwhile, librarians were looking for evidence that students knew how to use library resources, that they had thoroughly canvassed and organized the available source material, and that they were accurately documenting it. As both departments were facing a programmatic assessment requirement that year, the BP metaphor promised a coherent rubric under which to pursue each department's goals simultaneously. Further, the BP boundary object promised a way to integrate the discourses of "school" (academic argument) and "non-school" (social conversation) for our fyw students (Trainor 45). After all, one of the central goals of both fyw and the library is to help move students toward membership in the academy.

Burkean Parlor Curriculum

The collaborative BP curriculum we created consisted of four short modules: (1) Listening, (2) Catching the Tenor, (3) Mapping the Parlor/Putting in your Oar, and (4) Framing. Librarians and fyw instructors co-taught modules 1 and 2; fyw instructors took the lead on modules 3 and 4 with some assistance from librarians. Librarians also created and hosted the videos that supported the modules. All modules were built on a "flipped classroom" platform, a strategy characteristic of composition pedagogy (Milman), in which students read or watch material prior to class and then engage in hands-on applications or extensions of the material in class.

While there was no standard syllabus for English 102, most instructors taught the research process in discipline-standard ways:

1. Typical texts included the *Curious Researcher* (Ballenger), *They Say, I Say* (Graff and Birkenstein), and *Everything's an Argument* (Lunsford and Ruskiewicz).
2. Time spent writing the eight-to-ten page research paper ranged from five to eight weeks. For example, in a 102 section with the theme "models of mind," an instructor would guide students by forming them into writing groups that met weekly for several weeks to discuss the *ethos* of their sources and help each other broaden their research methodology.
3. The research writing process generally included several drafts and some contributing projects. For example, a themed course on "The Great (American?) Pastime: An Exploration of Baseball and Community" would scaffold the major research essay on an in-depth project proposal and an annotated bibliography.

As is apparent from these examples, the conversation metaphor was already latent in typical praxis. Our intervention was thus relatively minor:

1. We foregrounded the conversation metaphor as a unifying trope for all of the various phases of research writing.
2. We added a simple, concrete visualization exercise to the research process during which students collect and understand their source material.
3. We extended interactions between students and librarians during the research process.

These minor changes, however, produced significant results, as we will discuss below.

Forty-two English 102 instructors during the spring 2014 semester were divided alphabetically into two groups—a control group who would teach the research writing process as usual, and those who would teach this process by using the BP modules.[1] A few instructors opted out, leaving us with a final roster of eighteen instructors in the control group and twenty-one instructors in the BP module group. All activities were conducted with IRB approval (693124-1).

In keeping with the contemporary *ethos* of the fyw program at UNR, the assessment team did not mandate how the BP modules were taught, nor were BP instructors monitored while delivering the curriculum. However, we did ask for a commitment from BP instructors to teach at least module 3, the mapping module. What follows are outlines of modules as well as examples of how instructors operationalized them.

Module 1: Listening

By framing initial, exploratory research efforts as "eavesdropping" on a conversation rather than amassing citations, this module encouraged students to view research as a process that builds knowledge through dialogue. Students were assigned to watch an online video outlining our library resources and three short YouTube videos explaining the BP metaphor and its relationship to academic writing processes. They were also asked to explore Portland State library's online orientation. The methods for teaching "listening in on a conversation" varied: BP instructors reported use of scholarly debates, ranging from Richard Vatz and Lloyd Bitzer's famous clash over the rhetorical situation to current definitions of disability in academic settings to U.S. involvement in Middle Eastern conflicts. One instructor, whose ENG 102 was themed on "place, space, and the local," brought in a NPR segment on drought in California to illustrate how the journalist synthesized sources to create a cogent investigation. Students were encouraged to listen carefully and suspend judgment until after the rhetorical work of module two could be performed.

Module 2: Catching the Tenor

This module moved students from observation to rhetorical evaluation. As scaffolding for instruction, librarians posted videos that helped students assess sources using the CRAAP (currency, relevance, authority, accuracy, purpose) test and other metrics. Instructors added their own textual resources: One instructor noted that she asked students to find a "scientific claim" made on social media and then required students to bring in authoritative research relating to that claim for in-class evaluation; topics ranged from "the dangers of baby formula" to "scientists finally figure out the essence of 'cool.'" Similarly, an instructor who had spent time teaching in the Middle East showed a debate that originally aired on the American Broadcasting Company, titled "Should Americans Fear Islam?" The instructor asked students to investigate the *ethos* of the debaters and panelists, the political motivations of the organizations they represented, and the factual claims made during the debate. Several students reported drastic shifts in opinion after evaluating the veracity of claims and uncovering the political and personal agendas of debaters.

It was during this module—or module 1 in some cases—that BP sections visited the library for a session lasting between fifty and seventy-five minutes, during which a librarian first reviewed the key points made in the module videos and then helped students locate authoritative sources for their annotated bibliographies. Librarians continued to support student research through chat sessions (both online using IM and at the library help desk).

Module 3: Mapping the Parlor/Putting in Your Oar

This module was the crucial piece of the intervention. It centered around a map—created either by hand or by using the visual mapping software available at Bubbl.us—of the sources listed in students' annotated bibliographies (see Discussion for student examples). The map connected these sources along "argument lines" to clarify their interrelation.

The conceptualization and construction of this module epitomized the cross-disciplinary nature of our collaboration. The librarians immediately connected the idea of the BP conversation to knowledge webs used in Library and Information Science (LIS). They suggested the Bubbl.us application and created the instructional video to support it. Meanwhile, fyw personnel wrote the script for the video and contributed the concept of "argument lines" as a way to link students' sources into a networked conversation. Argument lines (otherwise known as common topics or *koinoi topoi* in the rhetorical tradition) represent vectors along which arguments on any subject can be effectively invented and then communicated to readers; these include schemes such as "compare/contrast," "change over time," or "definition and consequences." Research has shown that teaching the dominant argument lines of a discipline to fyw students shortens their time-to-mastery of discourse in that discipline (Wilder and Wolfe). The argument lines that fyw personnel contributed to the Parlor Map exercise were as follows:

1. Compare/contrast two or more opposing schools of thought on a topic.
2. Use cause/effect to show how the research problem evolved as researchers contributed to and refined their knowledge.

Other lines are, of course, possible, and instructors were encouraged to allow students to label lines with whatever connections that made sense to them; these two were simply common strategies in literature reviews.

Both librarians and fyw instructors taught students how to construct the parlor maps. This continued engagement was designed to respond to criticisms of previous fyw and library collaborations as "one-off" interactions that "provide just enough basic skill training for the student to find the 3-5 sources required to write their composition paper" but do not improve their information literacy (Artman, Frisicaro-Pawlowski, and Monge 94). In our design, students learned how to integrate their research sources into a coherent academic conversation with the help of librarians' LIS expertise.

Module 4: Framing

The final module focused on the technical practices required to enter a scholarly conversation. Mindful and ethical use of sources was taught through a video on plagiarism. Instructors added their own content, including a review of famous plagiarism cases and a familiar exercise called "The Quotation Sandwich." The quotation sandwich provided students with a variety of signal phrases and short definitions of their purpose (e.g., "'However' indicates a contradictory idea is about to be introduced"). It also provided several examples of citations, paraphrases, and summaries that were skillfully introduced and unpacked. Students were then asked to find six citations and paraphrases from their own research and to create a "quotation sandwich" by introducing the quote, writing the quote, and then explaining the quote's relevance in a final sentence. Afterward, often to their surprise, they would realize that they had written close to a page of their essay and done so in relevant, solidly framed language. In addition, several BP instructors asked students to workshop the quotation sandwiches and reported higher quality feedback regarding the framing of sources than is typical.

Outcomes and Student Work

In this section we discuss the results of our curricular intervention in terms of the three boundaries we aimed to bridge using the conversation metaphor: interdisciplinary boundaries, administrative boundaries, and non-school/school boundaries for students.

Interdisciplinary boundaries: FYW and the library

Quantitative and qualitative surveys are typical in both library and fyw portfolio assessments. Therefore, explicitly combining our approaches fit the spirit of the project while offering a comprehensive instrument. At this writing the fyw program has continued to support the BP modules developed in 2014 and to offer professional development to English 102 instructors geared toward teaching the modules; and the library has continued to support the module curriculum as well. The increased appreciation and respect that fyw personnel gained for librarians' expertise stands as another benefit of our collaboration.

Administrative Boundaries: Assessment

Assessment is now the dominant medium through which faculty and administrators communicate about what's going on in the classroom. The BP metaphor provided a rubric under which to organize assessments that would help both fyw and the library demonstrate the effectiveness of their pedagogy to the provost's office: a pre- and post- survey demonstrated improved confidence in library research (survey questions and results available upon email request to lead author); a rubric-based assessment of student research papers helped demonstrate the effectiveness of research writing instruction (see appendix for rubric); and a rhetorical analysis of selected student papers and parlor maps provided important context for the quantitative assessments (as discussed below).

In terms of survey results, librarians were able to demonstrate excellent participation rates by English 102 instructors during spring 2014: 91% of all 102 sections received at least one library session during the semester, and librarians worked with 88% of English 102 instructors overall. Librarians deemed this result a significant improvement over previous semesters and considered it a major accomplishment of the collaboration.

Fifty-four percent of students in the BP intervention who responded to the post-survey rated the BP modules as "important" or "very important" to the development of their research skills; 58% said they would use concept-mapping techniques such as the Parlor Map again. In *The Diffusion of Innovation*, the seminal text on rate of adoption for educational and other innovations, Everett M. Rogers sets the "tipping point" for sustainable adoption of an innovation within a population at around 34% (the "early majority") (264-79). By this standard, BP participants' reports of success with and intention to adopt the Parlor Map as a writing technique are very promising. Further, the BP group's post-responses to question 2a, which asked students to report their confidence in being able to "develop a general topic of interest into a research question and then into a thesis statement," were significantly higher than the pre-responses when the population means were compared using a T-test, which measures the odds (p) of the perceived difference in means being due to chance as opposed to the educational intervention. A p- value of less than .05 (5% chance) is considered significant, and a p- value of less than .01 (1% chance) is considered strongly significant. We measured $p=0.00015$ (.015% chance) for the observed difference in BP and control reports of student confidence during the research writing process.

For the portfolio assessment, all English 102 instructors were asked to provide unmarked, anonymous copies of final research papers and annotated bibliographies (and parlor maps, for BP sections) for a random sample of five to seven students, stratified by gender for each of the sections. This method corrected for a bias toward instructors who taught multiple sections and produced a sample of 252 portfolios, equaling 13% of the 1,896 students enrolled in English 102 in spring 2014; this sample size was calculated as reliable for the population (95% confidence level; 5% margin of error). Not all students turned in work, so the final sample for rating comprised 232 portfolios representing 12% of the total population. Portfolios were redacted for personally identifiable information, assigned random identification numbers, recorded as belonging to either a BP or a control section, and uploaded to SharePoint for access and rating.

A group of six raters, all experienced instructors from fyw and the library, evaluated the research papers in the portfolios over three two-hour sessions using a rubric generated by the assessment team (see appendix). The rubric was revised during this process to facilitate norming and to keep the rubric tied to fyw student learning outcomes.[1] Raters were reminded to use the full range of the rubric whenever possible, and they did so during the norming sessions.

Inter-rater reliability was calculated by using Intraclass Correlation Coefficient (ICC) scores (two-way, agreement, average). This method was selected due to the ordinal variable scale and our study design, in which all coders rated each participant during the norming phase but split up remaining participants to save time and effort (Hallgren). After norming, two raters read each paper independently, and the scores were averaged to produce one set of scores for each paper, a process that facilitated comparison between BP and control group ratings.

Results of T-tests on mean scores between BP and non-BP papers indicated that the BP intervention significantly improved students' ability to articulate a clear rhetorical purpose that acknowledged and extended previous work ($p=.04$). This result is supported by BP students' survey answers that reported increased confidence in working from research questions to a thesis statement.

Two other differences between average performances in BP and control groups evinced low probabilities of chance occurrence: BP participants showed better deployment of authoritative sources ($p=.11$) and better rhetorical framing ($p=.18$) of those sources than did control participants. These results were not statistically significant but indicate areas for future research, as will be addressed in the discussion section of this article.[2] There was no discernable difference in BP and control participants' ability to "document/cite source material," "acknowledge [their] own biases," or "acknowledge the wisdom of alternate perspectives," as demonstrated in table 1.

Table 1
Means Comparison for Final Paper Ratings between BP and Control Groups with Significant Differences (*)

	Control Mean Score	Control Standard Deviation*	BP Mean Score	BP Standard Deviation	T-test probability
Sources	3.50	1.09	3.68	1.10	0.11
Purpose	3.97	0.76	4.17	0.92	*0.04
Documentation and citation	3.32	1.21	3.25	1.20	0.32
Framing	3.37	1.07	3.50	1.09	0.18
Own biases	3.39	1.01	3.47	1.01	0.28
Other perspectives	3.08	1.09	3.09	1.15	0.48

To sum up our assessment efforts, we succeeded in demonstrating to our administration the improvements in student learning generated by this collaboration between FYW and the library. In fact, our Provost included our project in our university's accreditation package as a hallmark example of progressive assessment.

Non-School/School Boundaries: Student Membership in the Academy

In terms of student achievement, the BP curriculum did significantly help students to imagine themselves as part of the academy—as measured by their ability to articulate an effective research argument in the context of previous scholarship. It is impossible to say definitively which aspects of the BP curriculum produced this effect, but, after rhetorical analysis of student work, we suspect the Parlor Map exercise significantly helped students integrate "school" and "non-school" knowledge into a coherent intellectual identity. Below, we have selected several maps created by students who produced high-scoring thesis statements to dramatize the process by which these maps scaffolded school and non-school integration in the research writing process.

The map in figure 1 was created by a nutrition major, writing a research paper on the pros and cons of social media. The map was color-coded to group and compare the research the student found on the negative and positive effects of social media: sources showing negative effects are grouped to the left of the laptop, and those showing positive ones are grouped to the right, following an argument line of compare/contrast (visually depicted, not written). The "loading bar" in the student's central computer graphic makes the argument that 75% of the academic research she discovered reflected a negative bias toward social media. In a conference with her instructor, the student said she felt that her non-school identity as a social media user helped her see this bias. Without dismissing the criticism outlined against social media, she does offer an insider perspective on its benefits and proper employment. By arguing for the utility of social media in her discourse community, this student created a narrative that resisted the mainstream consensus, or a "counterstory," in the spirit of the interventions that Aja Martinez has imagined for the BP metaphor (Martinez 51-53).

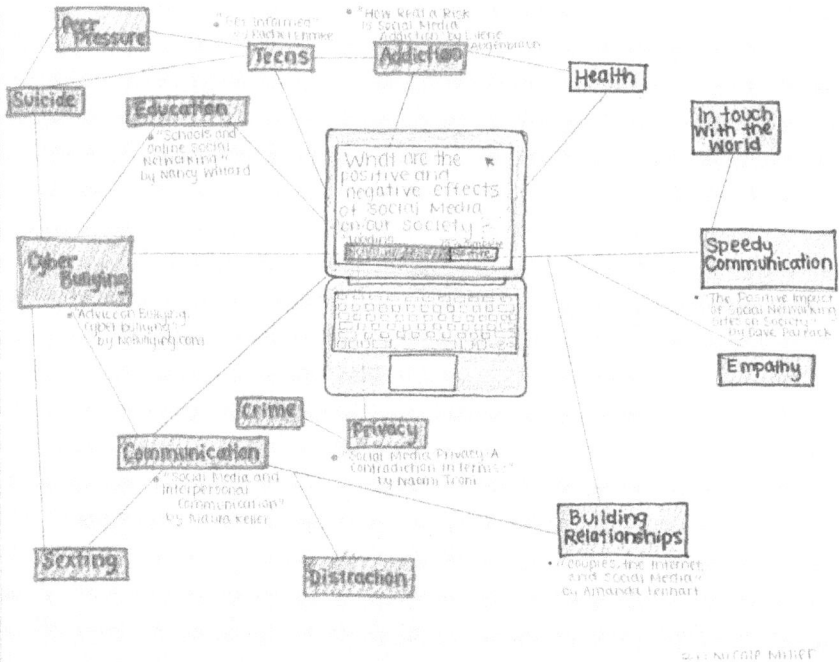

Fig. 1: Student map, "What are the positive and negative effects of social media on our society?"

The Parlor Map in figure 2 was created by an education major reacting to national news about recent problems with massive open online courses (MOOCs) at Stanford University. As is often the case, the student started out with a cut-and-dry for/against paradigm of the situation. But as he went through the mapping exercise, it helped him see that (a) no one provided a clear definition of "quality education" (on the right), and (b) not all his sources neatly fit the compare/contrast paradigm. These challenges prompted him to question the supposed superiority of traditional education and to open up a third category (indicated with the dotted argument lines) articulating "partial" support for MOOCs. His resulting thesis statement was much more nuanced, acknowledging both the limitations of traditional education and the situations in which MOOCs could succeed.

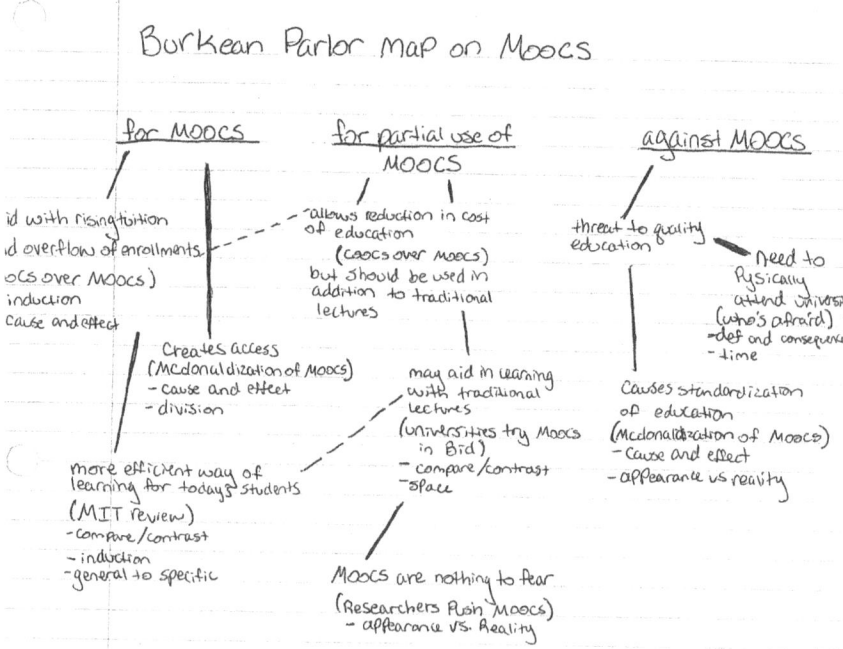

Fig. 2: Burkean Parlor Map on MOOCs.

If the map in figure 3 looks like a mess, this is because it was. The student who created it, an engineering major minoring in economics, was interested in the educational contributions made by casinos—both in the form of taxation and philanthropy. The project integrated the student's non-school experience with casino culture (he had family members who worked at casinos) with his academic interest in economics. However, he got bogged down in the research process because he found himself trying to "fix" the whole educational system.

The proliferation of argument lines in his finished map visually confronted him with the possibility that he was taking on too much material. In this way, the Parlor Map helped him to narrow his research approach toward a focused problem/solution project centered upon the type of financial support for education that the state should require from the gaming industry.

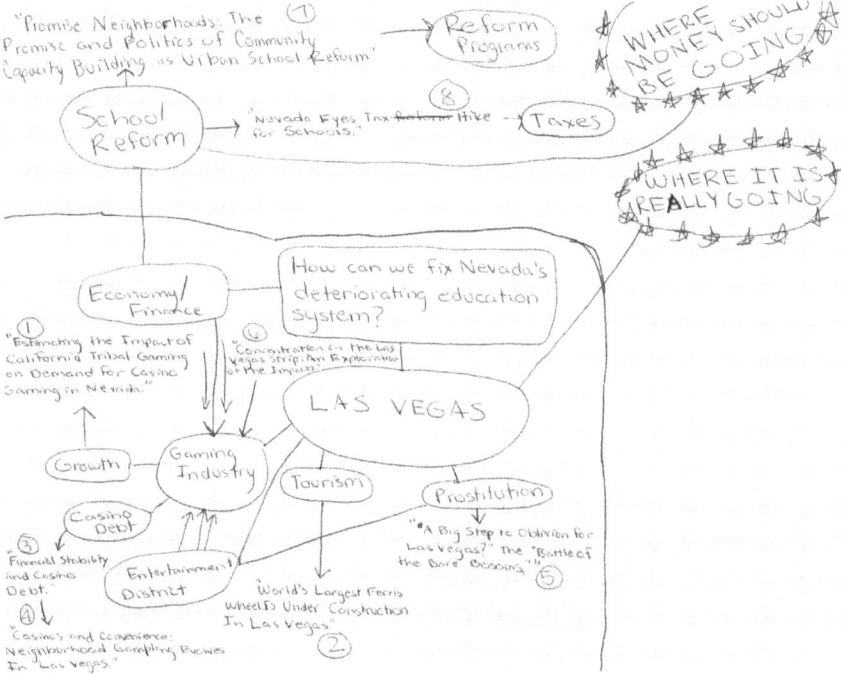

Fig. 3: Student map, "How can we fix Nevada's deteriorating educational system?"

The above examples demonstrate that even though not every student executed the Parlor Map exercise as instructed, the process was robust enough to help all of them in some way. Specifically, the maps appeared to help students (a) recognize the scope of a coherent research argument; (b) visualize entry points into a pre-existing academic conversation; and (c) enact boundary transgressions identified by Trainor (school/non-school) and Martinez (counterstory).

These observations correlate with the paper assessment, which demonstrated significant improvement in students' ability to articulate a research purpose in terms of a previous academic conversation. These quantitative differences can be dramatized by comparing the thesis statements written by the BP students who made the maps discussed above to low-scoring thesis statements on similar topics from the control group.

Table 2:
Examples of Student Statements of Research Purpose

Control group introductory context and thesis statement	BP group introductory context, thesis statement, and parlor map
A student paper on the misperception of salsa dancing begins with a dictionary.com definition of the dance style. The author then poses several rhetorical questions including whether the reader "thinks the dance is sexualized" and whether or not it "exploits women." After these questions comes the author's thesis statement: *"A good example of how some people see salsa would be when the movie* Dirty Dancing *came out. The audiences inside the movie saw this newborn (to America) dance as explicit and matriarchal. Yet the Hispanic culture saw this as another dance they wanted to transition to the states."*	A student paper explores issues surrounding social media including cyberbullying, academic bias against social media, and her own identity as a daily user of Facebook and Twitter. *"Although the negative impacts of social media seem to outweigh the positives, hopefully, one day, with the correct understanding and precautions, we will be able to use social media in a healthy, safe and productive way."*
A student paper on the definition and uses of lucid dreaming in therapy begins by introducing the psychiatrist who coined the phrase. Next, it claims that the "true father of lucid dreaming" was a psychiatrist who, years later, dedicated his life to the topic of lucid dreaming. This leads into the thesis statement: *"Some scientists and other people in the lucid dreaming community believe that lucid dreaming is not something that can be obtained."*	A student paper on the definition and use of MOOCs in higher education reviews definitions of traditional versus online education and presents expert arguments for and against MOOCs. Then, it concludes: *"Many argue for traditional lecture but fail to define what it is and its components in comparison to online education. This research paper discusses just what tradition and online education is. Online education simulates the academic community found in traditional education but cannot replace it."*

Control group introductory context and thesis statement	BP group introductory context, thesis statement, and parlor map
A student paper on the death of the "American Dream" begins by defining what constitutes the American dream and offers his own family's considerable financial success as a counterpoint to the opportunities of most U.S. citizens. His thesis states: *"This paper is not intended to explain how my parents succeeded in America and how they thrived in the middle-class. Instead, it explains why families like mine are the minority in America Today. It explains the current state of the United States and how America's youth have less and less chance to succeed. The Idea of the American dream is not realistic, and following the 2008 recession, it is not obtainable."*	A student paper begins with a general acknowledgement of the problems facing Nevada's educational system; it then directs its gaze toward the casino industry as a primary catalyst for many of the issues: *"By looking into greater detail at the casino and entertainment industries—specifically casino debt, how casinos and tourism are focused on more than education, the 2008-2009 recession, and gambling addiction—we can determine how much of a negative impact it is having on Nevada's educational system and determine a solution."*

As evident in column two of table 2, BP participants did a better job of establishing context for their thesis statements: they articulated a scholarly conversation with multiple points of view and engaged it explicitly, either by aligning themselves with one camp or by critiquing a gap in the conversation to date. Furthermore, two of these examples show students bringing their non-school lives and interests (social media and casino culture) to bear on scholarly conversations in ways that enriched both the papers and the overall conversations. By contrast, the low-scoring control examples fail to articulate non-school interests (salsa dancing, lucid dreaming, the American dream) with related scholarly conversations in a meaningful way: they either present no previous scholarship or assemble one or two sources into a brief history of the subject. Thus, their thesis statements seem unconnected to and unmotivated by their sources.

These differences between BP and control thesis statements dramatize the quantitative differences we found between a typical monologic approach to research writing, which focuses on the writer's knowledge and opinions, and the dialogic approach encouraged by the BP metaphor. The dialogic approach stresses not only the role the writer plays in an ongoing and broadening investigation of a subject but also their membership in the academic community.

We recognize that our collaboration, while very successful, did not overcome all of the challenges mentioned at the outset of this article. Both fyw personnel and librarians would have liked a few things done differently: librarians would have liked to standardize the delivery of BP modules; fyw instructors would have liked to spend more time on writing during library sessions. And, as we speculated about integrating librarians as writing instructors in fyw, institutional barriers in the form of pay and degree requirements came up.

In terms of student achievement, as discussed above, we found no quantitative differences in BP and control students' abilities to document and cite source material, acknowledge their own biases, or acknowledge the wisdom of alternate perspectives—even though BP instructors anecdotally reported seeing improvement in these areas. And indeed, these categories yielded the largest standard deviations in raters' quantitative assessments—indicating that the rubric might need refinement in these areas. But it may also be true that the conversation metaphor did not sufficiently unite module 4, which treats framing of source material in the actual research paper, with the other modules; future iterations would be well advised to emphasize the conversation metaphor during module 4.

Our survey results, however, remind us that border crossing is a process, not an achievement. Our librarians pointed out to us the ironic result that while students reported increased confidence in using the library, they also reported consulting librarians less frequently as the semester progressed—the opposite of our intentions to involve the library more with fyw. Similarly, students reported increased confidence in quoting and citing sources, but the paper assessment revealed these areas as essentially unimproved since the previous assessment. While the first result, at least, could be interpreted positively (i.e., students don't need mentors after they have mastered skills), the librarians raised the concern that our students might be underestimating the level of information literacy needed to succeed in the academy (i.e., they're confident but unskilled). Clearly, more than a semester's engagement between the library and fyw is necessary to help students transition to robust research habits.

Conclusion

It is our hope that the BP trope and similar boundary objects may serve as sites on which librarians, compositionists, and other disciplinary experts can build truly interdisciplinary writing programs. Our curriculum is simple to implement, and any fyw program is welcome to link to and use the BP modules we developed ((https://guides.library.unr.edu/c.php?g=684882&p=5834132). Library support varies from institution to institution, but the librarians on our team assured us that their colleagues at other universities are generally eager to become more involved with writing instruction, and indeed, the growing literature on library and fyw collaboration bears out this impression. Librarians help compositionists to be more reflexive about disciplinary biases regarding argument and research, and they help students see information in ways compositionists cannot. These new ways of seeing, made possible by parlor maps, are not a game—they represent the rapidly evolving knowledge structures that our students must navigate as they move through their degree programs and into their careers. It has never been a better time to seek out boundary objects between libraries and fyw to facilitate our students' acquisition of inquiry, critique, and engagement.

Notes

1. Our assessment model here was "between instructor" because it was not practical to deliver two different curricula in the same classroom, nor ethical to change teaching assignments for instructors—many of whom were adjuncts and teaching assistants—effectively from a one-prep to a two-prep with only a month's notice (Dimitrov and Rumrill Jr.). This design left our assessment vulnerable to instructor effects; however, we ensured that instructors' experience levels and gender were relatively equally distributed across the two groups.

2. An early iteration of our rubric subdivided the Sources categories into Source Credibility, Source Relevance, and Source Sufficiency. When we normed using this rubric and a subset of the student papers, ICC scores were in the Excellent range for all categories except for the three sources subcategories, which scored below the Fair range. We combined the three sub-categories into a single category and normed again, achieving Excellent inter-rater reliability (.907) on Sources.

Appendix: Assessment Rubric

	1-inadequate	2-minimal/marginal	3-weak	4-satisfactory	5-good	6-excellent
Sources	Sources are grossly insufficient in number and are problematically non-authoritative*, outdated, and/or irrelevant to main argument.	Sources are still inadequate in number and are generally non-authoritative, outdated, or irrelevant—though paper may exhibit a paragraph or two of competent support.	Works cited page shows mix of authoritative and non-authoritative sources and in the paper, student does not appear to distinguish among them in supporting argument. Sources speak to main argument but may be inaccurately or awkwardly deployed, and there may be slightly too few of them.	Paper employs a sufficient number of sources, and at least one relevant and authoritative source supports each major claim. Problems likely remain with over-reliance on single sources, outdated sources, or overall coherence of support.	Paper employs multiple, relevant and authoritative sources to support major claims. One or two sources may still be outdated, the student may lean too heavily on one source in one section of the paper, or the breadth of the student's claim may render comprehensive coverage of previous work unrealistic.	Paper uses multiple authoritative sources to support all major claims; sources derive from a relevant, coherent, and thoroughly researched field of work; some may be impressively advanced for a 102 student.
Purpose	Paper has no thesis statement and does not acknowledge previous work in this area.	Paper has no thesis statement or no acknowledgment of previous work in this area.	Paper has unclear thesis statement and does not sufficiently acknowledge previous work in this area.	Paper has clear, coherent thesis statement even though it is often too broad to defend in 10 pages; previous work is acknowledged but may not be explicitly connected to student's thesis.	Paper has clear, coherent thesis statement that explicitly relates to previous work. May gesture toward an original argument but not fully explain it. Scope of thesis may still be too broad for a 10-page paper.	Paper has clear, coherent, specific thesis statement that is reasonably scoped to a 10-page paper and extends previous work in an original direction to a degree reasonable for 102.
Documentation and Citation	Documentation and/or citation is missing altogether for many sources, resulting in inadvertent or deliberate plagiarism.	It is unclear if all sources used are cited; documentation when present is in the wrong format overall or is partial.	Documentation and citation are in place for all source material but contain many patterns of errors.	Documentation and citation are in place for all source material, though one or two patterns of error may still exist.	Documentation and citation are in place for all source material with a few very minor errors (no pattern of error).	Documentation and citation are functionally flawless according to the required style (one or two small punctuation goofs OK).

Framing	Quotations and paraphrases, if used at all, are not introduced or "unpacked" and frequently appear as the first sentence of a paragraph.	Quotations and paraphrases are inaccurately or only partially introduced and "unpacked" across the board.	Quotations and paraphrases are generally introduced or "unpacked" though part of the frame is still frequently missing or some sources appear to be misinterpreted.	Quotations and paraphrases are generally introduced and "unpacked" accurately though a few problems with consistency and sufficiency of frame may remain.	All quotations and paraphrases are introduced and "unpacked" such that they flow into the argument, though occasional lapses may remain.	All quotations and paraphrases are introduced and "unpacked" in a manner that integrates them nearly seamlessly with the overall argument.
Awareness of Own Biases	Paper states claim far more strongly than the assembled evidence permits and refuses to admit any limitations or bias to author's perspective. Never hedges (e.g., "seem," "perhaps," "some/most" etc.) or qualifies (amends argument in response to alternative perspectives).	Paper overstates claim and makes only a token attempt to hedge or qualify; thus, bias/limitations of author's perspective remain unaddressed and unaltered.	Paper overstates claim or makes inconsistent attempts to hedge/qualify claim, thus leaving reader worried that author does not realize the limitations of own perspective.	Scope/strength of main argument is justified overall by the evidence presented. Author hedges or qualifies claim, although these efforts may not fully reassure reader that the author fully realizes limitations of own perspective.	Paper evinces solid claim whose limitations are clearly marked with appropriate hedging and qualification strategies; however, author may stop short of establishing a clear, grounded ethos with respect to argument.	Paper clearly grounds or establishes the author's ethos and, from that position, makes a strong argument that conscientiously addresses its limitations; author casts own argument as one of several valid perspectives.
Awareness of Others' Perspectives	Paper either ignores differing perspectives or misrepresents them across the board, resulting in plagiarism, straw man fallacy, ad hominem, and/or stereotype.	When paper treats differing perspectives, it generally misrepresents or dismisses them with few exceptions.	Paper may mention differing perspectives neutrally/fairly but makes either limited or no response to these arguments.	Paper addresses differing perspectives respectfully but may still lack depth in analyzing or responding to them.	Paper addresses differing perspectives respectfully and analyzes the causes or effects of these perspectives in some depth.	Paper not only addresses differing perspectives respectfully but also casts main argument as a response to diverse perspectives.

The Burkean Parlor as Boundary Object   121

Works Cited

Artman, Margaret, Erica Frisicaro-Pawlowski, and Robert Monge. "Not Just One Shot: Extending the Dialogue About Information Literacy in Composition Classes." *Composition Studies*, vol. 38, no. 2, 2010, pp. 93-110.

Association of College and Research Libraries. "Framework for Information Literacy for Higher Education," 23 Sept. 2016, ala.org/acrl/standards/ilframework.

Barratt, Caroline Cason, et al. "Collaboration is Key: Librarians and Composition Instructors Analyze Student Research and Writing." *Portal: Libraries and the Academy*, vol.9, no.1, 2009, pp. 37-56.

Burke, Kenneth. *The Philosophy of Literary Form*. U of California P, 1974.

D'Angelo, Barbara J., and Barry Maid. "Moving Beyond Definitions: Implementing Information Literacy across the Curriculum." *The Journal of Academic Librarianship*, Vol. 30, no. 3, 2004, pp. 212-17.

Davidson, Jeanne R., and Carole Ann Crateau. "Intersections: Teaching Research through a Rhetorical Lens." *Research Strategies*. vol. 16, no. 4, 1998, pp. 245-57.

Davis, Robert, and Mark Shadle. "'Building a Mystery': Alternative Research Writing and the Academic Act of Seeking." *CCC*, vol. 51, no. 3, 2000, pp. 417-46.

Deyrup, Marta Mestrovic, and Beth Bloom, editors. *Successful Strategies for Teaching Undergraduate Research*. Scarecrow Press, 2013.

Dimitrov, Dimiter M., and Phillip D. Rumrill, Jr. "Pretest-Posttest Designs and Measurement of Change." *Work*, vol. 20, no. 2, 2003, pp. 159-65.

Elbow, Peter. *Everyone can Write: Essays Toward a Hopeful Theory of Writing and Teaching Writing*. Oxford UP, 2000.

Gieryn, Thomas F. "Boundary-Work and the Demarcation of Science from Non-Science: Strains and Interests in Professional Ideologies of Scientists." *American Sociological Review*, vol. 48, no. 6, 1983, pp. 781-95.

Goodburn, Amy, and Heather Camp. "English 354: Advanced Composition Writing Ourselves/Communities into Public Conversations." *Composition Studies*, vol. 32, no. 1, 2004, p. 89-108.

Graff, Gerald, and Cathy Birkenstein. *"They Say / I Say": The Moves That Matter in Academic Writing*. 3rd ed., W.W. Norton, 2014.

Hallgren, Kevin A. "Computing Inter-Rater Reliability for Observational Data: An Overview and Tutorial." *Tutorials in Quantitative Methods for Psychology*, vol. 8, no. 1, Jan. 2012, pp. 23–34, doi:10.20982/tqmp.08.1.

Howard, Rebecca, and Sandra Jamieson. "What Is the Citation Project?" *The Citation Project RSS*, Syracuse University, 28 July 2015, citationproject.net/.

Ivy, Robert T. "Teaching Faculty Perceptions of Academic Librarians at Memphis State University (Research Note)." *College and Research Libraries*, vol. 55, no. 1, 1994, pp. 69-82.

Lunsford, Andrea A., John J. Ruszkiewicz, and Keith Walters. *Everything's an Argument with Readings*. 6th ed., Bedford/St. Martins, 2013.

Manuel, Kate, et al. "An Ethnographic Study of Attitudes Influencing Faculty Collaboration in Library Instruction." *Reference Librarian*, vol. 43, no. 89/90, 2005, pp. 139-61.

Martinez, Aja Y. "A Plea for Critical Race Theory Counterstory: Stock Story Versus Counterstory Dialogues Concerning Alejandra's 'Fit' in the Academy." *Composition Studies*, vol. 42, no. 2, 2014, p. 33-55.

McMillen, Paula S., and Eric Hill. "Why Teach Research as a Conversation in Freshman Composition Courses?: A Metaphor to Help Librarians and Composition Instructors Develop a Shared Model." *Research Strategies*, vol. 20, no. 1-2, 2004, pp. 3-22.

Milman, Natalie B. "The Flipped Classroom Strategy: What Is It and How Can It Best be Used?" *Distance Learning*, vol. 11, no. 4, 2014, p. 9-12.

McClure, Randall, and James P. Purdy, editors. *The New Digital Scholar: Exploring and Enriching the Research and Writing Practices of NEXTGEN STUDENTS*. Information Today Inc., 2013.

Paretti, Marie, et. al. "Reformist Possibilities? Exploring Writing Program Cross-Campus Partnerships." *WPA: Writing Program Administration*, vol. 33, no. 1, 2009, pp. 74-113.

Purdy, James P., and Joyce R. Walker. "Liminal Spaces and Research Identity the Construction of Introductory Composition Students as Researchers." *Pedagogy*, vol. 13, no. 1, 2013, pp. 9-41.

Ragains, Patrick. *Information Literacy Instruction That Works: a Guide to Teaching by Discipline and Student Population*. ALA–Neal Schuman, 2006.

Rogers, Everett M. *The Diffusion of Innovations*. Simon & Schuster, 2003.

Shackley, Simon, and Brian Wynne. "Representing Uncertainty in Global Climate Change Science and Policy: Boundary-Ordering Devices and Authority." *Science Technology Human Values*, vol. 21, no. 3, 1996, pp. 275-302.

Sheridan, Jean. *Writing-Across-the-Curriculum and the Academic Library: A Guide for Librarians, Instructors, and Writing Program Directors*. Greenwood Press, 1995. *ERIC*, eric.ed.gov/?id=ED395601.

Star, Susan Leigh, and James R. Griesemer. "Institutional Ecology, 'Translations' and Boundary Objects: Amateurs and Professionals in Berkeley's Museum of Vertebrate Zoology, 1907-39." *Social Studies of Science* vol. 61, no. 3, 1989, pp. 387-420.

Thaiss, Chris, and Tara Porter. "The State of WAC/WID in 2010: Methods and Results of the U.S. Survey of the International WAC/WID Mapping Project." *CCC*, vol. 61, no. 3, 2010, p. 534-70.

Trainor, Jennifer. "Moving Beyond Place in Discussions of Literacy." *Literacy in Composition Studies*, vol. 1, no. 1, 2013, pp. 45-47.

Wilder, Laura, and Joanna Wolfe. "Sharing the Tacit Rhetorical Knowledge of the Literary Scholar: The Effects of Making Disciplinary Conventions Explicit in Undergraduate Writing About Literature Courses." *Research in the Teaching of English*, vol. 44, no. 2, 2009, pp. 170-209

Course Designs

Decolonial Theory and Methodology

Andrea Riley Mukavetz

Course Description

ENG 6800/ACS 6820: Decolonial Theory and Methodology was offered as a fully online course within the English department at Bowling Green State University (BGSU). The department offers two online master's programs: a general degree in English with three possible specializations, and another in professional and technical writing. In addition, BGSU offers a doctoral degree in rhetoric and writing.

Decolonial Theory and Methodology introduces students to decolonial thinking, situates the course materials within the historical and contemporary circumstances that necessitate a decolonial approach, and encourages students to develop a decolonial scholarly and pedagogical practice reflective of their intellectual and professional goals. This course was cross-listed with the Department of American Culture Studies. Due to these circumstances, the course roster included graduate students, both fee-paying and assistantship-supported, from a variety of humanities-based programs. Students did not need previous experience in decolonial theory to enroll. In addition to using the university platform, Canvas, we also used a Google+ community to interact with each other.

Institutional Context

BGSU was built on the settled, indigenous land of the Miami and Eastern Shawnee. Each semester, I provide students with an indigenous history of Ohio and encourage them to research the peoples—both past and present—of the land on which the students live and work. Drawing from Janice Gould, it is crucial to consider the role of indigenous spaces in institutional contexts as this information provides further understanding regarding the relationship between colonial impact and knowledge making.

I designed Decolonial Theory and Methodology for multiple audiences with varied professional goals, including doctoral students in rhetoric and writing, the online master's students in English, and graduate students from English education and American culture studies. The programs that offer an online component attract returning teachers who seek certification to teach at the community-college level or in the College Credit Plus program (an Ohio-based higher education initiative that offers high school students the opportunity to take college classes before graduation and receive college credit). Students come into this class with little to no knowledge about decolonial theory, cultural rhetorics, or the contemporary experiences of American Indians. Yet, they are drawn to this course because of their interest in adding multicultural voices to their curricula. Knowing this, I make sure to provide students with foundational theories while making space for them to consider how to apply these theories in situations they find meaningful—typically, their classrooms.

Currently, the English department does not consistently offer graduate courses on non-Western theories, histories, or perspectives (with the exception of an Ethnic American Literature course as an elective for master's students in literary and textual studies). As such, the decolonial theory course fills a much-needed gap in the curriculum. While the course's presence in the curriculum has many positive outcomes, I want to note that "filling a gap" puts marginalized faculty in difficult situations where we must navigate an institutional system that does not make space for us, underrepresented people, and our lived experiences. For example, departments at BGSU must follow a university-wide enrollment policy that requires all courses to meet a particular number to run. This requirement might seem reasonable and typical in many contexts, but in small departments special topics courses compete with each other to attract students who choose from a variety of electives. Facing these obstacles, faculty develop strategies to appeal to students to enroll in the course. To put additional pressure on faculty, when students elect to take a course where the lived experiences of people of color are at the center, they will most likely not encounter these intellectual traditions in the remainder of course work. This seemingly places these traditions on the periphery. To be plain, these negotiations are further representative of how institutions of higher education are sites of paracolonial tension.

One way to solve this problem is to develop curriculum where all faculty treat the histories, traditions, and perspectives of people of color and underrepresented backgrounds as equally important and worthy of study in all of their courses (Niemann 470). A euro-centered curriculum influences how students understand the world and what constitutes intellectual knowledge, advancing a colonial viewpoint that is wholly damaging to themselves and our communities. That is why this course provides students with the foundations of decolonial theory and methodology and encourages connections between course, programs of study, and professional goals. When students enter a course where the lived experiences of people of color form the framework of the course and where they realize that much of their educational history is rooted in colonial frameworks, they go through a series of feelings: confusion, embarrassment, shame, anger, frustration, and hopelessness. Anticipating this, I value an exploratory, experience-based approach to learning that allows students to join the conversation and contribute to their prospective disciplinary discourses.

Theoretical Rationale

Decolonial theory is heavily informed by the everyday practices of indigenous people, who engage in ongoing resistance and cultural continuance for self-determination, sovereignty, and healing from colonial impact (Driskill 69). Within decolonial frameworks, the ultimate goal is to create, sustain, and maintain a habitable space for present and future generations—practicing decolonial theory is a form of care and love for ancestors and relatives. When designing a curriculum that relies on and emphasizes indigenous worldviews, I operate under the assumption that students have limited knowledge of the contemporary lives of American Indians and that their understanding of American history is from a linear settler perspective. This assumption is informed by how the American educational system has narrated the lives and histories of American Indians as being located only in the past, as instrumental in sustaining narratives of American exceptionalism, as impoverished, as located on reservations, or as suffering from alcoholism (King 27). For example, after we discuss the history of indigenous peoples of Ohio, we talk about the implications of the region's dominant narrative that American Indians willingly left the area when they were actually systematically and violently removed.

Like other cultural rhetorics scholars, I frame decolonial theory as a rhetorical tradition—one that *constellates* with and around additional traditions. As scholars of The Cultural Rhetorics Theory Lab observe, "We believe it's important to keep all traditions/stories/histories in play as equally legitimate origins and progenitors of many simultaneous rhetorical traditions. Further, we believe there is rhetorical power in building relationships between multiple traditions, multiple histories, multiple practices" (7). Through constellation, we are provided multiple options and orientations for understanding rhetorical traditions without having to begin with or return to Aristotle. Malea Powell observes that this practice of constellating offers students the opportunity to critically explore the way that knowledge is valued and considered intellectual in relation to historical events, which gives them "the tools to see the real options open to them . . . as forces, discourses they can negotiate, as decisions that they can make" (401). Overall, my goal is to provide students with this constellated understanding of decolonial theory and to show its connections with postcolonial theory, indigenous studies, critical race theory, local knowledges and grassroots movements, and queer studies. Each week, we dwell in another decolonial orientation and thereby build a complicated understanding of what it means to practice decolonial thinking. This structure allows me to emphasize that writing, representation, and perspective are always interconnected and that to engage in decolonial theory is to develop an intellectual practice cognizant of how knowledge is made through one's relationship with space, bodies, and the universe.

To assist students in understanding relationality and dwelling, we begin the semester with Frantz Fanon and Aimé Césaire. I frame these intellects as anti-colonial thinkers who theorized decolonization as a violent phenomena and who were deeply aware of the roles community, land, and region play in relation to colonial impact. I highlight the relationships Cesaire and Fanon had with each other—as mentors and mentees—and how these relationships can further teach us about dwelling and relational accountability. To expand this discussion, we move to Linda Tuhiwai Smith and Emma Pérez who argue for reconstruction instead of deconstruction and emphasize the importance of decolonial futures. Smith and Pérez direct us to conversations about the role of citation practices, developing a decolonial language of critique, and working with and for communities. Throughout the semester, we return to these topics with additional perspectives to show the vastness of decolonial theory and to provide students with concrete examples of engagement in decolonial thinking and practice.

In addition to academic writing, poetry, and creative nonfiction, I assigned quite a few feature films, songs, and stand-up comedy sketches. These materials are produced by younger generations of intellectuals, like Supaman, Ryan McMahon (creator of the "Red Man Laughing" podcast), Christi Belcourt, or the 1491s who work with their communities, conduct educational workshops, and are prominent activists. Drawing from Walter Mignolo, we learn how to listen to and learn from delinking and epistemic disobedience activities central to local movements. When students engaged with these artists and their pieces, I asked them to pay attention to how they theorized their making practices in relation to land, time, culture, and bodies. In addition, I wanted students to hear how these artists listened to their elders, took teachings, and used particular modes like fashion, comedy, or hip-hop to speak to younger generations *as* community-based research. My hope was that these artists would be models for non-hierarchical work with, for, and alongside communities.

I designed experiential assignments to provide additional opportunities for students to practice relational accountability, interconnectedness, and embodiment. Throughout the semester, students engaged in low-stakes activities where I prompted them to do things like "tell me a story" or "spend time outside." For one activity, I asked students to map their intellectual genealogy by naming their scholarly relatives and ancestors, which gave students the opportunity to build a rhetorical tradition that exemplified their histories, subject positions, experiences, and intellectual goals. Students completed these assignments independently and reported their experiences and observations via our Google+ community. This created a classroom structured around relational accountability where students could publicly provide support and stand witness to each other.

In addition to these low-risk activities, students wrote weekly responses, responded to peers in discussion forums on Canvas and Google+, and produced two projects, a rhetorical fieldwork assignment and a self-directed final project. The rhetorical fieldwork assignment was designed for students to put into practice their theoretical questions about the roles of outsiders (in this case, researchers from dominant backgrounds) entering underrepresented communities. This assignment allowed students to experience what it felt like to observe, engage with the land, and work with underrepresented communities as a starting point for relational research. Students selected an independent experience or attended the organized field trip to the Octagon Earthworks, the largest earthen enclosures in the world, which are currently being used as a golf club in Newark, Ohio. In preparation for the fieldwork, they researched the place they wanted to visit and the people who created or maintained that space. The purpose of this assignment was for students to understand that indigenous space is always connected to ongoing colonial impact and to feel that interconnectedness. This, in turn, helped them understand how decolonial practice is always localized and affective. After the fieldwork, students completed a short narrative, situated within decolonial discussions, that detailed what they did to prepare for the experience and recounted their embodied reactions when engaging with the people and the community.

To meet students' wide range of interests and goals, I created a self-directed final project. Each student submitted a proposal and met with me so I could answer questions and provide guidance. Student projects included a video tracing the history of a town where one student grew up to explore his complicity in colonial rhetorics, an exploratory narrative incorporating decolonial practices within the first-year writing classroom, curriculum plans for incorporating indigenous and decolonial theories within high school English classrooms, and a variety of annotated bibliographies that explored decolonial theory as it intersects with a subject of the student's choice. Through these projects, each student found a way to thoughtfully engage with relationality, interconnectedness, embodiment, and land-based methods.

In *The Darker Side of Western Modernity*, Walter Mignolo argues that there is a different type of reward that comes with delinking from the logics of modernity. Seeking such a reward, I strove to create an evaluation and assessment system that reflected decolonial thinking. I met with each student to determine individual goals and expectations. During our meeting, we discussed how to use the course to meet their goals. Evidence of practice, completion, and engagement with course concepts were the key criteria I used when reading and evaluating student projects. Additionally, students submitted a writer's memo that explained their rhetorical situation, the process of making and completing the project, and the feedback they wanted from me. The memo was designed to provide students a space to think reflectively and critically about their own process while giving consent and direction for how their work would be engaged. This approach allowed me to invite in-process and exploratory projects that did not end with the semester. I was able to assist students in envisioning the next steps whether it was conducting further research, creating curricular materials for their own classrooms, or identifying a journal for publication.

Critical Reflection

Since most students came from a euro-centric background, the majority of the online discussion centered around concerns about how they could or should participate in decolonial thinking. While the class engaged in thoughtful discussion, it was limited by their apprehension about whether they had the authority to contribute to the discourses of decolonial thinking and practice. I responded in a variety of ways, from encouraging them that they each have a place in the conversation to explaining that we are all affected by colonial rhetorics, or that we can all benefit from decoloniality. These responses aimed to provide students with support and solace while giving them permission to engage with the ideas of the course. Rather than solely worry about their subject positions, I wanted the students to imagine what it would look like for them to engage in decoloniality in their own lives. I realize now that this expectation was unfair and that the class needed to express their concerns in a cyclical way—throughout the semester. Looking back, I hear the class trying to theorize and understand their responsibility and privilege as euro-Americans and academics by voicing apprehension and concern. Learning from this experience, when I teach this course again I will create openings for these conversations and treat these concerns as absolutely reasonable and theoretically on point. I will frame these discussions as a way to explore our complicity in colonial practices and further understand how to delink from the logics of modernity. I think the struggle will always be to help students understand that I do not expect them to leave this course fully delinked from the colonial matrix of power or completely knowledgeable about how to do decolonial theory. In fact, that is a completely unrealistic expectation for anyone.

Often, I think about how I could provide more applications of decolonial theory throughout the semester. I would continue to assign low-stakes ongoing decolonial practices for students to experience and then connect to the readings. Sometimes I dream about reaching out to a community with whom I have a connection, asking what they might need, and then, depending on the scope, achieving a task for that community during the semester. This could mean designing a flyer or website, or assisting with set-up or clean-up for a local event, as all labor is important and necessary, especially when working with local communities. I think a lot about Standing Rock and how the protesters really needed folks to cook and clean the dishes. This is unrewarded decolonial work that women and queer people especially have always done. I wonder what it would feel and look like to bring a group of graduate students to work with a community without a research project in mind. The work they do with the community could help them think about their role within the university and how they might use that role for community engagement and transformative change. I am being diffident here because this type of activity is not easily arranged; it depends on connections the instructor has with the community and with the students.

Overall, students expressed that they enjoyed the course and wished it were face-to-face in order to have more opportunities to engage in direct discussion. I think this desire stems from my emphasis on embodiment, experiential learning, and relationality. But also, many of us struggled with the technology—Google groups, discussion boards, the Google+ community—and with adequate internet access for video conferences and downloading video lectures. I have alleviated some of these conflicts by using Canvas only, which now offers a conference feature that allows students to video conference with each other and me and allows me to record lectures.

If I were to teach this course face-to-face, I would further emphasize the experiential learning component, which aligns with the emphasis on practice within decolonial and indigenous theories. I would ask students to make something like a basket or to do beadwork, we would map during class, or students would pass their notebooks around and respond in one another's notebooks. During the first snow, we would spend the day solely telling stories and participating in talking circles. Also, I would want us to do more fieldwork together like go to a museum, visit a historical site, or work in the archives. The field trip to the Earthworks deeply and positively impacted both the students who attended and myself. I was able to model what it looked like to be a good visitor and relative by displaying the practices used when acknowledging indigenous space in a way that could not happen in the classroom. Because these types of experiences are central to the course and not supplementary, an embodied, relational learning should be prioritized and rewarded. Overall, what excites me about engaging with this content in the classroom is that it creates a space for both teacher and student to learn with and from each other, their peers, the land, and the universe, where knowledge is not claimed but received, as a gift, and requires responsibility and care.

Works Cited

Belcourt, Christi. "My Heart is Beautiful." *YouTube*, 2 May 2012, www.youtube.com/watch?v=JwNHNm9dw6Y.

Césaire, Aimé. *Notebook of a Return to the Native Land*, translated by Clayton Eshleman, Wesleyan UP, 2003.

The Cultural Rhetorics Theory Lab (Malea Powell, Daisy Levy, Andrea Riley Mukavetz, Marilee Brooks-Gillies, Maria Novotny, and Jennifer Fisch-Ferguson). "Our Story Begins Here: Constellating Cultural Rhetorics." *enculturation: a journal of rhetoric, writing, and culture*, 25 Oct. 2014, enculturation.net/our-story-begins-here.

Driskill, Qwo-li. "Doubleweaving Two Spirit Critiques: Building Alliances Between Native and Queer Studies." *GLQ: A Journal of Lesbian and Gay Studies*, vol. 16, no. 1-2, 2010, pp. 69-92.

Fanon, Frantz, *Wretched of the Earth*. Grove, 2005.

Gould, Janice. "The Problem of Being 'Indian': One Mixed-Blood's Dilemma." *De/Colonizing the Subject: The Politics of Gender in Women's Autobiography*, edited by Sidonie Smith and Julia Watson, U of Minnesota P, 1992, pp. 81-87.

King, Lisa. "Sovereignty, Rhetorical Sovereignty, and Representation: Keywords for Teaching Indigenous Texts." *Survivance, Sovereignty, and Story: Teaching American Indian Rhetorics*, edited by Lisa King, Rose Gubele, and Joyce Rain Anderson, U of Colorado P, 2015, pp. 17-34.

McMahon, Ryan. "Red Man Laughing." *Indian and Cowboy Radio*, 2013, www.redmanlaughing.com.

Mignolo, Walter. *The Darker Side of Western Modernity: Global Futures, Decolonial Options*. Duke UP, 2011.

Niemann, Yolanda Flores. "Lessons from the Experiences of Women of Color in Working in Academia." *Presumed Incompetent: The Intersections of Race and Class for Women in Academia*, edited by Gabriella Gutiérrez y Muhs, Yolanda Flores Niemann, Caren G. González, and Angela P. Harris, Utah State UP, 2012, pp. 446-99.

Pérez, Emma. *The Decolonial Imaginary: Writing Chicanas into History*. Indiana UP, 1999.

Powell, Malea. "2012 CCCC Chair's Address, Stories Take Place: A Performance in One Act." *CCC*, vol. 64, no. 2, 2012, pp. 383-406.

Smith, Linda Tuhiwai. *Decolonizing Methodologies: Research and Indigenous Peoples*. Zed, 1999.

Supaman. "Prayer Loop Song." *YouTube*, 20 Feb. 2014, www.youtube.com/watch?v=_0jq7jIa34Y.the1491s. "the 1491s." *YouTube*, 26 Mar. 2010, https://www.youtube.com/user/the1491s.

Syllabus

ENG 6800/ACS 6820 Decolonial Theory and Methodology
Fall 2014
Andrea Riley Mukavetz

Course Description

This course is designed as an introduction to decolonial theory and methodology. Specifically, we will draw from both academic and nonacademic intellectual communities to understand the traditions, practices, and histories associated with decolonization and decoloniality. Since this course is an introduction, I will try to "hold the space" for you to explore, examine, practice, understand, and play with decolonial theory.

What We'll Do

Read, write, talk, write to each other, visit places, listen to music, watch movies, and practice forming decolonial relationships with each other and to the subject material.

Throughout the semester, I will ask you to consider the following:
- How do decolonial scholars practice decolonization? And what can we learn from them as scholars, teachers, and human beings?
- How do decolonial scholars theorize healing? What does survival look like?
- How do decolonial scholars form relationships with colonial histories? What does decolonial history and historiography look like?
- How does colonialism and paracolonialism impact decolonization and decolonial practice?

Required Readings

Articles and Books

Bird, Gloria, and Joy Harjo. *Reinventing the Enemy's Language: Contemporary Native Women's Writings in North America*. W.W. Norton, 1997.
Brooks, Lisa. *The Common Pot: The Recovery of Native Space in the Northeast*. U of Minnesota P, 2008.
Césaire, Aimé. *Notebook of a Return to the Native Land,* translated by Clayton Eshleman, Wesleyan UP, 2003.
Driskill, Qwo-li. "Doubleweaving Two Spirit Critiques: Building Alliances Between Native and Queer Studies." *GLQ: A Journal of Lesbian and Gay Studies,* vol. 16, no. 1-2, 2010, pp. 69-92.

Driskill, Qwo-li, Chris Finley, Brian Joseph Gilley, and Scott Morgensen, editors. *Queer Indigenous Studies: Critical Interventions in Theory, Politics, and Literature.* U of Arizona P, 2011.

Driskill, Qwo-li, Daniel Heath Justice, Debora Miranda, and Lisa Tatonetti, editors. *Sovereign Erotics: A Collection of Two-Spirit Literature.* U of Arizona P, 2011.

Erdrich, Louise. *Books and Islands in Ojibwe Country: Traveling Through the Lands of My Ancestors,* National Geographic, 2003.

Ettawageshik, Frank. "My Father's Business." *Unpacking Culture: Art and Commodity in Colonial and Postcolonial Worlds,* edited by Ruth B. Phillips and Christopher Burghard Steiner, U of California P, 1999, pp. 21-29.

Fanon, Frantz, *Wretched of the Earth.* Grove, 2005.

Gutiérrez y Muhs, Gabriella, Yolanda Flores Niemann, Caren G. González, and Angela P. Harris, editors. *Presumed Incompetent: The Intersections of Race and Class for Women in Academia.* Utah State UP, 2012.

hooks, bell. *Teaching to Transgress: Education as a Practice of Freedom.* Routledge, 1994.

Jackson, Shona N. *Creole Indigeneity: Between Myth and Nation in the Caribbean.* U of Minnesota P, 2012.

King, Thomas. *The Truth About Stories: A Native Narrative.* U of Minnesota P, 2005.

Kuppers, Petra, "Decolonizing Disability, Indigeneity, and Poetic Methods: Hanging Out in Australia." *Journal of Literary and Cultural Disability Studies,* vol. 7, no. 2, 2013, pp. 175-93. *EBSCO.* doi:10.3828/jlcds.2013.13.

MacKay, Gail A. "A Reading of Eekwol's 'Apprentice to the Mystery' as an Expression of Cree Youth's Cultural Role and Responsibility." *American Indian Culture and Research Journal,* vol. 34, no. 2, 2010, pp. 47-65. *UCLA American Indian Studies Center Publications,* doi:10.17953/aicr.34.2.y02775k6713t0573.

Maracle, Lee. *Oratory: Coming to Theory.* Gallerie, 1990.

Mignolo, Walter. *The Darker Side of Western Modernity: Global Futures, Decolonial Options.* Duke UP, 2011.

Million, Dian. "There is a River in Me: Theory from Life." *Theorizing Native Studies,* edited by Andrea Smith and Audra Simpson, Duke UP, 2014.

Miner, Dylan. "Red (Pedal) Power: Natives, Bikes, and Ant-Colonial Art." *Do Not Park Bicycles!: Aboriginal Bike Culture,* edited by Jenny Western, Art Gallery of Southwest Manitoba, 2007, pp. 1-15. *Academia.edu,* www.academia.edu/1964418/.

—. "Straddling la otra Frontera: Revisioning Chicana/o Art History through MiChicana/o Visual Culture." *Aztlan: The Journal of Chicano Studies,* vol. 33, no. 1, 2008, pp. 89-122.

Miranda, Deborah. *Bad Indians: A Tribal Memoir.* Heyday, 2013.

Moraga, Cherríe. *A Xicana Codex of Changing Consciousness Writings, 2000-2010.* Duke UP, 2011.

Navarro, Jenell. "Solarize-ing Native hip-hop: Native Feminist Land Ethics and Cultural Resistance." *Decolonization: Indigeneity, Education & Society,* vol. 3, no. 1, 2014, pp. 101-18, decolonization.org/index.php/des/article/view/20812.

Pérez, Emma. *The Decolonial Imaginary: Writing Chicanas into History.* Indiana UP, 1999.

Powell, Malea. "Dreaming of Charles Eastman: Cultural Memory, Autobiography, and Geography in Indigenous Rhetorical Histories." *Beyond the Archives: Research as a Lived Process,* edited by Gesa E. Krisch and Liz Rohan, SIUP, 2008, pp. 115-27.

—. "Listening to Ghosts: An Alternative (Non)Argument." *ALT DIS: Alternatives to Academic Discourse,* edited by Christopher Schroeder, Helen Fox, and Patricia Bizzell, Boynton/Cook-Heinemann, 2002, pp. 11-22.

Sefa Dei, George. "Indigenous Anti-Colonial Knowledge as 'Heritage Knowledge' for Promoting Black/African Education in Diasporic Contexts." *Decolonization: Indigeneity, Education and Society,* vol.1, no.1, 2012, pp. 102-19, decolonization.org/index.php/des/article/view/18631.

Simpson, Leanne. *Island of Decolonial Love.* Arbeiter Ring, 2013.

Smith, Linda Tuhiwai. *Decolonizing Methodologies: Research and Indigenous Peoples.* Zed, 1999.

Thiong'o, Ngugi Wa. *Decolonising the Mind: The Politics of Language in African Literature.* James Currey LTD/Heinemann, 1986.

Villanueva, Victor. "On the Rhetoric and Precendents of Racism." *CCC,* vol. 50, no. 4, 1999, pp. 645-61.

Wilson, Shawn. *Research is Ceremony: Indigenous Research Methods.* Fernwood, 2008.

Film, Music, Comedy, Websites

Atanarjuat: The Fast Runner. Directed by Zacharias Kinuk, Sony Pictures, 2002.

A Tribe Called Red. "A Tribe Called Red." MuchFACT, 2012, atribecalledred.com/releases/tribe-called-red-tribe-called-red/.

Belcourt, Christi. "My Heart is Beautiful." *YouTube,* 2 May 2012, www.youtube.com/watch?v=JwNHNm9dw6Y.

Beyond Buckskin. "Home." http://shop.beyondbuckskin.com/category/new.

Eekwol. "Too Sick." *YouTube,* 5 May 2009, www.youtube.com/watch?v=0XuYikRUl7g.

Justice, Daniel Heath. "Carrying The Fire." http://nationsrising.org/carrying-the-fire/.

Keen, Adrienne. "Native Appropriations." http://nativeappropriations.com/.

McMahon, Ryan. "Red Man Laughing." *Indian and Cowboy Radio,* 2013, www.redmanlaughing.com.

the1491s. " the 1491s." *YouTube,* 26 Mar. 2010, https://www.youtube.com/user/the1491s.

The Lesser Blessed. Directed by Anita Doron, Monterey Media, 2012.

McMahon, Ryan. "Red Man Laughing." *Indian and Cowboy Radio,* 2013, www.redmanlaughing.com.

Sacramento Knoxx. "The Rise of the Turtle." *BandCamp,* 2012, sknoxx.bandcamp.com/album/the-rise-of-the-turtle.

Selena. Directed by Gregory Nava, Warner Home Video, 1997.

Supaman. "Prayer Loop Song." *YouTube,* 20 Feb. 2014, www.youtube.com/watch?v=_0jq7jIa34Y.

Walking with Our Sisters. "About." walkingwithoursisters.ca/.

Required Software/Technologies (and how we will use them…)

Google account: We will be using a Google+ community and Google group. Once you create a Google account, please add me to your circle and then I will invite you to our community and group.

Google+ community (BGSU_Decolonial Theory and Methodology): I will use this space to share relevant information including course materials and communicate with you. You should use this space to do the same.

Google group (BGSU_decolonial theory and methodology): You will use this space to post your weekly writings and respond to classmates.

Email: Since this is an online course, I expect you to check (and respond to) email regularly. Please let me know your desired email address for communication.

Canvas: We will use Canvas as an archive for assignments, assignment guidelines, and syllabus and schedule details.

Scheduled Face-to-Face Sessions (and my expectations…)

In order to give everyone the opportunity for some face-to-face time, I will offer the following opportunities:

- A group field trip for the Rhetorical Fieldwork Assignment (this is optional and will be discussed at a later time).
- Monthly Google Hangout sessions to discuss and synthesize the material (this is required).
- Group movie watching session: I will schedule a time, on BGSU's campus, to watch the required movies. (This is optional, but there will be popcorn.)
- Office hours will be held via Google Hangouts by appointment. Additionally, I will be on campus once a week and will happily meet with students face-to-face!

Assignment Descriptions

Rhetorical Fieldwork 20%

You will visit a place that engages with or enacts decolonial practices or ideas. While visiting this place, you should try to be mindful of or engage with decolonial practices while you observe and inhabit the space. Afterwards, you will write something that discusses the place you visited—the rhetorical practices and histories at play and how you see decolonial theory or practice at work. You may use any narrative style to do so. (Please see assignment guidelines below.)

Rhetorical Fieldwork Assignment Guidelines
For this assignment, you will do rhetorical fieldwork (experiential observation) at an event or space/place that engages with or uses decolonial theories and practices. After you visit the space/place/event, you will write a narrative that further examines what you experienced and observed. I will schedule an optional field trip for those who are local (details TBD).

The narrative should trace your experience inhabiting the space and examine the decolonial practices, traditions, and histories of the space. While writing, please consider the following questions:

- Why did you select this event/space/place?
- What is its significance to the surrounding communities?
- Who participates?
- What does participation look like (i.e., practices)?
- How is the space decolonial (i.e., practices, strategies)?
- What tensions did you notice or experience (i.e., paracolonial fissures)?
- How did visiting and inhabiting the space help you understand course materials and class discussions?
- How did it feel to engage in this fieldwork experience?
- What did you realize or learn along the way?

Before Attending

- Research the space/place and community of people.
- Gather your materials (notebook, tickets, appropriate materials necessary to engage with community).
- Freewrite on your expectations and concerns.

When Attending

- Take notes.
- Observe.
- Listen.
- Pay attention to and be aware of your body.
- Talk to people and ask questions.
- Take your time.
- Buy something (optional, but important).

Additional Information
- 5-6 pages following MLA style.
- *Peer-reviewed, secondary resources are optional.*

Weekly Writing 50%

Since this is an online course, the majority of our interaction will be through online discussion. Each week, you are responsible for writing something in response to the readings. These discussions are mainly exploratory—an intellectual space for you to think through the ideas from the course materials and consider how you and your research interests fit into the conversation. You are not expected to use these discussions to prove that you have read or understood the material (i.e., summary and synthesis). Instead, I would like you to use the discussions to continue the conversation from the reading—to show what you are grappling with.

In addition to writing a weekly discussion, you will respond to one classmate each week. This discussion is designed to replicate conversation that occurs during a face-to-face seminar. In addition, you are welcome to provide a video response to replace a written one. *Generally, the weekly writings should be about two pages.* If you draw from class materials, please make sure to follow the MLA style guide.

Deadlines
Unless previously notified, all weekly writing should be posted on Thursdays by midnight. The writing should be uploaded to our Google group.

Unless previously notified, you should respond to one classmate on Mondays by midnight. These responses should be uploaded to our Google group.

Spotlight Discussion 10%

Once during the semester, you will write a longer response generated from the reading and your peers' responses. Like the weekly responses, you are not expected to summarize the readings or your classmates' responses. Instead, you are expected to draw attention to and further theorize any threads that you see among the responses and want to grapple with. In addition, you should post this discussion to our Google+ community. Spotlight discussions should be about *four or five pages long and follow the MLA style guide.*

Deadline
The spotlight discussion is due Friday by midnight.

Self-Directed Final Project 20%

Ultimately, I would like you to complete a final project that is useful and interesting to you. The options are just suggestions and not requirements. In fact, you can combine or modify them to meet your interests.

Options:
- Tell me a story that examines your relationship to decolonial theory and practice.
- Give me a little razzle-dazzle (i.e., something multimodal, material, aural, or visual).
- Go investigative (research and further understand a historical space/place, a public intellectual, or an event that you believe deserves further research and discussion).
- Engage with a community.
- Develop a project that is pedagogical (e.g., an annotated syllabus or curriculum rationale arguing for decolonial theories and practices).
- Develop a project that is a work in progress (e.g., an annotated bibliography that incorporates decolonial texts).

<u>Additional Guidelines</u>

Before you develop your proposal, please schedule a meeting with me to discuss your project.

In preparation for that meeting, develop a 300-500 word proposal. The proposal is due Week 13 and should include

- a brief description of your project,
- identification of the rhetorical situation: audience, purpose, forum (the location where audience will access piece) and context, and
- any questions that you have for me.

Schedule

Week 1	Césaire: *Notebook* Fanon: *Wretched* ("Preface")
Week 2	Pérez: *Decolonial Imaginary* (selections) Smith: *Decolonizing Methodologies* (selections) Optional but recommended: *Selena*
Week 3	Mignolo: *Darker Side* (introduction, part 1, part 2)

Week 4	Jackson: *Creole Indigeneity* (introduction, creole indigeneity) Thiong'o: *Decolonising the Mind* (all but "Language of African Theater") Google Hangouts session
Week 5	Powell: "Listening," "Dreaming" Driskill: "Doubleweaving" King: *Truth* (sections 1 and 2) Simpson: *Island* (selections) Million: "There is a River" Maracle: *On Oratory*
Week 6	Erdrich: *Books and Islands (selections)* Bird and Harjo: *Reinventing* (selections)
Week 7	Brooks: *Common Pot* (selections) Erdrich: *Books and Islands (selections)*
Week 8	Miranda: *Bad Indians* Google Hangouts session
Week 9	*Lesser Blessed* *Atanarjuat* Meet in 206 East Hall (I'll bring the popcorn), or watch movies on your own.
Week 10	Moraga: *Xicana Codex*
Week 11	Driskill, Justice, et al.: *Sovereign Erotics* (selections) Driskill, Finley, et al.: *Queer Indigenous Studies* (selections)

Week 12
 Due:
   Rhetorical
   Fieldwork
	Wilson: *Research*

Week 13	Sacramento Knoxx: "Rise" (selections) A Tribe Called Red: "A Tribe Called Red" Supaman: "Prayer Loop Song" Eekwol: "Too Sick" "Red Man Laughing" (selections) the1491s: (selections) MacKay: "Reading" Navarro: "Solarize-ing"
Week 14, Thanksgiving Break	Spend some time on and with the land

Week 15	Miner: "Red (Pedal) Power," "Straddling" Ettawageshik: "My Father's Business" Kuppers: "Decolonizing" Visit the website *Walking with Our Sisters* Belcourt: "My Heart" Optional but recommended: Visit the websites *Beyond Buckskin* and *Native Appropriations Examining Representations of Indigenous Peoples*
Week 16, final week of classes	Justice: "Carrying" Sefa Dei: "Indigenous Anti-Colonial Knowledge" Gutiérrez y Muhs, et al.: *Presumed Incompetent* (selections) hooks: *Teaching to Transgress* (selections) Optional but recommended: Villanueva: "Precedent"
Week 17, exam week Due: Final Project	

Course Design

Writing and Rhetoric 3326: Legal Writing

Drew M. Loewe

Course Description

Writing and Rhetoric 3326: Legal Writing is an introduction to legal analysis and writing. It is offered at St. Edward's University in Austin, Texas, a Holy Cross liberal arts university of approximately 4,300 students, mostly undergraduates. The university's mission includes preparing students through "training in critical and creative thinking as well as moral reasoning to analyze problems, propose solutions and make responsible decisions" ("Mission"). The mission also focuses on students' preparation "to express themselves articulately in both oral and written form," "to confront the critical issues of society," and "to seek justice and peace" ("Mission").

The only prerequisite to the course is completion of the university's two first-year writing courses. The course, which fulfills a requirement in the political science pre-law track, is an elective within the degree plans for the departments of writing and rhetoric and communications. The undergraduate catalog describes the course this way:

> This course focuses on applied rhetoric, and is designed to give undergraduate students experience in writing clear, effective plain-language legal documents. The course offers a range of realistic legal writing problems, but does not presume any specialized legal knowledge. The writing assignments will help students to improve their writing and editing skills and to refine their abilities to analyze and develop arguments within a legal context.

Institutional Context

At St. Edward's, one section of Legal Writing is offered every year and typically enrolls 12–18 students in a course that meets twice a week. It is housed in the university's writing and rhetoric department and bears that department's WRIT course prefix. The course serves a mixed population of undergraduates, drawn primarily from among four majors: criminal justice, political science, writing and rhetoric, and communications. Students who take the course are often considering law school or professional writing careers and thus enroll out of professional interest, curiosity, or the desire for an upper-division elective different from other humanities courses. The course has been offered for over ten years; I have taught it nine times since 2010.

I have designed and refined the course in an effort to respond to three challenges. First, as mentioned above, the course's only prerequisite is a 1000-level general education course, Rhetoric and Composition II. Rhetoric and Composition II focuses on helping students develop transferable knowledge about research, source use, and argumentation in academic writing. But that course asks students to work within scholarly genres more common to academic writing as a whole rather than to the specialized world of legal writing. Second, there is no required state or national curriculum that students must complete to be admitted to law school, a larger reality mirrored by the curriculum at St. Edward's. The political science major at St. Edward's does offer a pre-law track of three courses, with students required to complete (a) either Criminal Law I or a business course titled Legal Environment of Business, and (b) two other courses out of three possibilities, one of which is Legal Writing. St. Edward's also offers philosophy courses in legal ethics and philosophy of law, as well as the business course mentioned above (and another on constitutional law), but those courses focus on scholarly analysis. Third, although most students who take the course have no legal writing experience, a few students have interned for state legislators or in law firms and do have some exposure to legal writing and analysis.

The course tries to meet these challenges by not being too elementary or too advanced; it is designed to help students gain practical experience in thinking and writing effectively within common legal situations and in everyday legal genres. It is not a course in doctrinal law or in academic law review style analysis. Rather, it borrows from professional writing courses and from law school legal writing courses that immerse students in realistic scenarios, common writing situations, and everyday genres to teach writing as solving a problem on behalf of a client.

Theoretical Rationale

The rationale for the course's design is influenced by my experience as a practicing attorney[1]; the open pathway into the course; the mix of students who take the course; and repeated calls from the bench, bar, and legal scholars to reform legal education. These factors led me to make three major pedagogical choices.

First, I designed the course to simulate everyday legal practice. I structure the course this way because lawyers and judges have been complaining for years that beginning lawyers are not prepared for the day-to-day realities of law practice. The American Bar Association (ABA) has long urged providers of legal education to make that education more relevant to the actual work that lawyers do. For instance, the ABA's 1992 "Statement of Fundamental Lawyering Skills and Professional Values," found in the so-called "MacCrate Report," describes the skills that legal education ought to help students develop; these skills include "problem-solving," "legal analysis and reasoning," and "communication" (138-41). As a result of continued criticisms of law schools' "reliance on passive learning in the classroom," "focus on appellate cases," and "failure to prepare law students for the real-life experience of representing clients and practicing law" after the 1992 statement, the ABA passed a resolution in 2011 urging providers of legal education "to implement curricular programs intended to develop practice-ready lawyers" (2). The ABA called upon law schools to reform curricula and clinical experiences to focus on the "skills, aptitudes, values and habits a contemporary lawyer should optimally possess" (3).

While this is an undergraduate course, its focus is on simulating real legal practice as best as can be done in fifteen weeks. The course positions students as associates in a fictional law firm, representing clients in mock Texas cases set in the local county. The mock cases include extensive facts that evolve as the semester progresses, as investigations and discovery proceedings evolve. The case file includes intake materials, deposition excerpts and summaries (with conflicting facts and testimony), evidence, memoranda, correspondence, and selected legal authorities. The legal authorities are abridged Texas appellate court opinions, statutes, and court rules. Students receive direct instruction in how to read legal opinions, reason analogically from precedent, synthesize and analyze caselaw and disputed facts, and revise their writing. To make the mock case materials publicly available, I share them online, including through the file-sharing site GitHub.

Immersion in a realistic scenario allows students to experience much of what the ABA's 1992 Statement and 2001 Resolution urge, particularly problem-solving, legal reasoning, litigation and dispute resolution, and—most centrally—communicating clearly to various audiences. Because the unauthorized practice of law is illegal, this course cannot provide the clinical experiences that law schools provide, nor can it involve external client or service-learning projects, as are common in professional writing courses. However, the course gives students a chance to experience some of the writing situations typical for a practicing lawyer.

In addition to the focus on simulated law practice within a realistic, immersive scenario, the course is designed to answer calls by some to embed legal writing throughout legal education. After all, legal advocacy is an activity mediated by writing, so reducing legal writing to "skills" or teaching students to write in ways that do not match actual legal discourse are missed opportunities. Teri McMurtry-Chubb contends that law school curricula overvalue one-shot, all-or-nothing final exams in so-called doctrinal courses (courses in torts, contracts, etc.) at the expense of helping students learn legal discourse through common genres. She argues that relying only on exams "evaluates what students know by divorcing that knowledge and its acquisition from what lawyers do" (85). Thus, she concludes, "it should be of little surprise that the bench and bar have critiqued legal education as disconnected from the work of practicing attorneys" (85).

One of the fundamental ways to help students learn what practitioners do is to guide them in analyzing and practicing common genres. As Wanda J. Orlikowski and JoAnne Yates urge, "to understand a community's communicative practices, we must examine the set of genres that are routinely enacted by members of the community" (542). Indeed, "genre knowledge is a form of situated cognition, inextricable from . . . procedural and social knowledge" (Berkenkotter and Huckin 487). A one-shot analysis of a convoluted fact pattern to be completed in two to three hours may be what law school courses have taught students to value, but it's not what lawyers actually do (or clients actually value) as "procedural and social knowledge." McMurtry-Chubb advocates for a restructuring of law school curricula to foreground "the most common legal genres that occur in practice," making those common genres "the genres through which legal knowledge is taught" (90).

I agree; thus, although this is an undergraduate course, the core of the course is everyday legal genres and the discourse of practicing lawyers attempting to solve legal problems for their clients. The course does not have students write scholarly (law review style) analyses or appellate briefs. Those forms of writing are relatively rare in the profession. Students who go on to attend law school, join law review, and gain judicial clerkships (nationwide, very few students) will have opportunities to learn such genres. But according to the ABA, 49% of American attorneys are solo practitioners, just 1% work in education, and 76% of firms are small, employing between two and five attorneys ("Lawyer Demographics-Year 2016"). While specialized solo and boutique practices exist, they are rare; this course attempts to introduce students to a realistic simulation of a much more typical lawyer's daily work.

To help students understand the communicative practices that everyday legal genres mediate, the course asks students to write for different audiences and purposes, just as practicing lawyers must do. Thus, in building the mock cases, I strive to blend challenging material, accessibility, and wide applicability. For instance, the fictional firm has represented individuals and businesses in dram shop[2] cases, injury car wrecks, defamation suits, dog bite injuries, fraud in real estate sales, and legal malpractice claims. These common types of cases allow for substantive learning about selected everyday legal concepts and typical genres, but are not idiosyncratic to Texas law or so esoteric as to be unapproachable by a mixed student population.

As an example of the kinds of work the class asks students to do, the most recent version of the course put students in the role of lawyers defending an attorney in a malpractice suit arising from a missed statute of limitations. One feature of various iterations of the course, and a frequent topic of discussion as the cases progress, is how to wrestle with being a good advocate for a less-than-ideal client—as clients usually are in actual practice. In this instance, students had to represent someone who was undeniably liable for at least some of the plaintiff's claimed damages. Major assignments included initial correspondence (engagement letter and notice of representation), a responsive pleading with discovery requests, and a mediation statement. I structured each project with readings on the relevant law and facts, quizzes, examples, activities that use legal precedent and synthesize caselaw, drafting workshops, graded peer review workshops, and revision opportunities. This approach allows me to intervene frequently, to offer advice to students at each stage, and to forestall procrastination. These particular genres and activities gave students the chance to write to their clients, their adversaries, a court, and their supervising partner, so they could learn how to write to audiences with different levels of legal sophistication and with different aims.

A third pedagogical choice—one that departs from ABA recommendations—is that the course requires no legal research. This choice reflects the fact that this is an undergraduate course, not a law school writing and research course. I simply give students all the statutes, court rules, and abridged appellate opinions they need, rather than take time to teach them how to do legal research using electronic databases or other means. Of course, students who go on to become paralegals or to attend law school will need to learn how to research the law. But in the context of this particular course, teaching legal research would take too much time away from helping students acquire the genre knowledge, basic legal reasoning skills, and revision practices that they need at this level. Taking away the research responsibility allows us to focus on understanding and working with the law to serve a client's needs within the possibilities of a given situation and genre.

Time saved by not teaching legal research makes it possible to pay close attention to the fact that the writing proficiencies, self-concepts, and experiences that beginning legal writers bring with them are often contrary to the expectations of effective legal writing. Effective legal writing not only accomplishes a particular purpose in an instrumental sense but also enacts a professional ethos of care toward the client. Mark Osbeck argues that good legal writing is clear, concise, engaging, elegant (64), and—above all—focused on helping "readers…obtain from legal documents information that will assist them with their professional decision-making" (67). Bryan Garner's legal-writing consultancy,

Law Prose, contends that good legal writing is simple, direct, straightforward, credible, and shows "empathy for the reader" ("Philosophy").

While those traits of good legal writing might sound straightforward, students often struggle mightily with learning legal discourse, meaning that the course must address transfer, not only forward into law school and law practice, but also within the context of students' other writing practices. Rebecca Nowacek defines five principles of transfer that help illuminate students' efforts to connect disparate writing and learning experiences. She argues that transfer "is not only mere application; it is also an act of reconstruction," "can be both positive and negative," has "a powerful affective dimension," is given exigence through genres, and, finally, is affected by "meta-awareness," "an important, but not a necessary, element of transfer" (21-30). Students in the course often struggle with the precise, pragmatic, rationalistic stance of legal writing and with adapting what they have previously been rewarded for doing in their writing.

Indeed, even students who have committed to law school experience these struggles. Miriam E. Felsenburg and Laura P. Graham surveyed beginning law students at two schools about the types of writing they were experienced in, their conceptions of legal writing, their composing practices, and their self-concepts as writers (225). Before the semester, students identified as strengths such items as their "elevated" writing, "vivid imagination," "the ability to be verbose," "unique voice," "creativity," and "a large vocabulary" (286). Those traits may have been rewarded in other writing situations, but can cause problems in legal writing situations. Indeed, on a second survey, students reported that legal writing had turned out to be more difficult and less formulaic than they had anticipated (253). As Felsenburg and Graham put it, "A disconnect seemed likely to occur when the [beginning legal writing] students were told not to do the very things they thought they did well" (285).

The undergraduates who take this course are often experienced in writing academic arguments using scholarly sources or writing analyses using some method of textual criticism. They also report experience with personal reflections and summaries. Some have experience in legal writing through internships or part-time jobs, but most do not. I start the course by asking students to discuss the kinds of writing they are experienced in doing (both inside and outside the classroom), what they consider their strengths and weaknesses, and what they know or think they know about legal writing specifically. Generally, students in this course echo what Felsenburg and Graham reported in their survey data, but even the first assignment (correspondence to multiple audiences) results in the kind of "disconnect" that Felsenburg and Graham found. Nowacek provides a useful formulation of how to make the "disconnect" productive, contending that "transfer is best understood as an act of recontextualization" (8). Much of the course, especially in the early weeks, but including the students' evolving experiences within the fictional life cycle of the mock case, is expressly about recontextualization. Each assignment presents a new situation, a new purpose, and a new genre, with class time devoted to connections and differences; in Nowacek's terms, each assignment creates a new "exigence for transfer" (28) where students' efforts at recontextualizing their writing knowledge can be put to use. Those efforts form the basis of in-class discussions, office-hours consultations, extensive work with in-process texts mentioned above, and commentary on original or revised submissions.

Legal writing affects us all, from legislative drafting to landlord-tenant disputes and consumer contracts. Thus, the need to help students develop as adept, ethical communicators is especially acute in legal writing courses, whether as part of an undergraduate curriculum or in law school. To help students develop as legal communicators, the course enacts the three major choices discussed above: simulating real law practice, teaching everyday genres, and eschewing legal research in favor of focusing on transfer.

Critical Reflection

Student evaluations conducted each time the course is taught, as well as the occasional emails and letters from former students, show that the course works as intended to help students begin to learn the discourse of law practice. Students who go on to attend law school report that the course gave them an advantage because, compared to their peers, they had already begun to learn some of the situated knowledge of law-trained readers and writers.

I have refined the course over the eight times I have taught it to have fewer major projects and more opportunities to work with in-process texts. Previous versions of the course had as many as five major projects, which was too many for most students to do well while also learning the ways of thinking and writing that the course entails. Having so many projects also did not allow enough time for work with in-process texts and for students to apply feedback and revision suggestions optimally. Now the course has three major projects and more in-class workshops. For these undergraduate beginning legal writers, fewer major assignments with more sequenced support has been a better way to meet course goals.

One area where the course could be improved is in its scope. Because my entire career as a practicing lawyer was in civil litigation, all the mock cases and legal genres that I have used in the course are scenarios in which someone is suing someone else for damages, and students are either prosecuting or defending the suit. Building the mock cases as civil suits has four advantages: (1) it allows me to use my direct experience to guide students, (2) litigation is common and most students are somewhat familiar from popular media with basic ideas of what a civil suit entails, (3) working on the same matter throughout the semester creates continuity, and (4) civil suits allow us to work with core substantive and procedural law. However, despite these advantages, the course has thus far neglected the opportunity to teach students about legal writing outside of civil litigation over money damages. Law practice and legal writing are more capacious than just litigation over money damages; lawyers craft transactional, civil rights, administrative, criminal justice, and myriad other genres in a wide variety of settings ("Fields of Law").

One opportunity to expand the scope of the course arises from a fundamental challenge of teaching legal writing: the persistent challenge of transforming students into (beginning) competent users of legal discourse while also helping them to develop critical consciousness. As Aidan Ricketts contends, "[t]he very idea of teaching students to think like a lawyer invokes the idea that students need to transform their thought processes, and it is strongly suggestive of a counter-intuitive form of discourse that is central to the discipline's self-image" (6). Our cultural *mythos* of the impartial rule of law is supported by rules of procedure, statutes, regulations, written decisions and opinions, an adversarial court system, etc. Beginning legal writers are preoccupied, quite understandably, with trying to understand legal sources and become competent legal technicians. They are looking for what Douglas Litowitz calls a "conversion experience . . . when they begin to see the world in terms of property, contracts, torts, and remedies" (709). If that conversion happens, Litowitz points out, "it is only a matter of time until the existing legal framework seems natural and inevitable" to the student (709). Because legal writing is how that framework is continually called into being, it can, Litowitz argues, "obscur[e] and mystify . . . power relations," "narrow [the writer's] range of thought and emotion," reinforce "the tyranny of formal rationality," and perpetuate the public's need to turn to specialists to understand the law (723). Gerald López dubs this lawyer-centered view of legal services the "regnant" view because the lawyer is the expert and the client is a consumer of professional advice (23). Even when legal writing courses involve projects written for lay audiences (e.g., the client letters in this course), the regnant model can still intrude if "the attorney's expertise is still the focus" (Edwards and Vance 70).

In this course, beginning legal writers have tended to invest a great deal of affect in a cognitive conversion, particularly if they intend to go on to law school. The law's role in normalizing power should be folded back into the rhetorical core of the course more explicitly. The course has always featured discussions about how legal genres create particular roles and expectations. Moreover, the ethical mandates of "The Texas Lawyers' Creed: A Mandate for Professionalism" are part of each project. Yet more needs to be done to prevent the course from inadvertently reinforcing the regnant model. After all, much of what lawyers do through the written word meets professional ethical expectations but nevertheless elides the law's role in creating and constraining power and agency.

In particular, the course can be modified to feature factual scenarios and mock cases centering on social justice concerns, while still teaching sound legal skills (Edwards and Vance 70). These new scenarios can likely be made just as approachable to students in this open pathway course as the scenarios used in the past. Legal standards for injunctive relief or other types of nonmonetary relief can be made as approachable as standards for recovering money damages. Common situations such as rental agreements, employment matters, consumer contracts, zoning matters, and the like could enhance the course's efforts to teach writing as problem solving on behalf of a client—*lawyering*, not just *law*—but add a social justice dimension. Such a shift, already underway for the next iteration of the course, could align the course more closely with St. Edward's mission of preparing students "to confront the critical issues of society and to seek justice and peace."

Notes

1. Before earning a PhD in rhetoric and composition and becoming a writing professor, I practiced civil litigation (mostly insurance defense) in California and in Texas from 1993-2002. I remain a member of both states' bars on voluntary inactive status.

2. Dram shop cases involve claims against bars and restaurants for selling alcohol to an obviously intoxicated adult, who goes on to injure the plaintiff as a result of being overserved.

3. In the mock case scenario described in the syllabus below, the third project was a mediation statement, a typical legal genre that attempts to resolve a case before trial. As I have done in the past, I listed the third project on the syllabus as "Surprise for now" until it came time to assign it. In addition, though it was planned out, the calendar for the final project was not filled in or visible to students at the beginning of the course. I take these measures because the mock case typically unfolds over about 18 months of fictional time. Students should not know where the case is headed early in the semester, just as a lawyer cannot know early in the life of a case how it will evolve.

Works Cited

American Bar Association House of Delegates. "Resolution 10B Adopted by the House of Delegates August 8-9, 2011." American Bar Association, 2011. americanbar.org/content/dam/aba/directories/policy/2011_am_10b.authcheckdam.pdf.

American Bar Association Section of Legal Education and Admissions to the Bar. "Legal Education and Professional Development—an Educational Continuum. Report of The Task Force on Law Schools and the Profession: Narrowing the

Gap." American Bar Association, 1992. americanbar.org/content/dam/aba/publications/misc/legal_education/2013_legal_education_and_professional_development_maccrate_report).authcheckdam. pdf.

Berkenkotter, Carol, and Thomas N. Huckin. "Rethinking Genre from a Sociocognitive Perspective." *Written Communication*, vol. 10, no.4, 1993, pp. 475–509.

Edwards, Pamela, and Sheilah Vance. "Teaching Social Justice Through Legal Writing." *Legal Writing: The Journal of the Legal Writing Institute*, vol. 7, 2001, pp. 63-86. legalwritingjournal.org/wp-content/uploads/2015 /06/volume7.pdf.

Felsenburg, Miriam E., and Laura P. Graham. "Beginning Legal Writers in Their Own Words: Why It's so Tough and What We Can Do About It." *Legal Writing: Journal of the Legal Writing Institute,* vol. 16, 2010, pp. 223-311. legalwritingjournal.org /wp-content/uploads/2015/07/ volume16.pdf.

"Fields of Law." Law School Admission Council. lsac.org/jd/thinking-about-law-school/fields-of-law.

"Lawyer Demographics Table—2016." American Bar Association-Legal Profession Statistics, 2016. americanbar.org/content/dam/aba/administrative/market_research/lawyer-demographics-tables-2016.authcheckdam.pdf.

Litowitz, Douglas. "Legal Writing: Its Nature, Limits, and Dangers." *Mercer Law Review*, vol. 49, no. 3, 1998, pp. 709-39. law.mercer.edu/lawreview/ getfile.cfm?file=49302.pdf.

López, Gerald P. *Rebellious Lawyering: One Chicano's Vision of Progressive Law Practice.* Westview Press, 1992.

McMurtry-Chubb, Teri A. "Toward a Disciplinary Pedagogy for Legal Education." *Savannah Law Review,* vol. 1, no. 1, 2014, pp. 69-101. savannahlawschool.org/wp-content/uploads/volume1number1-article04.pdf.

"Mission." St. Edward's University. stedwards.edu/mission.

Nowacek, Rebecca. *Agents of Integration: Understanding Transfer as a Rhetorical Act*. Southern Illinois UP, 2011.

Orlikowski, Wanda J., and JoAnne Yates. "Genre Repertoire: The Structuring of Communicative Practices in Organizations." *Administrative Science Quarterly,* vol. 39, no. 4, 1994, pp. 541-74.

Osbeck, Mark K. "What Is 'Good Legal Writing' and Why Does It Matter?" *Drexel Law Review*, vol. 4, Spring 2012, pp. 417-67. drexel.edu/~/media/Files/law/law%20review/spring_2012/Osbeck.ashx.

"Philosophy." Law Prose. lawprose.org/training/lawprose-philosophy/.

Ricketts, Aidan. "Threshold Concepts in Legal Education." *Directions: Journal of Educational Studies*, vol. 26, no. 2, 2006, pp. 2-12. directions.usp.ac.fj/collect/direct/index/assoc/D1175070.dir/doc.pdf.

Supreme Court of Texas and Texas Court of Criminal Appeals. "Texas Lawyer's Creed: a Mandate for Professionalism." 1989. *Texas Center for Legal Ethics*. legalethicstexas.com/Downloads/Texas-Lawyers-Creed/Texas_Lawyers_Creed.aspx

Syllabus

Course Description

The undergraduate catalog describes this course as follows:

> This course focuses on applied rhetoric, and is designed to give undergraduate students experience in writing clear, effective plain-language legal documents. The course offers a range of realistic legal writing problems, but does not presume any specialized legal knowledge. The writing assignments will help students to improve their writing and editing skills and to refine their abilities to analyze and develop arguments within a legal context.

This really is a course in applied rhetoric. While not "law school in 15 weeks" or "law-school Legal Research and Writing in 15 weeks," this course will give you the chance to experience thinking, reading, writing, and arguing in particular legal contexts and genres—all within a highly realistic case scenario. You might even have fun.

Course Texts

Please note: The course texts are listed below in MLA style. You will learn proper legal citation style for legal authorities, which differs from MLA style.

Court of Appeals of Texas, Dallas. *Kelley & Witherspoon, LLP v. Hooper*. 9 May 2013. *GoogleScholar*. scholar.google.com/scholar_case?case=8516008157009519313&q= 401+SW+3d+841+&hl=en&as_sdt=6,44.

Enquist, Anne. "Teaching Students to Make Explicit Factual Comparisons." *Perspectives: Teaching Legal Research and Writing*, vol. 12, no. 3, 2004, pp. 147-50. legalsolutions.thomsonreuters.com/pdf/perspec/2004-spring/2004-spring-2.pdf.

Garner, Bryan. *The Redbook: a Manual on Legal Style*, 3d ed, West, 2013.

Hanna, Jett. "Do You Really Write Engagement Letters?" *Texas Lawyers' Insurance Exchange*. tlie.org/article/do-you-really-write-engagement-letters/.

Kerr, Orin S. "How to Read a Legal Opinion: A Guide for New Law Students." *The Green Bag*, vol. 11, no. 1, 2007, pp. 51-63.

Schiess, Wayne. "Writing to the Trial Judge-Part One-For Motions." *Michigan Bar Journal*, vol. 54, 2004, pp. 54-56. michbar.org/file/generalinfo/plainenglish/pdfs/04_jan.pdf.

Supreme Court of Texas. *Browning-Ferris Indus., Inc. v. Lieck*. 19 Nov. 1992. *Google Scholar*. scholar.google.com/scholar_case?case= 1393624135552036508&q=881 +S.W.2d+288+(1994)&hl=en&as_sdt=6,44.

—. *Douglas v. Delp*. 25 Mar. 1999. *Google Scholar*. scholar.google.com/scholar_case?case=12973857601572136688&q=987+SW+2d+879&hl=en&as_sdt=6,44.

—. Texas Disciplinary Rules of Professional Conduct. 2005. *Board of Disciplinary Appeals*. http://txboda.org/sites/default/files/TDRPC.pdf.

—. Texas Rules of Civil Procedure, Amended. 1 Sept. 2016. *Texas Judicial Branch*. txcourts.gov/media/1435952/trcp-all-updated-with-amendments-effective-912016.pdf.

Supreme Court of Texas and Texas Court of Criminal Appeals. "Texas Lawyer's Creed: a Mandate for Professionalism." 1989. *Texas Center for Legal Ethics*. legalethicstexas.com/Downloads/Texas-Lawyers-Creed/Texas_Lawyers_Creed.aspx.

Projects, Activities, Grade Weights

- Project One–Initial Letters: 150 points
- Project Two–Responsive Pleading with Discovery: 250 points
- Project Three–Mediation Statement: 375 points
- 3 Peer Reviews at 25 points each: 75 points
- Quizzes and Graded Activities: 150 points
- Total: 1000 points

Project 1: Initial Letters (150 pts)

Overview

In this project, you will write two letters, each with different audiences and purposes. The first letter is an engagement letter to the client, which helps to manage expectations, to build the relationship necessary to serve the client well, and to protect your firm. The second letter is a notice of representation letter addressed to the adverse parties (your adversaries, not your blood enemies). This one helps to manage expectations, build respect, and protect your client. Each letter requires a strong factual and rhetorical performance: you need to get the audience's attention, shape the audience's attitude toward your message, and follow through on the message. You are responsible for the choices you make in how you do all of that; there are better and worse ways, though there is no One Perfect Way. We will discuss audiences, purposes, and genres.

Advice

In addition to all the advice in assigned readings (e.g., reread §15 in the Garner text several times), be sure to make the letters:

- reader-centered
- action-oriented
- concise
- recognizable as well-formatted business letters
- alert to tone

- free of sneering, condescending, or threatening moves
- designed to induce response (or to show why failing to do the desired response will have bad consequences)
- consistent with Texas Lawyer's Creed and ethical rules
- truthful
- accurate
- useful
- dignified

Polish, cut, rework, and revise your letters so that they are clear and easy to read aloud. The language should sound like a human being communicating about the law, not "like a lawyer." These letters are expressions of your professional and rhetorical competence as an advocate. Misspellings and poor sentences harm your professional ethos. Sweat the big stuff and sweat the small stuff. Misspelling people's names, especially your own client's name, is a killer. Please note: Many of the example letters you'll find online are poorly done and full of legalese. As Bryan Garner reminds us, "[t]he novice legal writer yearns to acquire legalese . . . but the expert yearns to eliminate it."

Grading Criteria

Content and Focus Criteria

(85%-128 pts)

Engagement Letter	Excellent	Strong	Fair	Weak	Failing
Audiences and Purposes: Fulfills all the specific purposes of engagement letters as brought up in class. Meets the needs of all of its audiences.					
Confirmation: Confirms services, limitations on scope of services, and fee basis.					
Confidentiality: Preserves confidentiality and informs client about information security/retention.					

Engagement Letter	Excellent	Strong	Fair	Weak	Failing
Time for Completion: Estimates time for completion. Estimate is reasonable and does not create misunderstandings.					
Bridge to Client Contact: Creates a bridge to client contact (the #1 complaint from clients is lack of contact); creates ethos of "professional and caring."					
Manages Expectations: Manages client expectations; does not create extra liabilities or misunderstandings; does not promise the moon. Deals effectively with all relevant facts and contexts.					
Notice of Representation/Spoliation Letter	Excellent	Strong	Fair	Weak	Failing
Audiences and Purposes: Fulfills all the specific purposes of representation and spoliation letters as brought up in class, including a reasonable list of items to preserve. Meets the needs of all of its audiences.					
Ethics: Complies with Texas Lawyer's Creed and other readings; no saber rattling or chest-pounding bombast. Creates ethos of "tough, smart, and capable."					
Accuracy: Accurate on law and facts. Does not create misunderstandings.					

Form, Nuts and Bolts Criteria
(15%-22 pts)

	Excellent	Strong	Fair	Weak	Failing
Appropriate Letterhead and Format: Typical business letter format and sections (see §15.5 of Garner text); 1.15-spaced text; 1.2 inch margins; professional-looking serif font; signed.					
Length: Engagement letter: 2.5 pages maximum; Representation letter: 1.5 pages maximum					
Voice: Sounds like a human being communicating about the law to other human beings, not "like a lawyer." Avoids verbosity, legalese, zombie nouns, and troublesome words. (See §§10.44, 11, and 12 of Garner text; § 12 is a usage glossary; please refer to it).					
Editing and Proofreading: Shows careful attention to editing and proofreading (see §§ 13.1-13.5 of Garner text).					
Mechanics: Unhampered by **disruptive** errors (e.g. comma splice, fused sentence, sentence fragment), **careless** errors (e.g., dropped quotes, it's/its), and **mistakes** (e.g., repeated words, typos).					

Project 2: Responsive Pleading and Discovery (250 pts)

"No case can have a meaning by itself! Standing alone it gives you no guidance. It can give you no guidance as to how far it carries, as to how much of its language will hold water later. What counts, what gives you leads, what gives you sureness, that is the background of the other cases in relation to which you must read the one. They color the language, the technical terms, used in the opinion. But above all they give you the wherewithal to find which of the facts are significant, and in what aspect they are significant, and how far the rules laid down are to be trusted."

--K.N. Llewellyn

Overview
- In this project, you will prepare your client's response to the lawsuit filed against them. Texas allows a first pleading to do several things, so this document will
    - (a) Answer the lawsuit, preventing a default judgment against your clients and putting the case "at issue";
    - (b) Request basic information and documents;
    - (c) Specially except to non-cognizable claims (basically, object to claims that the law does not recognize and should not be asserted); and
    - (d) Move to dismiss non-cognizable claims (same as b, but a newer procedure, with more "teeth" in it)
- Your audiences include your boss, your adversary, the judge/judge's staff, and anyone who reads the publicly available court file.

Advice
In addition to all the advice in assigned readings, be sure to make the document:

- legally sufficient (i.e., it has to "say the magic words" without ambiguity or language that backfires on your client);
- well-analyzed and synthesized in its use of legal authorities;
- organized and useful;
- complete yet concise;
- alert to tone; and
- consistent with Texas Lawyer's Creed and ethical rules.

Polish, cut, rework, and revise the project so that it is clear and easy to read aloud. It should read like a human being communicating about the law, not "like a lawyer." This is a publicly available document that should express your professional and rhetorical competence as an advocate.

Strong, effective analysis, synthesis, argumentation, and citation will help your clients fend off some of the Plaintiffs' claims. *It does not matter if you have not done legal analysis before; we will practice and learn the basics together.* Be precise and follow through in the ways that our invention activities help you learn to do. In particular, the "Enquist chart" activity will likely help you. You can do this!

Follow the basic skeleton in the case file in terms of what goes where, and how it should look. NB: As before, please bear in mind that many of the examples you'll find online are poorly done and full of legalese.

Grading Criteria

Content and Focus Criteria
(85%-213 pts)

	Excellent	Strong	Fair	Weak	Failing
Completeness/All Parts: Summary, Answer, Requests for Disclosure, Special Exceptions, Motion to Dismiss.					
Summary: Fulfills all of the purposes of a "bold synopsis" as discussed in class and in assigned readings; signposts heart of argument and "what you want/why you should win it."					
Answer: Puts case at issue, puts plaintiffs to their burden of proof and stops possibility of default judgment.					
Requests for Disclosure: Works with TRCP 194.2, but don't regurgitate legalese unnecessarily.					
Special Exceptions: Uses the TRCP and caselaw effectively and ethically, with synthesis and careful argument, to show defects in Original Petition. Answers the "why are we here and why do you win this round?" questions.					
Motion to Dismiss: Uses the TRCP and caselaw effectively and ethically, with synthesis and careful argument, to show why defects in Original Petition are grounds for dismissal of those particular claims. Answers the "why are we here and why do you win this round?" questions.					
Organization: Entire document is easy for judge and court staff to navigate and understand.					

Form, Nuts and Bolts Criteria
(15%-37 pts)

	Excellent	Strong	Fair	Weak	Failing
Citations: Legal citations are effective and in proper form for the particular purpose (reread Garner sections on citations).					
Format: Appropriate format, with headings and typography (see examples). Signed.					
Voice: Sounds like a human being communicating about the law to other human beings, not "like a lawyer." Avoids verbosity, legalese, zombie nouns, and troublesome words? (See §§10.44, 11, and 12 of Garner text; § 12 is a usage glossary; please refer to it).					
Mechanics: Unhampered by **disruptive** errors (e.g., comma splice, fused sentence, sentence fragment), **careless** errors (e.g., dropped quotes, it's/its), and **mistakes** (e.g., repeated words, typos).					
Editing and Proofreading: Shows careful attention to editing and proofreading (see §§ 13.1-13.5 of Garner text).					

Project 3: Mediation Statement

Overview

Most lawsuits are not tried to a jury. This one might be, but perhaps it can be resolved in mediation. Your purpose is to write a mediation statement setting forth your position for the mediation and, one hopes, helping to resolve the case on favorable terms. Even if mediation fails, your purpose will be to show that you are ready to try the case. You have four audiences here:

- Mediator (neutral, but you want her to see your position in the best light)
- Plaintiffs and their attorney (the adversaries)
- Your clients (show them that you are prepared, meticulous, and effective)
- Your boss (show her that you are doing effective, high-quality work)
- Advice
- Read and re-read this entire packet of materials, taking notes and asking questions.
- Know the facts "backwards and forwards."
- Reread §15 in the Garner text.
- There are many samples of mediation statements on the web. Take all of them with a giant grain of salt. You rely on online examples at your own peril.
- Remember that your development of the details, your ability to package a case, and your level of prose style and polish all count.
- If you can package a case for mediation, you might be able to do so for a trial. Conversely, if you can't package a case for mediation, you'll never do so for a trial.
- Leverage all the work you've put into the case so far. Effective legal writers are smart, efficient, purposeful users of their own resources.

Evaluation

Content and Focus Criteria

(85%- 319 pts)

	Excellent	Strong	Fair	Weak	Failing
Balancing Priorities/Purposes: The statement is developed, yet succinct. It is straightforward, yet is effective advocacy. It sets up the possibility of settlement, yet educates everyone on the true posture of the case. It meets the needs of all four of its audiences. Overall ethos should be: "We are prepared and realistic."					

	Excellent	Strong	Fair	Weak	Failing
Completeness/All Parts: Introduction, Factual Background, Claims and Defenses, Contested Legal Issues, Settlement Position and Rationale.					
Factual Background: Develops case themes; honest; does not hide facts.					
Claims and Defenses: Deals effectively and ethically with *all* of the important facts within the legal frameworks of Plaintiffs' causes of action, burden of proof, and our defenses.					
Contested Legal Issues: Mini-brief on admissibility of expert's opinions uses law and facts accurately, effectively, clearly, and succinctly, with citations.					
Settlement Position: Grounded in facts and law; reasonable; uses case themes; anticipates other side's responses.					

Form, Nuts and Bolts Criteria
15% (56 pts)

	Excellent	Strong	Fair	Weak	Failing
Appropriate Letterhead and Format: Typical business letter format and sections (see §15.5 of Garner text); 1.15-spaced text; 1.2 inch margins; professional-looking serif font; signed. Include correct case number, file number, court information, and addresses.					
Citations: Legal citations are effective and in proper form for the particular purpose (reread Garner sections on citations).					

	Excellent	Strong	Fair	Weak	Failing
Format: Appropriate format, with headings and typography (see examples). Signed.					
Voice: Sounds like a human being communicating about the law to other human beings, not "like a lawyer." Avoids verbosity, legalese, zombie nouns, and troublesome words. (See §§10.44, 11, and 12 of Garner text; § 12 is a usage glossary; please refer to it).					
Editing and Proofreading: Shows careful attention to editing and proofreading (see §§ 13.1-13.5 of Garner text). Proofread and edited meticulously, both for all major disruptive errors and minor errors.					

Calendar

Week 1

- Introduction to course and each other; what is legal writing/what does it do/who does it?
- Read: Intake Memo from senior partner; news articles on legal writing mistakes and complaints about legal writing.
- Activities: Inventory of writing experiences and strategies.

Week 2

- Read: Project 1 (Initial Letters) assignment; Kerr, "How to Read a Legal Opinion: A Guide for New Law Students"; Hanna, "Do You Really Write Engagement Letters?"; Garner §§ 15.1-15.5; assigned caselaw.
- Activities: How to understand and use a reported case; genre, purposes, and audiences of initial letters; writing to different audiences.
- Read: The Texas Lawyer's Creed; Garner §§ 11.1, 11.2, 11.3, 10.44, and 10.45; Texas Disciplinary Rules of Professional Conduct sections: "A Lawyer's Responsibilities"; "Truthfulness in Statements to Others"; sample engagement letters.
- Activities: Discuss ethical obligations and advocacy; discuss sample engagement letters; practice in class.

Week 3
- Activities: Work on project in class. Bring whatever you need to work on the project, e.g., your laptop, notes, course documents, textbook, etc. Ask me questions.
- Write: 250 words on how you spent your workshop time (this will be easy if you ask me questions and show me your text-in-progress) and two questions about this project that I can answer for everyone next meeting.

Week 4
- Activities: Graded peer review "good faith drafts" of Project #1 in class. A good faith draft is a draft of the entire assignment, made as good as the writer can make it at that time.
- Write: Please bring two hard copies of draft of each letter; one copy is for your partner and the other is for me. I will read the drafts and give feedback to the entire class.
- Read: Garner §§ 13.1-13.5; bring Garner text for other questions about polishing project (e.g., Part 1 and 2 of Garner).
- Activities: Editing and polishing workshop; answers to questions about in-progress texts; developing strategies for reviewing your own legal writing.
- Due: Project #1 due for a grade by 11:59 pm tonight, uploaded to Canvas.

Week 5
- Read: Project #2 (Responsive Pleading with Discovery); case file updates and glossary of terms; Garner §§ 21.1-21.4 and 22.1-22.4; Texas Rules of Civil Procedure sections for Project 2 on pleadings and discovery.
- Activities: invention and discussion; mini-lecture on pleadings and procedure.
- Read: Enquist, "Teaching Students to Make Explicit Factual Comparisons" caselaw for Project #2.
- Activities: Invention and discussion; "Enquist Synthesis Chart" activity assigned and discussed.

Week 6
- Read: Garner §8.1, 8.2(d), 8.5, 8.7, 8.8, 8.9, 8.10, 8.11, 8.12, 8.13, 8.14, 8.15, 8.16, 8.17, 8.18, 8.20, and 8.22 re: citations; Schiess, "Writing to the Trial Judge."
- Activities: invention activity; in-class practice with reasoning by analogy; work on Enquist chart.
- Activities: Work on project in class. Bring whatever you need to work on the project, e.g., your laptop, notes, course documents, textbook, etc. Ask me questions.

- Write: 250 words on how you spent your workshop time (this will be easy if you ask me questions and show me your text-in-progress) and two questions about this project that I can answer for everyone next meeting.

Week 7
- Activities: Work on project in class. Bring whatever you need to work on the project, e.g., your laptop, notes, course documents, textbook, etc. Ask me questions.
- Write: 250 words on how you spent your workshop time (this will be easy if you ask me questions and show me your text-in-progress) and two questions about this project that I can answer for everyone next meeting.
- Activities: Graded peer review "good faith drafts" of Project #2 in class.
- Write: Please bring two hard copies of draft of each letter; one copy is for your partner and the other is for me. I will read the drafts and give feedback to the entire class.

Week 8
- Read: Garner §§ 13.1-13.5; bring Garner text for other questions about polishing project (e.g., Part 1 and 2 of Garner).
- Activities: Editing and polishing workshop; answers to questions about in-progress texts; develop strategies for reviewing your own legal writing in this genre.
- Due: Project #2 due for a grade by 11:59 pm tonight (upload to Canvas dropbox).
- Read: Case update packet and assignment for Project #3 (Mediation Statement). Please note: update packet contains items from different sources; be sure you know where each came from (in the fictional world of our case).
- Activities: Quiz on new facts; discussion of new genre, audiences, and purposes.

Week 9
- Read: Texas Rules of Evidence/*Robinson*/*Gammill* handout (see case file); other assigned cases. Please note: Read those materials in the order listed; it'll help you keep them clear in your mind.
- Activities: Quiz on caselaw; invention, discussion of challenges to expert testimony.
- Read: Handout titled "Applied Rhetoric: Valuation, Theory of Case, and Persuasive Themes."
- Activities: Invention and discussion of themes, theory of the case, and valuation.

- Write: Four potential themes and two value rationales.

Week 10
- Activities: Discuss themes and value rationales; review of damages. Begin to work on project in class.
- Write: 250 words on how you spent your workshop time (this will be easy if you ask me questions and show me your text-in-progress) and two questions about this project that I can answer for everyone next meeting.
- Same as previous meeting; work on project in class and write 250 words/two questions.

Week 11
- Read: Handout for "silent auction" peer review activity.
- Activities: Bring draft in progress (one hard copy) to class for "silent auction" review activity. It'll be fun and valuable; I promise. This only works, though, if you have tried to do the entire project, even though, of course, it'll be quite rough at this point.
- Read: handouts on negotiation and settlement dynamics.
- Activities: group activities on genre and settlement dynamics; work plans from "silent auction" peer review.

Week 12
- Activities: Graded peer review "good faith drafts" of Project #3 in class.
- Write: Please bring two hard copies of draft of each letter; one copy is for your partner and the other is for me. I will read the drafts and give feedback to the entire class.
- Read: Bring Garner text for other questions about polishing.
- Activities: Editing and polishing workshop; answers to questions about in-progress texts; developing strategies for reviewing your own legal writing in this genre
- Due: Project #3 due for a grade by 11:59 pm tonight (upload to Canvas dropbox).

Week 13
- Course recap; planning revisions to Project #3.

Week 14
- Conferences

Week 15
- Conferences

Finals Week
- Revisions of Projects 2 and 3 due; be sure to write revision memos and to send me a Microsoft Word "compare" document showing all the differences between the submissions of a revised graded project.

Book Reviews

Securing Composition's Disciplinarity: The Possibilities for Independent Writing Programs and Contingent Labor Activism

A Minefield of Dreams: Triumphs and Travails of Independent Writing Programs, edited by Justin Everett and Christina Hanganu-Bresch. UP of Colorado, 2017. 375 pp.

Labored: The State(ment) and Future of Work in Composition, edited by Randall McClure, Dayna V. Goldstein, and Michael A. Pemberton. Parlor Press, 2017. 324 pp.

Reviewed by Nick Sanders, University of Maine

For some time, composition has struggled to declare an identity separate from "English." For instance, in 1987 Stephen North noted that unlike other knowledge-making disciplines (i.e., literary studies) with, what he calls, "methodological homogeneity" (North 367), composition often sits on the periphery in English departments. Still regularly viewed as lacking content knowledge, writing professionals are frequently characterized as teachers of general skills. Outside the profession, even in our own departments, little is known about what we know, what we do, and how we do it. While recent scholarship, particularly Linda Adler-Kassner and Elizabeth Wardle's *Naming What We Know*, has begun to settle this question of what we know as a discipline, what remains is how we enact this epistemological question through "methodological … axiological, pedagogical, and processual" modes (Fulkerson 681). As we continue to define who we are and what we know, we must now consider how we might sustain the disciplinary identity we have attempted to articulate as a field. The books reviewed in this essay offer ways to foster such a disciplinary identity in strategic ways. The first, *A Minefield of Dreams: Triumphs and Travails of Independent Writing Programs*, edited by Justin Everett and Cristina Hanganu-Bresch, illustrates how Independent Writing Programs (IWPs) can establish a concrete, identifiable presence for writing on and across campuses. By developing the curriculum in fyw and undergraduate writing programs, IWPs are able to move beyond the field's writing-as-skill typecasting. The other collection, *Labored: The State(ment) and Future Work in Composition*, edited by Randall McClure, Dayna V. Goldstein, and Michael A. Pemberton, argues for data-centered discussions around contingent labor activism in the twenty-first century. While labor conditions and IWPs might be considered separately, they converge to illuminate that our future must invest in the people who teach in and ultimately sustain our discipline.

Published in 2002, *Field of Dreams* addressed the "'what-ifs' and 'if-onlys,' in which compositionists imagine professional lives institutionally separate from an English department" (Crow and O'Neill 2). Fourteen years later, *A Minefield of Dreams* reflects a substantially different world, where these hypothetical what-ifs have morphed into (mostly) attainable realities. In their introduction, Justin Everett and Cristina Hanganu-Bresch position the IWP as a way to "achieve a higher disciplinary status" (9). An IWP, they propose, provides ways to secure "legitimacy and equality with other programs" (9). In these cases, as writing specialists we can control the fyw curriculum, a luxury that is not always afforded to us in literature-dominated English departments. In separating from English, IWPs must consider the obstacles associated with quests for independence: How can we establish an identity within the university, counter institutional perceptions that writing instruction is a "how to" pedagogy, and ensure program sustainability? Independent writing programs can wield their power to promote writing studies in the university. Writing studies, then, is able to become recognizable on university campuses, convincing other departments, including English, to see "that what we do is valuable" (ix). In other words, writing studies becomes more legitimate through a departmental presence.

Minefield's first section, "Mythos," narrates various histories of IWPs, featuring programs that foster cross-disciplinary collaborations as a way to increase the visibility of writing on campuses. Dan Royer and Ellen Schendel explain, for instance, that the Department of Writing at Grand Valley State operates as an academic unit lateral to English, uniting faculty in writing studies, creative writing, and professional and technical writing. While the authors acknowledge that the inclusion of creative writing in an IWP might not be feasible everywhere, a creative writing partnership further focuses writing classes on textual production and draws undergraduate students to the writing major. Keith Hjortshoj, similarly, explains that the Knight Institute for Writing in the Disciplines at Cornell has historically employed an interdisciplinary model for writing instruction outside of English. At Cornell, writing instruction is the responsibility of everyone, across the different colleges, echoing contemporary wishes of Writing Across the Curriculum initiatives. Cornell offers "an 'interdependent' program, valuable and valued because it helps teachers to solve problems they care about, with strategies we've learned from other teachers in other fields" (80). Hjortshoj reminds us that, at its core, "writing" isn't owned by anyone and "what we know and do as composition specialists will depend on our grasp of what other disciplinary and cross-disciplinary specialists currently know and do" (83).

Essays in the subsequent section, "Topoi," focus on the ongoing development of writing teachers as a key component to the continual professionalization of writing studies. W. Brock MacDonald, Margaret Procter, and Andrea L. Williams' "Integrating Writing into the Disciplines" report on the IWP at the University of Toronto, "a program that works across disciplines and is not limited to its own departmental perspective or structure" (111). Toronto's Writing Instruction for Teaching Assistants (WIT) presents a WAC-centered perspective where "students must learn to write within their disciplines" (114). Participating departments receive funding for one Lead Writing Teaching Assistant (LWTA), who serves as a writing and pedagogical consultant for faculty in that department. These LWTAs are mentored by the WIT Coordinator, a full-time writing specialist. The authors explain that the "hub" of communication between the LWTA, course instructors, and the WIT Coordinator has shifted the culture of writing from "student deficiency to one that emphasizes teaching responsibilities" (125). In chapter six, Georgia Rhoades, Kim Gunter, and Elizabeth Carroll focus our attention on contingent faculty advocacy in their current struggle for independence at Appalachian State. They reveal trials and tribulations related to integrating non-tenure track faculty (NTT) in department life but insist that the professionalization of NTTs must be a priority in the turbulent quest for independence. On their campus, NTT faculty attend professional development opportunities led by visiting scholars.

As a way to sustain our programs and discipline, the section "Techne" directs our attention to pedagogical approaches employed in IWPs. Michelle Filling-Brown and Seth Frechie discuss the process for developing a vertical model of writing instruction that "inscribes justice" throughout an intensive writing sequence at Cabrini University. When the curriculum reforms of the 1980s were reevaluated in the early 2000s, the demand for a more centralized writing education became apparent. This lead the IWP at Cabrini to replace the lateral English department-WAC initiative with a vertical model of writing instruction. The vertical model includes a freshman-level class focused on issues of power, privilege, and difference, a sophomore-level class that "require[s a] service-learning component that allows students to reflect upon the college social justice mission in light of real world realities" (186), and a junior-level class that develops understandings from the sophomore-level class to civically engage with systemic issues often through community-based research. The strong connections across the courses represent the "attempt to move writing and an informed understanding of justice and inclusivity center stage" (192). In chapter nine, Christina Hanganu-Bresch describes the implementation of a writing about writing (WAW) pedagogy, a pedagogical movement that fosters the "disciplinary integrity" (197) of writing studies and promotes transfer by making writing and rhetoric studies the content of first-year writing (fyw). She explains that rhetorical education might productively enrich WAW because both "aim to educate rhetorically-skilled citizens who can understand, assess, and adapt their communication to a variety of circumstances" (207). The rhetorical dexterity promised in a WAW-rhetorical education focused fyw class allows teachers of writing to encourage communicators to reassess their own rhetorical situations.

The final chapters focus on the transformative nature of IWPs achieved by creating and managing an identity on campus. Valerie Ross explains that transforming the discipline does not just happen; instead, it must be brought into existence and managed. She examines how identity must be conceptualized as a social fact in order for an IWP to "create a durable, recognizable identity that propels the organization toward becoming a social fact" (247). Ross invites us to envision IWPs as ongoing identity projects, where all interactions communicate this identity, concretizing the IWP into existence. Keeping in line with Ross's thesis that transformations ought to be managed, Justin Everett's chapter describes the "strategic planning" for University of the Sciences' writing programs, including branding, generating a mission statement, and developing a strategic plan. Everett recounts the "frustrating" (279) process of drafting, assessing, and revising a strategic plan that "sold" the identity of the writing program. The plan aligned with institutional outcomes and objectives. Such assessments enabled the "market" (e.g., students) and "shareholders" (e.g., administrators and other faculty members) to understand what the writing program is doing and what it accomplishes. In many ways, branding, mission statements, strategic plans, and assessments are ways to make the identity of an IWP a concrete, identifiable reality. Lastly, William Lalicker proposes that transformations do not have to be splits and separations, but that mutual respect between literature and composition can exist in English departments. He theorizes what he calls the "five equities" for composition to exist in harmony within English: hiring, governance, writing and rhetoric as core components of the English major; writing studies specialization and graduate studies as key elements in rhetoric and composition. He reminds us that disciplinary harmony benefits our students by "serv[ing] [them] with the best practices our discipline offers" (319). Ultimately, *A Minefield of Dreams* advances practical ways to sustain composition's disciplinarity, including the ongoing development of teachers in the program, innovative pedagogical and curricular design, and program identity management.

The co-edited collection *Labored*, alternatively, centers around the 1989 *Statement of Principles and Standards for the Postsecondary Teaching of Writing*. The *Statement* sought "to examine the conditions which undermine the quality of postsecondary writing instruction" (329) and was the first attempt, after the *Wyoming Resolution*, to make visible unfair working conditions for writing teachers without a tenure appointment. Even in 2018, it's no surprise that working conditions for NTT professionals have remained, as the *Statement* declares, "the worst scandal in higher education" (330). NTT teaching positions typically offer limited if any job security, office space, material resources, and opportunities to participate in professional governance—as such, faculty in these positions are forced to accept an "itinerant existence" (330). As Joseph Harris notes in his afterword, the *Wyoming Resolution* is a "labor grievance" (285) while the *Statement* is leveraged as "providing a quality education" (286). He goes on to suggest that the *Statement* reflects a "sense that teaching writing is a true profession" (286). The professionalization of composition studies provides a reason why the *Statement* boldly supports tenure as a disciplinary imperative. *The Statement* functions, then, as an emblem of disciplinarity and, in many ways, attempts to counter many of the same institutional beliefs about the teaching of writing that IWPs have battled, including the traditional notion that anyone can teach writing.

The problem, however, for McClure, Goldstein, and Pemberton was that the *Statement* needed revisions for the twenty-first century. Chapters in *Labored* focus on the *Statement* as a text-in-progress, one needing further focus on part-time faculty. Such a focus, it seems, was absent from the 2013 revision of the *Statement*, which condensed mention of labor conditions to a two-paragraph bullet late in the document. In many ways, the collection takes the form of a call-to-action, pleading for specific data-driven arguments that respond to the reality of contingent labor in the twenty-first century. Framed through Chaïm Perelman and Lucie Olbrechts-Tytrcha's concept of the "loci of the preferable," the editors' final chapter calls for empirical data to operationalize labor improvements. Using quantitative data, administrators can establish a research agenda that advocates for improved contingent faculty labor conditions. "A concrete research agenda" (282), they argue, is central, if we are to improve contingent labor conditions. Following their call for concrete research on contingent faculty, the editors provide a "data-enhanced" *Statement*, pointing to research conducted at the national level that substantiates the claims in the 1989 document, ultimately calling for "empirical exemplars of equitable, successful labor conditions" (290). Improving labor conditions and studying labor with an emphasis on quantitative data would allow program administrators to make persuasive arguments "to those who make decisions that directly impact the working conditions of writing instructors" (271).

Section one of *Labored* positions the *Statement* in context, emphasizing the gap between what the *Statement* had hoped to change and realities of the profession in the twenty-first century. As an indirect product of the *Wyoming*

Resolution, the *Statement* began to acknowledge the unfair working conditions for part-time faculty who teach writing. In stories about the Wyoming Conference in the summer of 1986 (Trimbur and Cambridge), many remember that discussions about labor conditions were propelled by a graduate student following James Sledd's talk about writing instruction, power, and oppression. Narratives recalling the genesis of the *Resolution* for years referred to this graduate student as the "anonymous graduate student." Susan Wyche, in chapter one, reflects on being the anonymous graduate student who got everyone talking about labor conditions at the Wyoming Conference. While the chapter focuses on the conference, Wyche places the event in context, describing her and a fellow TA being strong-armed at her home institution into teaching an upper-division writing class without pay. Thus, the *Wyoming Resolution* and subsequent arguments for labor conditions remind us how integral graduate student working conditions are in discussions about contingent labor. Further, in the form of a Faustian dialogue, Chris Anson situates the *Statement* as articulating the need for disciplinarity in writing studies, where specialists in composition (not in literature) teach composition classes and pursue research to concretize the discipline. He advocates for initiatives that build in support for NTT faculty, including longer renewable appointments, space and time to work with students, and opportunities for conferencing. Both Valerie Balester (chapter three) and Jeanne Gunner (chapter four) take issue with the *Statement* for its scope and what it represents to professionals in the discipline. Balester's "War on the *Statement*" criticizes the 1989 document's representation of writing centers as mere support services for "actual" (43) classroom teaching. By arguing for an explicit acknowledgment that writing centers are sites of teaching and learning, she proposes that writing center administrators must be thought of as writing program administrators. Balester sees the work of writing centers as serving institutional goals, not departmental ones. To develop the institutional presence of writing centers, revisions of the *Statement* should acknowledge the serious learning and teaching that occur in writing and reading centers. In chapter four, Jeanne Gunner's dissatisfaction with the *Statement* stems from the cycle of revisions the *Statement* has undergone, which has defocused the initial intentions of the *Wyoming Resolution*. She suggests that the *Statement* might be eulogized as a failed model since it subverts "the *Resolution*'s original goals and voices in order to serve the interests of the then more culturally-powerful tenure-line professional" (53). By supporting tenure and relegating NTT faculty to lower classes, labor conditions in 2018 seem to be unintentionally perpetuated by the 1989 document. In response, scholars in *Labored* recommend increased departmental governance that includes NTTs, increased pay for NTT faculty, and more stable appointments.

Section two of *Labored* attempts to map labor conditions in the present, ultimately displaying the changed nature of contingent labor in the twenty-first century. The contributors focus their discussions around contingent faculty as a means to integrate teachers into department life and legitimize the teaching of writing. James McDonald locates the *Statement* alongside other professional labor documents from MLA, AAUP, and AWP, urging composition faculty to use the *Statement* in conjunction with these other position statements. Like several scholars surveyed in this review (Anson; Rhoades, Kim, and Carroll; Royer and Schendel), McDonald asks for revisions of the *Statement* that do not "defend tenure at the expense of helping contingent faculty" (86). Instead, he urges institutions to provide space, compensation, and professional respect to those working in our programs. In comparison, Timothy Dougherty widens the scope of "contingent" to include non-tenure track writing program administrators. Through interviewing several NTT administrators, he advises that the *Statement* should provide "benchmarks" for programs to move toward "tenured paradise" (108). His recommendations point to clear job descriptions and a fair evaluation structure. Risa Gorelick, following the overarching purpose of *Labored*, calls for the Research Network Forum (RNF) at *CCCC* to invite speakers and foster new research ideas about NTT working conditions in order to move the field forward. Following her call, RNF at the 2018 *CCCC* featured plenary speeches from Seth Kahn and Amy Lynch-Biniek, both of which focused on labor-activism research. In chapter eight, Casie Fedukovich, Susan Miller-Cochran, Brent Simoneaux, and Robin Snead propose that a revision of the *Statement* should address the trend of hiring more NTT than tenure-track faculty. They focus their recommendation around the *CCCC Writing Program Certificate of Excellence*, which, as they note, implicitly supports unethical hiring practices and thereby "normalizes and promotes practices against which many in the discipline are stringently fighting" (139). Holly Hassel and Joanne Baird Giordano further direct our attention to two-year colleges and the demands of NTTs serving diverse populations. They endorse a "program mentality where all department members contribute to the program's development regardless of employment status" (154). Collectively, these scholars advocate for changing the realities of contingent labor in our programs, championing fairer evaluation structures, and fostering more inclusive departmental governances. By fostering the continual development of writing professionals, these changes would continue to challenge pervasive beliefs that writing is a set of skills that anyone can teach.

Labored, also, alerts us to the material, technological, and pedagogical changes in our discipline since 1989, drawing our attention to how we might articulate the needs of professionals in the future. The last chapters forecast the possibilities for a revised statement that acknowledges shifts in technology and pedagogical models. In doing so, contributors offer future directions, not only for contingent faculty activism but also for the discipline. Evelyn Beck, for instance, explains that teaching online is more equitable and even liberating for adjunct faculty. She provides recommendations to foster an inclusive online classroom community. Barry Maid and Barbara D'Angelo offer an alternate scenario for NTT faculty. They overview ways that faculty, curriculum, course load, and evaluation can be leveraged to illustrate that tenure-line jobs are no longer essential, and that we should embrace permanent NTT jobs. They propose that their chapter can be used to recognize and negotiate realities at local institutions. In addition, Maid and D'Angelo advocate for accountable hiring practices by suggesting that "faculty working conditions need to become outcome-based so they, too, can be assessed" (206). As the contributors put forth, labor conditions might be better conceptualized as at the center of our work rather than separate from it. They note that contingent labor activism is inherently linked to our future as a discipline. In developing accountability practices, acknowledging the positive potential for online adjunct instructors, and making visible the realities of contingent labor, we can guide our discipline to a socially just future.

Labored and *A Minefield of Dreams* point to the possibilities for institutional transformation that composition can lead and actively engage in. If *Naming What We Know* was the field's attempt to advance our epistemological disciplinary core, then *Labored* and *Minefield* propose ways that we foster this disciplinarity, particularly through investing in those who teach in and ultimately sustain our programs. Independent writing programs provide a place in the university community that acknowledges and recognizes writing studies as a genuine field of study, not just a general education staffing program. However, as we work hard to construct and shift these concrete realities, we must recognize that if we continue to overlook unfair working conditions for contingent faculty, we continue to be part of the problem. Instead, we need to invest in contingent faculty development, offer adequate office space and materials, and provide contingent faculty governance roles in our departments. As we continue to transform our discipline, we must remember that transformations do not always come easy or amount to an ideal situation (i.e., independent writing programs with trained composition specialists all holding tenure-line positions). These volumes remind us that our disciplinarity must be strategically managed, further reminding us that the best resources we have, for our programs and for our students, are the people who work in our programs: devoted teacher-scholars of composition. If we are to dispel myths that anyone can teach writing, if we are to reinvigorate university life with writing across the curriculum, if we are to take up space in the university, then, we need to continually invest, support, and develop the teachers who teach the most important classes at the university.

Orono, Maine

Works Cited

Adler-Kassner, Linda, and Elizabeth Wardle. *Naming What We Know: Threshold Concepts in Writing Studies*. UP of Colorado, 2015.

CCCC Executive Committee. *Statement of Principles and Standards for the Postsecondary Teaching of Writing*. *CCC*, vol. 40, no. 3, 1989, pp. 329-36. cccc.ncte.org/library/NCTEFiles/Resources/Journals/CCC/1989/0403-oct1989/CCC-0403Statement.pdf.

Crow, Angela, and Peggy O'Neill. "Introduction: Cautionary Tales about Change." *A Field of Dreams: Independent Writing Programs and the Future of Composition*, edited by Peggy O'Neill, Angela Crow, and Larry W. Burton, Utah State UP, 2002, pp. 1-18.

Fulkerson, Richard. "Composition at the Turn of the Twenty-First Century." *CCC*, vol. 56, no. 4, 2005, pp. 654-87. cccc.ncte.org/library/NCTEFiles/Resources/Journals/CCC/0564-june05/CO0564Summary.pdf.

North, Stephen. *The Making of Knowledge in Composition: Portrait of an Emerging Field*. Boyton/Cook Publishers, 1987.

Trimbur, John, and Barbara Cambridge. "The Wyoming Conference Resolution: A Beginning." *WPA: Writing Program Administration*, vol. 12, no. 1-2, 1988, pp. 13-18. wpacouncil.org/archives/12n1-2/12n1-2trimbur.pdf.

Mikhail Bakhtin: Rhetoric, Poetics, Dialogics, Rhetoricality, by Don Bialostosky. Parlor P, 2016. 191 pp.

Reviewed by Ben Wetherbee, University of Science and Arts of Oklahoma

Mikhail Bakhtin: Rhetoric, Poetics, Dialogics, Rhetoricality collects and reorganizes Don Bialostosky's work on rhetoric and the Bakhtin circle in a single, tight volume. It's a valuable book, in no small part because it spurs intertextual connections among four decades of work that, by my estimation, represent the most incisive and consummate corpus of scholarship on Bakhtin as a rhetorician. Variously labeled a literary critic, linguist, philosopher, semiotician, ethicist, and anti-Stalinist luminary, Bakhtin is, in Bialostosky's hands, most centrally a theorist of *human discourse*, of language in motion among discrete speakers and auditors. It is this attention to the particulate, communicative detail of speech and text that allows Bialostosky to reconfirm Bakhtin, and his colleagues V.N. Vološinov and Pavel Medvedev, as theorists of rhetoric. The relationships among formalized persuasive discourses (rhetoric), mimetic literary discourses (poetics), speaker-auditor dynamics (dialogics), and the rhetorical currents underlying organic everyday communication (rhetoricality) occupy Bialostosky's commentary in this rich, challenging, and rewarding book.

I should also acknowledge what this book is *not*. To begin, Bialostosky provides no general introduction to Bakhtin's scholarship; many of Bakhtin's most well-traveled concepts (chronotope, carnivalesque, polyphony, etc.) take a back seat to the specific extrapolation of Bakhtinian discourse theory in relationship to critical conversation, writing pedagogy, and everyday rhetorical practice. But neither does Bialostosky's book—unlike, for example, Kay Halasek's *A Pedagogy of Possibility*—position itself as a comprehensive introduction to Bakhtin studies for rhetoricians or compositionists in particular. Rather, Bialostosky's chapters read as vignettes representing conversations among rhetoricians, compositionists, and literary theorists. This is not a bad thing. The result is a series of encounters with the work of figures like Aristotle, Wayne Booth, Michael Billig, Jeanne Fahnestock, Helen Rothschild Ewald, and Peter Elbow, which cumulatively illustrate the reach and power of Bakhtin's insight through case-based induction rather than top-down deduction. Instead of toppling existing rhetorical paradigms, Bialostosky takes a modest but arguably more productive approach; he adjusts the terms of conversation through the forceful but nuanced application of Bakhtinian vocabulary and attention to the intersections of rhetoric and poetics. It's a fittingly dialogic way of doing criticism.

It's also a feat few could perform. While *Mikhail Bakhtin* chiefly comprises revised versions of previously published work, its largely autobiographical introduction newly illuminates all the book's content. Bialostosky recounts his own unusual academic upbringing as a disciple of Booth who never quite shook the Chicago School's preoccupation with neo-Aristotelian criticism and the arts of the trivium, but who finally internalized Bakhtin as "a new center of intellectual gravity" and followed Bakhtinian revisions to rhetorical theory and pedagogy into the disciplinary conversation of rhetoric and composition (3-9). The self-avowed "peculiarity" (6) of Bialostosky's position as a latecomer to the discipline is apparent in chapters two and three. In chapter two, "Dialogics as an Art of Discourse," the author offers Bakhtinian sensitivity to person-ideas—or "specific persons who voice their ideas in specific texts and contexts" in order to anticipate and answer each other (22)—as an alternative to dialectic, which Bialostosky links with abstract truth, and to rhetoric, which he confines to the competitive discourse of victory and loss. Chapter three riffs on a similar argument, this time in relation to Booth's rhetorical theory of the novel and his subsequent model of critical pluralism. In his old mentor, Bialostosky sees both an American analog to the Soviet rhetorizing of the novel that Bakhtin decried and a hopeful pluralist clambering toward the dialogic heterogeneity Bakhtin envisions and celebrates.

Chapters four, five, and six demonstrate a distinct shift in Bialostosky's thinking toward rhetoric. Like Bakhtin himself, the early Bialostosky denigrates rhetoric's winner-take-all agonism; but these chapters play out the author's transitioning focus from such traditionally disciplined rhetoric—an enemy of dialogics—toward what John Bender and David E. Wellbery term "rhetoricality," or the "pre-disciplinary" currents of persuasion underlying everyday action and communication—which is largely synonymous with dialogics (Bialostosky 74, 82, 146; Bender and Wellbery 22-39). In chapter four, Bialostosky proposes a rhetorical school of literary criticism that couples stylistic figures—his well-chosen guide here is Fahnestock's *Rhetorical Figures in Science*—with Bakhtinian speech genres to parse the texture of poetical discourse. Chapter five, abstracted from a 1992 exchange with Halasek and Michael Bernard-Donals in *Rhetoric Society Quarterly* (see Halasek, et al.), sharpens the author's position on Bakhtin in relation to rhetoric; Bialostosky lands somewhere between Halasek's zealous embrace of a dialogic rhetoric and Bernard-Donald's perhaps overcautious segregation of rhetoric from scientific materiality. The model of Bahktinian rhetoricality that Bialostosky locates between his interlocutors' positions takes further shape in chapter six, which links Bakhtin to Billig's use of the sophist Protagoras to explain thinking itself as a rhetorical negotiation among contrary positions.

Chapters seven and eight focus on the Bakhtin school's early phenomenological and sociological texts, particularly *Toward a Philosophy of the Act*, with an eye toward composition, rhetoric, and poetics. Framed as a rejoinder to

Ewald's "Waiting for Answerability: Bakhtin and Composition Studies," chapter seven rereads Bakhtin's early writings not as an "ethical and individualist" statement on human responsibility (Bialostosky 86), but as a formulation of questions about language and action that Bakhtin would answer more fully in his later works on utterance and dialogics. Chapter eight untangles the same thread in more theoretical depth, casting rhetoric and poetry as "evaluative" and "contemplative" discourses that accompany action (114-18). From there, the book progresses toward two especially incisive chapters (nine and ten) that reread Aristotelian rhetoric and poetics (and the relationship between them) in light of Bakhtin's discourse theory, resuscitating the roles of delivery, arrangement, and style in rhetorical utterance and reconfiguring Aristotelian poetics as an artistic imitation of such rhetoric. These Bakhtin-and-Aristotle essays, in particular, ought to circulate widely in upper-level and graduate courses in rhetorical theory.

The final chapter, "Liberal Education, Writing, and the Dialogic Self," speaks most directly to matters of composition pedagogy. Here, Bialostosky invokes Bakhtin to trouble the Elbowian notion of "authentic voice," instead advocating for a classroom wherein "individual ideological development can become not just the accidental outcome of encounters with disciplinary languages," but a space where students reflect critically on their own Bakhtinian assimilation of others' voices (149-51, 153). Many readers of *Composition Studies*, no doubt, have already encountered the final chapter—which astutely mediates the positions of Elbow and David Bartholomae—in the landmark 1991 collection *Contending with Words* (Harkin and Schilb) where it originally appeared. But it is a pleasure to rediscover Bialostosky's statement on student writers, now couched in the full intellectual breadth of his thinking on Bakhtin, rhetoric, and poetics, where it reads as the pedagogical translation of a much larger theoretical project. Twenty-seven years later, the piece resonates anew.

Among Bialostosky's strengths, as I note above, is how thoughtfully he addresses interlocutors like Elbow, Bartholomae, and Ewald. But one also notes the age of such conversations. (Barring two titles from the author himself, the most recent bibliographic entry is from 2006; most are two or three decades old.) This is chiefly because the "Bakhtin bandwagon," as Bialostosky concedes, has slowed drastically since its heyday in the '80s and '90s (4). *Mikhail Bakhtin*, thus, reads with an almost anachronistic charm—an echo of composition's heady, high-theory old days—that some will also count as the book's main weakness. But I would raise the converse argument: That is, why *shouldn't* Bakhtin remain at home in the postmillennial landscape of rhetoric and composition? Rather than dismissing Bialostosky as a relic, I would point to his peculiar strengths as a half-outsider and late-comer to composition. The author joins elite company with three other Bs—Bakhtin himself, Booth and

Kenneth Burke—whose critical acumen derives from the Aristotelian coupling of rhetoric and poetics, which we have, of late, taught ourselves to partition along subdisciplinary lines. If one regards his book as an utterance before the sea of voices and ideas constituting rhet comp scholarship, Bialostosky makes a tacit but compelling case for the reintegration of English studies around common interest in the core rhetoricality of human utterance—both, as Vološinov once put it, "discourse in life" (the rhetorical, evaluative speech that accompanies action) and "discourse in art" (the poetical "aesthetic isolation of rhetorical communication") (Bialostosky 117; Vološinov 96-102). The logical extension of Bialostosky's argument might go like this: Rhetorical education, in first-year composition and beyond, should equip students to parse a world of complex multi-voiced texts—editorials, Facebook threads, and Pepsi ads, but also the latest Paul Thomas Anderson film or Margaret Atwood novel—as both critics and dialogic respondents. Bakhtin's example, with its core emphasis on rhetorical utterances and person-ideas in both life and art, suggests that teacher-scholars in rhetoric, composition, and literature alike might unite in such a project. If Bialostosky makes no such explicit call in his book, I am glad to raise the matter here.

Chickasha, Oklahoma

Works Cited

Bender, John, and David E. Wellbery. "Rhetoricality: On the Modernist Return of Rhetoric." *The Ends of Rhetoric: Theory, History, Practice*, edited by John Bender and David E. Wellbery, Stanford UP, 1990, pp. 3-39.

Ewald, Helen Rothschild. "Waiting for Answerability: Bakhtin and Composition Studies." *CCC,* vol. 44, no. 3, 1993, pp. 331-48.

Fahnestock, Jeanne. *Rhetorical Figures in Science*. Oxford UP, 1999.

Halasek, Kay. *A Pedagogy of Possibility: Bakhtinian Perspectives on Composition Studies*. SIUP, 1999.

Halasek, Kay, Michael Bernard-Donals, Don Bialostosky, and James Thomas Zebroski. "Bakhtin and Rhetorical Criticism: A Symposium." *Rhetoric Society Quarterly,* vol. 22, no. 4, 1992, pp. 1-28.

Harkin, Patricia, and John Schilb, editors. *Contending with Words: Composition and Rhetoric in a Postmodern Age*. MLA, 1991.

Vološinov, V.N. "Discourse in Life and Discourse in Art." In *Freudianism: A Critical Sketch*, edited by Neil H. Bruss, translated by I.R. Titunik, Indiana UP, 1987, pp. 93-116.

The Framework for Success in Postsecondary Writing: Scholarship and Applications, edited by Nicholas N. Behm, Sherry Rankins-Robertson, and Duane Roen. Parlor P, 2017. 299 pp.

Reviewed by Jessi Thomsen, Florida State University

In a political climate that continues to privilege standardization, assessment, and accountability in education, *The Framework for Success in Postsecondary Writing: Scholarship and Applications* (hereafter "the collection") features the voices of teacher-scholars who have a different vision of pedagogical practices—a vision driven by key habits and experiences that make rhetoric and composition an essential force in students' learning and lives. The sixteen essays in the collection, edited by Nicholas N. Behm, Sherry Rankins-Robertson, and Duane Roen, engage with the 2011 resolution *Framework for Success in Postsecondary Writing* ("*Framework*"), published by the Council of Writing Program Administrators (CWPA), the National Council of Teachers of English (NCTE), and the National Writing Project (NWP). The *Framework* describes eight habits of mind deemed critical for college success and applies those habits to reading, writing, and thinking in the fyw classroom. To contextualize the collection, Peggy O'Neill, Linda Adler-Kassner, Cathy Fleischer, and Anne-Marie Hall's foreword reflects on the origins of the *Framework* as a response to growing concerns from educators surrounding the finalization of the Common Core State Standards (CCSS) that were dominating policy decisions in 2010. The *Framework* has persisted beyond its original exigency, and the collection succeeds at further extending and developing the vision and scope by serving as both a "scholarly resource" and motivation for "readers to counteract and complicate the reductive and problematic conceptualizations of writing" (Behm, et al. xxxi). As rhetoric and composition continues to define and shape itself, this collection serves as a useful model for enacting a framework to engage with students, develop meaningful research agendas, and articulate disciplinary identity and values.

The *Framework* functions within a lineage of resolutions, position statements, and platforms issued by NCTE, CCCC, and CWPA—all intended to promote teaching, learning, and research within English studies. Similarly, the collection addresses a rich history of scholarship that grows out of these position statements, notably *Class Politics: The Movement for Students' Right to Their Own Language*; *Labored: The State(ment) and Future of Work in Composition*, which considers the CCCC Position Statement on *Principles and Standards for the Postsecondary Teaching of Writing*; and *The WPA Outcomes Statement—A Decade Later*. Much like the "decade later" perspective on the WPA Outcome Statements, this collection considers the state of the *Framework* "six years out" (O'Neill, et al. ix). Additionally, but less explicitly than *Naming What We Know: Threshold Concepts in Writing Studies* or *Keywords in Writing Studies*, this collection invites the reader to consider disciplinary identity and expertise as well as core values and concerns that connect across educational levels, research interests, and writing contexts.

Although the collection, mirroring the title of the *Framework*, designates "postsecondary" as its focus, it addresses a broad audience including professors and college writing instructors, teacher educators, writing program and departmental administrators, and secondary education teachers and administrators. To appeal to a diverse readership, the collection includes eight essays on scholarship and eight essays on applications. The scholarship section provides both theoretical discussions of the *Framework*—examining and critiquing its content—and qualitative studies—designed primarily to investigate the "habits of mind" outlined in the *Framework*. The section on applications addresses pedagogical choices, curriculum and program design, and implementation of the *Framework* in secondary and postsecondary classrooms. The collection considers the scholarship on and applications of the *Framework* as avenues for change, and woven into the essays is a model for considering the ways frameworks, more generally, serve significant purposes for shaping classrooms, pedagogies, and scholarship in rhetoric and composition.

Often, professionals create task forces to develop goals, statements, and frameworks, but engagement with the ideals that serve as the basis for such goals sputter out after statements have been crafted. This collection tells a different story, demonstrating the *Framework*'s utility and lasting power as a living document within rhetoric and composition studies. Contributors to the collection explore the strengths and adaptability of the *Framework* to better articulate experiences, skills, and knowledges across diverse classroom and program contexts. Essays address the *Framework* as a key component of curriculum and program design (Townsend; Ingraham; Johnston Myatt and Shelton). Alternatively, Andrea Feldman considers the *Framework* in relation to second language learners, and Beth Brunk-Chavez and Angela Clark-Oates both use the *Framework* in online spaces, further exploring the breadth of the *Framework*.

The collection depicts the *Framework* as a living document, requiring flexibility for evolving needs and understandings of the discipline. The *Framework* was initially developed to articulate success in *writing*, but numerous essays in the collection give increased attention to the relationship between writing and literacy. Ellen C. Carillo acknowledges that, although the *Framework* does briefly include reading assignments, it does not fully address "the instructor's job to deliberately and consistently 'foreground and teach' the connections between reading writing" (39). Alice S. Horning goes a step further and recommends an entirely new section to the *Framework* for "Developing Critical Reading and Information Literacy Abilities," increasing the focus on reading as an essential component for success in writing courses (63). Offering a critique of a different kind, Rebecca Powell celebrates the *Framework* for "prescribing actual ways of being in the world," but, drawing on her study at a rural high school, realizes that the *Framework* falls short of this ideal (118). She says, "currently the *Framework* describes an ideal habitus shaped by ideal writing experiences provided by an ideal teacher. The structure to support those ideals is missing" (134). These essays offer critiques but suggest that the contributors perceive the *Framework* as a dynamic document, which invites revision.

The collection also points to new directions for continued implementation of the *Framework*. Although the *Framework* was initially written to support student success, Dawn S. Opel, Rodrigo Joseph Rodríguez, and Angela Clark-Oates each apply the habits of mind to teacher preparation, opening possibilities for the *Framework* beyond secondary and fyw classrooms. Faith Kurtyka examines the habits of mind in the context of a sorority, emphasizing the social aspect of writing and revealing insights into the habits that might transfer between the extracurriculum and the classroom. Amy C. Kimme Hea, Jenna Pack Sheffield, and Kenneth C. Walker use the *Framework* as a tool for (re)articulation of values, agency, and power dynamics, making practices in a program "visible" (31). They suggest that the *Framework* is robust enough to be used as a tool in diverse contexts to productively transform programs and curriculums (Kimme Hea, et al. 35). The essays of the collection make a call for applying the *Framework* to a range of classrooms and programs, using the habits of mind to structure research studies, and exploring the reach of the *Framework*—in essence, offering a model for how a framework might be used for pedagogical and scholarly purposes within the discipline.

The *Framework* was created as "a border-crossing kind of document" that would strengthen connections across educational levels (O'Neill, et al. xi). The outcomes of the document focus on fyw students' knowledge and skills, but the *Framework* is positioned to ensure the success of those students *as they enter* the fyw classroom, suggesting the habits of mind should be learned and practiced during students' secondary educational experience. Within the collection, the idea of "border-crossing" appears to an extent, culminating in the final essay by Lori Ostergaard, Dana Driscoll, Cathy Rorai, and Amanda Laudig on basic writing as a bridge between secondary and postsecondary education. However, the collection could have more fully addressed teaching and research at the secondary level, especially considering the focus of the *Framework* on the transition from secondary to postsecondary education. To fill this gap, scholars may take up questions such as the following: How do secondary English language arts teachers incorporate the language of the *Framework* into classrooms that are overloaded with fluctuating vocabulary from educational policy, Advanced Placement, district curriculum, and school-wide initiatives? And, more importantly, how might the discipline assist secondary education teachers in using the *Framework*, particularly in terms of the supportive structures that Powell suggests are currently missing?

In a different consideration of scope, the collection does not directly address the habits of mind from the *Framework* in terms of disciplinarity. The habits of mind certainly play essential roles in the teaching and learning of writing, but they also apply to education more broadly, raising questions about the responsibility of English language arts teachers and fyw instructors to teach these habits. What is the scope of rhetoric and composition, and to what extent, if at all, do the habits of mind extend beyond that scope? The collection provides a foundation for asking disciplinary questions, but it falls short of fully developing answers. Despite this limitation, or perhaps because of it, the collection promotes the continued life cycle of the *Framework* as a dynamic and applicable document capable of fueling another generation of research.

The collection—particularly through the contrast between Kristine Johnson's and Peter Khost's chapters, which foreground the scholarship and applications sections, respectively—reveals a larger tension within rhetoric and composition: the tension between being and doing everything *and* clearly defining the scope of the discipline. Johnson cautions the discipline regarding the abundance of frameworks whereas Khost calls for action, advocacy, and the beginning of a movement, including "bumper stickers" to reach those not already on board with the *Framework* (147). Khost suggests making the *Framework* the agreed upon stance with which we push against uninformed decisions regarding standardization, assessment, and other concerns upheld by external stakeholders. We respect academic freedom, but it would also help us, as a discipline, to use a clear voice when questioning policies from external sources, a voice speaking with the authority of consensus. The collection productively challenges us, as teachers of rhetoric and composition, to further develop and implement the *Framework*. Underlying that challenge is the larger challenge to continue to define and shape our discipline, taking into consideration our areas of expertise, our responsibility across educational levels, and our balance between individual and collective strengths. The collection urges us to consider the positioning of the *Framework*, and implicitly any framework we use, as we negotiate tensions of our disciplinary identity, both articulated through and constructed beyond the *Framework*.

Tallahassee, Florida

Works Cited

Adler-Kassner, Linda, and Elizabeth Wardle. *Naming What We Know: Threshold Concepts of Writing Studies*. Utah State UP, 2015.

Behm, Nicholas N., et al. *The WPA Outcomes Statement—A Decade Later*. Parlor P, 2012.

Conference on College Composition and Communication. *Principles and Standards for the Postsecondary Teaching of Writing*. NCTE, 1989.

Council of Writing Program Administrators. "WPA Outcomes Statement for First-Year Composition." CWPA, 2014.

Council of Writing Program Administrators, National Council of Teachers of English, and National Writing Project. *Framework for Success in Postsecondary Writing*. CWPA, NCTE, and NWP, 2011.

Heilker, Paul, and Peter Vandenberg. *Keywords in Writing Studies*. Utah State UP, 2015.

McClure, Randall, et al. *Labored: The State(ment) and Future of Work in Composition*. Parlor P, 2017.

Park, Stephen. *Class Politics: The Movement for Students' Right to Their Own Language*. NCTE, 1999.

Writing in Online Courses: How the Online Environment Shapes Writing Practices, edited by Phoebe Jackson and Christopher Weaver. Myers Education Press, 2018. 327 pp.

Reviewed by Bob Mayberry, California State University Channel Islands

The online writing environment both shapes writing instruction and is shaped by it, that is the contention in Phoebe Jackson and Christopher Weaver's collection of essays, *Writing in Online Courses*. The authors claim that teaching writing classes online compelled them to "rethink how writing functions" in their classes (xi). The collection examines how technology has changed the writing process, how students negotiate identity online, and how academic discourse is learned in online environments. The collection is not a "how to" or "best practices" guidebook, but rather a fresh examination of the principles and theories of process pedagogy from an online perspective. To that end, the landmark process work of Donald Murray, Janet Emig and Peter Elbow, the social constructionist theories and practices of Kenneth Bruffee and David Bartholomae, and the discourse community theories of Patricia Bizzell are re-explored, re-interpreted, and re-discovered. The technological insights of Gail Hawisher, Cynthia Selfe, Paul Takayoshi and Brian Huot are reconsidered for what they might reveal about how technology changes our teaching. It's an exciting and revealing collection.

Back in the Dark Ages of Education—before cell phones, the internet, Wi-Fi or online classes—I taught a distance learning class for the University of Alaska Southeast. My dozen students were scattered all over the archipelagos of Alaska: from the Pribilof Islands in the northern Bering Sea, to Baranoff Island (where I lived and taught), to Wrangell Island so far south it nearly touches the state of Washington. Most lived on isolated islands where the only access was by ferry or seaplane. To reach these students, the university relied on fax machines and long distance telephone operators. Before each weekly class meeting, I would phone the operator to announce that I was ready, and the operator would connect me with the students in a conference call. The phone lines often crackled with interference, students disappeared into silence from time to time as the phone carrier switched from one satellite to another, and the pace of our conversations was dictated by that slight pause between your speech and someone else's response, rather like a poor cell phone connection today. It was a crude technology, but it was all we had. Freshman comp by telephone.

I expected problems. I anticipated that I would end up doing more of the talking than I normally did in my writing classes, and I was prepared for our hour and a half of weekly class time to fade into long silences during the waning hours of the evening. But none of that happened.

For the very first phone call, I had read the student essays ahead of time (hence the fax machine) and selected passages for discussion. But that proved unnecessary. The first time I read a selected passage aloud, someone asked, "Who wrote that? It's wonderful!" When the writer identified herself, someone else asked the writer to read the whole essay. Aloud, over the phone! And the moment a writer finished reading, someone would begin asking questions. "When did that happen to you?" "Why did you choose to write about it?" "I had a similar experience, but have you ever …"

And so our sessions began week after week, with students reading their essays aloud and others chiming in with comments, questions and praise, every night for fifteen weeks, with class extending well beyond the proscribed ninety minutes most weeks.

What surprised me most about that experience, and why it's pertinent to this book review, was the enthusiastic, extemporaneous, detailed responses the students gave to each other's essays. I've taught dozens of workshops in the usual classroom settings, and invariably I have to plead with students to respond to their peers' writing, or structure activities or create criteria to direct their feedback. But not with my isolated Alaska students.

Why, I wondered during that semester in Alaska, were their responses so different in kind and quantity than any other workshop I've taught? I asked them at the end of the last class, why had they responded so immediately, so enthusiastically and so consistently to hearing their classmates read their papers over the telephone?

They told me: because they craved contact with others, because the anonymity of the phone made it easy, because—as one student put it—"I couldn't wiggle in my desk, I had to listen hard." The very characteristics of our distance class which I anticipated would create problems for a workshop generated instead the best student feedback I've known in my forty- year career of teaching writing.

Anonymity, the need to connect, and forced focus made the workshop hum. Not coincidentally, these are the same qualities touted as the virtues of online writing instruction in essay after essay of Phoebe Jackson and Chris Weaver's anthology, *Writing in Online Courses: How the Online Environment Shapes Writing Practices*.

While the traditional classroom pushes strangers together in a (usually) cramped room, online classes leave students in their individually selected spaces. This anonymity, H. Mark Ellis, Kristine Larsen and Liane Robertson suggest in their essays, creates a "safe space" for students, where they feel secure enough to engage the material and classmates in ways inhibited by face-to-face contact in a traditional classroom. Larsen describes how the safe space of her online science classes permit non-science majors to ask questions they might not ask in a traditional classroom. Ellis argues that anonymity and the safe space of online instruction encourages "dispositional changes" in student thinking in his sociology classes. Robertson joins both of them in claiming that students in online writing courses have more agency in their own educations, precisely because online instruction is anonymous and "safe."

Agency, it would appear from the majority of the essays in this collection, is a significant and consistent benefit of online instruction. Andy Buchenot argues that online composition classes promote agency by "complicating" the experience of reading and writing. Phoebe Jackson echoes that assertion in descriptions of her online literature classes in which students experience "continuous engagement" with literary texts, with critical texts about literature, and with their classmates' written responses to both.

Patricia Webb Boyd invites students in her online business writing classes to construct, reflect upon and enact their professional identities during the course. The online environment, she claims, allows students time to "formulate and edit" their responses to their classmates' newly constructed professional identities. The personal interaction encouraged by digital discussion groups and online chat groups Linda Di Desidero calls "facework": She argues that the online environment has the potential to be a powerful tool for facilitating both learning and personal growth through such facework.

Christopher Justice makes a similar claim for his online ecology classes, suggesting that the convergence of hybrid courses, writing in the disciplines and ecocriticism might be the "brightest place yet" for composition's future.

Likewise, Chris Weaver, in his essay on using recorded comments in writing classes, sees "exciting possibilities" for online writing teachers, especially in the potential for online courses to create learning spaces that are "experimental, tentative and playful rather than just evaluative." Those possibilities seem especially rich to Chris Anson because of their potential to help retain at-risk students and reach students with varied learning styles. Anson's essay describes his experiment with screen capture technology that replaces written or face-to-face teacher commentary.

Reading this collection of essays makes it obvious that technology is guiding pedagogy these days, and while an old compositionist like me might be skeptical, the passion and enthusiasm in this collection of essays gives me pause. And hope.

Nick Carbone admits, in the collection's first essay, that as new software tools are developed, teachers are left wondering how to keep up. "The trick," as Carbone calls it, is to determine "what you want students to do." Keeping the focus on students, and not on the technology, reveals many of the promising possibilities the other essays in the collection celebrate, potential that derives from the underlying characteristics of online instruction: anonymity, safety and the agency derived from them.

Camarillo, CA

Works Cited

Bartholomae, David. "Inventing the University." *When a Writer Can't Write*, edited by Mike Rose. Guilford, 1985.

Bizzell, Patricia. *Academic Discourse and Critical Consciousness*. U of Pittsburgh P, 1992.

Bruffee, Kenneth. *Collaborative Learning: Higher Education, Interdependence and the Authority of Knowledge*. Johns Hopkins UP, 1993.

Elbow, Peter. *Writing Without Teachers*. Oxford UP, 1973.

Emig, Janet. "Writing as a Mode of Learning." *CCC*, vol. 28, no. 2, pp. 122-28.

Hawisher, Gail, Paul LeBlanc, Charles Moran, and Cynthia Selfe. *Computers and the Teaching of Writing in American Higher Education, 1979-1994: A History*. Ablex, 1996.

Murray, Donald. *A Writer Teaches Writing*. Holt, Rinehart, Winston, 1990.

Takayoshi, Pamela, and Brian Huot, editors. *Teaching Writing with Computers*. Houghton Mifflin, 2003.

Expanding Literate Landscapes: Persons, Practices, and Sociohistoric Perspectives of Disciplinarity Development, by Kevin Roozen and Joe Erickson. Computers and Composition Digital P/Utah State UP, 2017. http://ccdigitalpress.org/expanding/index.html.

Reviewed by Leslie Taylor, Georgia State University and Dalton State College

Though a composition classroom may not always afford opportunities for in-depth literacy reflection, *Expanding Literate Landscapes: Persons, Practices, and Sociohistoric Perspectives of Disciplinarity Development*, by Kevin Roozen and Joe Erickson, does. This book provides readers with the opportunity to consider literacy broadly and specifically by presenting five detailed case studies that consider both the vernacular literacies and academic literacies of five people in various stages of life. The authors present these case studies in response to what Anne Beaufort describes as the "dominant metaphor of writing development," a metaphor that is "one of seeing writers moving from outsider to insider status in particular discourse communities or activity systems" (1.02). Roozen and Erickson acknowledge that this metaphor, developed over the last thirty years, has sought to explain how writers develop within disciplines. They draw on the work of Charles Bazerman, Anne Beaufort, David Bartholomae, and many others to explain that "the dominant stories about disciplinary development" tend to "depict newcomers entering an unfamiliar disciplinary territory and moving from the periphery toward some more central location. At the center are the core discourse, practices, knowledge, and values shared by all members of the community" (1.02). According to the insider-outsider metaphor, becoming literate in a discipline is "a fairly straightforward process" (1.02) wherein a writer learns the conventions of the discipline.

While the dominant insider-outsider metaphor may reveal much about disciplinary writing, Roozen and Erickson aim to move conversations about disciplinary development away from the dominant metaphor. They draw from scholarship such as Paul Prior's and Prior and Jody Shipka's that "point to the situated and dispersed nature of disciplinary writing, learning, and socialization" as a means for challenging the dominant metaphor (1.04). Roozen and Erickson claim that what happens outside of the discipline is crucial: "Those histories outside the supposed borders, the paths people trace across lifeworlds, and that flow into and emanate from disciplinary sites, are vitally important," and they examine those histories as a means of enriching our understanding of literacy and improving the way we teach composition (1.02). Most importantly, Roozen and Erickson successfully use their case studies to argue and demonstrate that "the development of disciplinary ways of being needs to be understood in relation to, rather than apart from, learner's broader literate lives" (Home). Each of their case studies skillfully illustrate this argument.

This innovative book is an open access multimodal text published by Computers and Composition Digital Press. *Expanding Literate Landscapes* includes a traditional academic text enriched with audio and video clips, drawings, and writing samples that illustrate various components of each case study. Student experiences and processes are sometimes presented to readers through videos so that readers can hear directly from the subject, unmediated by the authors. Readers are also given artifacts such as drawings or notes from students that exemplify their processes and products and help make concrete the concepts being discussed. Though the text is meant to be experienced in multiple modes, each recording helpfully includes a transcript. The approach and included artifacts make the text and its ideas widely accessible. The authors acknowledge that the text's innovative format was inspired by Patrick Berry, Cynthia Selfe, and Gail Hawisher's *Transnational Literate Lives*, a book-length multimodal project.

Expanding Literate Landscapes opens with two video clips that show two people engaging in literate activities, an entry point for connecting and understanding the relationship between vernacular literacy practices and disciplinary literacy practices. It is here that Roozen and Erickson carefully identify the central assumptions guiding their study: "Disciplinary development is not homogeneous and linear, but is heterogeneously situated among varied historical trajectories that reach across the expansive literate landscapes a person inhabits" (1.01). Equally important, they write, "Disciplinary writing, learning, and socialization are mediated by the many discourses, practices, artifacts, and identities of a person's life" (1.01). They set out to illustrate and prove these ideas by examining the results of their ethnographic study of five people of different ages and with different backgrounds, careers, and educational goals. Before moving into those ethnographies, however, the writers begin by situating their research in the context of other conversations about how people become literate in a discipline. As Roozen and Erickson's research shows, people bring their everyday literacies into their disciplines, and seeing those connections offers additional insight into how disciplinary literacy develops: inside *and* outside of a discipline.

Chapter two identifies the theories and methods used in the ethnography. Drawing heavily on mediated discourse theory and the scholarship of Prior, the authors create case studies that examine how literate practices created and enacted outside of disciplinary settings influence, conflict, and entangle each other. The case studies consider literate activity, literacy histories, focused interviews, sample texts, and activities and practices. This variety of narratives comes from a range of media and times of the participants'—or "co-researchers," as Roozen and Erickson describe them—lives as a means of demonstrating the complexity and variation of literacy development. Chapter three follows Charles, a student placed in basic writing who also has a history of award-winning writing for newspapers. Chapter four focuses on Kate, an English studies student and writer of fan-fiction who went on to earn an MA and PhD in rhetoric and composition. Chapter five considers Lindsey, a graphic design student turned language arts teacher. Chapter six studies Terri, a nurse who is also a prolific writer of poetry and religious devotionals. Chapter seven looks at Alexandra, an engineering student, puzzle-solver, and fan-fiction writer.

All of these chapters lead to the conclusions and implications presented in the final chapter. The authors conclude that "disciplinary development is a product of people's acting with a dynamic and heterogeneous nexus of practice assembled from a lifetime of literate engagements" (8.01). Understanding this has broad implications for both teaching and researching in the field. Perhaps most useful from a pedagogical standpoint is the way Roozen and Erickson use case studies to show how literate activities outside the classroom can enrich disciplinary literacy. Such is the case with Alexandra, the engineering student who quickly becomes adept with Excel because of her experience with the game Minecraft. The tables in Minecraft work much like those in Excel, helping Alexandra to transfer her game playing skills to using Excel, an essential program in her discipline. In contrast, literate activities outside the classroom can block students from adopting new practices that can help them. For example, Charles, the newspaper writer whose reporting relied heavily on surveys he conducted, may have relied so heavily on statistics that it "perhaps kept him from exploring other means of developing and supporting his arguments" (8.02.02). The case studies raise important questions for those of us who teach composition. More specifically, how can we identify and encourage non-disciplinary habits that might benefit students if they can adapt and transfer them? At the same time, how can we encourage students to attempt and adopt new practices for new tasks?

Roozen and Erickson also conclude that "although disciplinary and everyday activities may appear worlds apart, in reality they are always woven together" (8.02.05). Since many who teach writing ask students to write literacy narratives, perhaps that is one way to highlight how students' disciplinary and everyday activities are "woven together." Though one assignment is unlikely to provide the kind of insight Roozen and Erickson's in-depth case studies provide, it is a good pedagogical tool for connecting students' various literacies. Not realizing the ways these literacies are woven together makes it easy to misunderstand the way disciplinary literacies develop; for example, without tracing Charles's literate activities—both in and out of the classroom—the authors might have left their study not understanding how Charles's disciplinary development was so heavily influenced by his newspaper writing. Such a dual focus is a step towards "generating [the] richer, fuller accounts of disciplinary writing, learning, and enculturation" (8.03) that Roozen and Erickson set out to illuminate. They also see this approach as taking us beyond the idea that people merely participate in a variety of literate activities; their work helps us see that the boundaries we imagine between disciplinary and non-disciplinary writing do not exist. Literacy develops on a continuum, or a literate landscape, and knowing this helps us better understand how disciplinary literacy truly develops and exists alongside vernacular literacy.

Dalton, GA

Works Cited

Bartholomae, David. "Inventing the University." *When a Writer Can't Write: Studies in Writer's Block and Other Composing-Process Problems,* edited by Mike Rose, Guilford Press, 1985, pp. 134-65.

Bazerman, Charles. "What Written Knowledge Does: Three Examples of Academic Discourse." *Philosophy of the Social Sciences,* vol. 11, no. 3, 1981, pp. 361-87.

Beaufort, Anne. *College Writing and Beyond.* Utah State UP, 2007.

—. "Developmental Gains of a History Major: A Case for Building a Theory of Disciplinary Writing Expertise." *Research in the Teaching of English*, vol. 39, no. 2, pp. 136-85.

Berry, Patrick W., Gail E. Hawisher, and Cynthia L. Selfe. *Transnational Literate Lives in Digital Times.* Computers and Composition Digital P/Utah State UP, 2012.

Prior, Paul. *Writing/Disciplinarity: A Sociohistoric Account of Literate Activity in the Academy.* Erlbaum, 1998.

Prior, Paul, and Jody Shipka. "Chronotopic Lamination: Tracing the Contours of Literate Activity." *Writing Selves, Writing Societies: Research from Activity Perspectives,* edited by Charles Bazerman and David R. Russell. The WAC Clearinghouse and Mind, Culture, and Activity, 2003, pp. 180-238.

 # CALL FOR NEW EDITOR(S) OF *Composition Studies*

Composition Studies is seeking a new editor, to begin with the fall 2019 issue (the editorial transition will begin in late fall 2018). Initial appointment is one three-year term, with possibility for renewal. In publication since March 1972, *Composition Studies* is the oldest independent journal in the field of writing studies. Published biannually, the journal is dedicated to sponsoring a broad range of scholarship: postsecondary writing pedagogy and theory; theorizing rhetoric and composing; administering writing programs; preparing the field's future teacher-scholars; and related topics.

Eligible applicants will have an active research agenda in writing studies as well as interest in and appreciation of diverse research and research methods in the field. Previous journal editorial experience a plus but not required. Applicants need strong organizational and management skills, relative comfort working with technology (Adobe products, google drive, online submission manager, and email), ability to work well with others—staff members, contributors, reviewers, advertisers, and publisher—and a commitment to publishing high quality, relevant, and engaging scholarship that advances knowledge in the field.

A complete application will include the following:
- A letter of support from someone who can speak to the applicant's qualifications sent directly to current editor Laura Micciche at compstudies@uc.edu.
- A 2-3 page letter of application, explaining the applicant's interest in the editorship; qualifications and unique qualities that have bearing on the position; potential institutional support; and readiness at this point in their career to serve as editor of a national journal.
- A current CV.

Application materials are due to Laura Micciche at compstudies@uc.edu by **October 1, 2018**. Editorial Board members will review applications and make a selection by October 15, 2018. If you have questions about the position, feel free to contact Laura.

Contributors

Jacob Babb is assistant professor of English and writing and writing coordinator at Indiana University Southeast. He is associate editor of *WPA: Writing Program Administration* and co-editor of *WPAs in Transition: Navigating Educational Leadership Positions*. His work has been published in *Composition Forum*, *Harlot*, and *WPA: Writing Program Administration*.

Beth L. Brunk-Chavez is dean of Extended University and professor of rhetoric and writing studies at the University of Texas at El Paso. Beth oversees online course development and program delivery at UTEP. Her research examines writing program administration, second-language writers and writing, and teaching with technologies.

Jeffrey T. Grabill serves Michigan State University as the associate provost for Teaching, Learning, and Technology, where he is a professor of rhetoric and professional writing. His research focuses on how digital writing is associated with citizenship and learning. That work has been located in community contexts, in museums, and in classrooms at both the K-12 and university levels. Grabill is also a co-founder of Drawbridge, an educational technology company. In his role as Associate Provost, Grabill is responsible for facilitating innovation in learning via his role as director of the Hub for Innovation in Learning and Technology and educator professional development through MSU's Academic Advancement Network.

Michael Griffith's most recent novel, *Trophy* (Northwestern University Press, 2011), was named one of that year's Best Books in Fiction by *Kirkus Review*. He is professor of English at the University of Cincinnati.

Edward Hahn is visiting assistant professor of first-year writing at the University of Wisconsin, Eau Claire. His work has appeared in *Rhetoric Review*, *Composition Forum*, and *Rhetoric Society Quarterly*.

Drew M. Loewe is associate professor in the writing and rhetoric program at St. Edward's University in Austin, Texas. He also directs the university's writing center. His scholarly and teaching interests include rhetorical theory and criticism, argumentation, prose style, legal writing, writing centers, and the first-year writing sequence.

Bob Mayberry is a former editor of *Freshman English News*, retiring associate professor of English, and playwright. His recent book is *Unteaching: A Writing Teacher's Odyssey*.

Jessie L. Moore is director of the Center for Engaged Learning and professor of professional writing and rhetoric at Elon University. Jessie coordinates the center's research seminars, which support multi-institutional inquiry on high-impact pedagogies. Her research examines transfer of writing knowledge, multi-institutional research, and high-impact pedagogies.

Andrea Riley Mukavetz is assistant professor in the Department of Liberal Studies at Grand Valley State University. Selections of her work can be found at *Rhetoric, Professional Communication, and Globalization* and *enculturation*. She is co-founder of The Cultural Rhetorics Research Lab and a co-chair of The Cultural Rhetorics Conference.

Stacey Pigg is assistant professor of English at North Carolina State University, where she is associate director of professional writing and a core faculty member in the communication rhetoric and digital media PhD program. Her research traces the impact of digital, mobile, and networked writing practices on how we work, think, and learn.

Michelle Rachal is head of public services at Savitt Medical Library. Previously Michelle was the health sciences librarian at the University of Nevada, Reno, where she also taught library research classes for the core writing program. Michelle earned her Master of Library and Information Science degree from the University of Wisconsin, Milwaukee.

Patrick Ragains is business and government information librarian emeritus at University of Nevada, Reno. Ragains is editor of *The New Information Literacy Instruction: Best Practices* (2016, coedited with M. Sandra Wood) and *The New Information Literacy Instruction That Works: A Guide to Teaching by Discipline and Student Population* (2013).

Brian Ray is assistant professor of rhetoric and writing at the University of Arkansas at Little Rock. He also directs the composition program.

Paula Rosinski is director of writing across the university and professor of professional writing and rhetoric at Elon University. Paula leads the writing excellence initiative at Elon, which enhances the teaching and learning of writing across the curriculum. Her research examines multimodal rhetorical theories and practices and the technologically mediated writing lives of students.

Nick Sanders is a second-year MA candidate in English (writing studies) at the University of Maine. His research interests include anti-racist writing program administration and assessment. Beginning in fall 2018, Nick will begin his doctoral coursework in writing and rhetoric at Michigan State University.

Heidi Slater, M.Ed., taught information literacy skills for 16 years as a K-12 public school librarian before she moved to the University of Nevada, Reno, where she spent four years as the lead instruction librarian for freshmen composition classes.

Leslie Taylor is a graduate student at Georgia State University and associate professor of English at Dalton State College.

Jessi Thomsen is pursuing her PhD in English with an emphasis in rhetoric and composition at Florida State University where her golden retrievers—Mardi and Janeway—supervise all of her scholarly endeavors and occasionally answer her emails.

Julia Voss is assistant professor of English at Santa Clara University, where she studies collaborative multimodal composing, the possibilities and responsibilities of classroom design, and WPA work as a discipline-defining practice of writing studies. Her work has also appeared in *Across the Disciplines, Computers and Composition*, and the *Stories That Speak To Us* collection

Lynda Walsh is associate professor of English at the University of Nevada, Reno. She has served as a writing program administrator at both UNR and at New Mexico Tech, and she works on the public reception of technoscience, particularly visual arguments.

Ben Wetherbee is assistant professor of English and interdisciplinary studies at the University of Science and Arts of Oklahoma. His research and teaching interests include rhetorical theory and history, writing pedagogy, and film.

Courtney Adams Wooten is assistant professor and first-year writing program administrator at Stephen F. Austin State University in Nacogdoches, TX. She is the book review editor for *WPA* and is co-editor of *WPAs in Transition*. Her work has also appeared in *Composition Studies, Harlot,* and *WPA*.

Adrian Matthew Zytkoskee is a fourth-year rhetoric and composition PhD student at the University of Nevada, Reno, with research interests in trauma studies, narrative medicine, reflective writing, and the intersections between these areas of inquiry. He is currently conducting research at the university's medical school.

DEPAUL UNIVERSITY
Chicago, IL

DEPARTMENT OF
WRITING, RHETORIC, & DISCOURSE

Master of Arts Degree in
WRITING, RHETORIC, & DISCOURSE
with concentrations in
PROFESSIONAL & DIGITAL WRITING
TEACHING WRITING & LANGUAGE

Graduate Certificate in TESOL

Combined BA/MA in
Writing, Rhetoric, & Discourse

GRADUATE FACULTY
Julie Bokser
Antonio Ceraso
Lisa Dush
Timothy Elliott
Jason Kalin
Jason Schneider
Peter Vandenberg
Erin Workman

WRD.DEPAUL.EDU

Help Students Cite Any Source Easily

MLA HANDBOOK, 8TH EDITION

"This is the most succinct and sensible revision to MLA documentation style in my long career."
—Andrea A. Lunsford, Stanford University

Lower-priced, shorter, and redesigned for writers at all levels, this groundbreaking edition of the *MLA Handbook* recommends one universal set of guidelines, which writers can apply to any type of source.

Paperback edition
146 pp. • 6 × 9
List price: $15.00

Large-print edition
146 pp. • 8 × 12
List price: $20.00

Also available in e-book formats.

style.mla.org • www.mla.org

DISCOVER MORE RESOURCES ONLINE

style.mla.org

Create, share, and store your work.

HUMANITIES COMMONS

The nonprofit interdisciplinary network for the humanities

Imagine a humanities network with the sharing power of *Academia.edu*, the archival features of an institutional repository, the community experience of the best academic conferences, and a commitment to open-source software. Now imagine that this network, a nonprofit run by scholars, doesn't want to sell your data or generate profit from your intellectual property. That network already exists: *Humanities Commons*.

Sign up at hcommons.org

PARLOR PRESS
EQUIPMENT FOR LIVING

New, in Living Color!

Type Matters: The Rhetoricity of Letterforms edited by Christopher Scott Wyatt and Dànielle Nicole DeVoss

Rhetoric and Experience Architecture edited by Liza Potts and Michael J. Salvo

New Releases

The Framework for Success in Postsecondary Writing: Scholarship and Applications edited by Nicholas N. Behm, Sherry Rankins-Robertson, and Duane Roen

Cross-Border Networks in Writing Studies edited by Derek Mueller, Andrea Williams, Louise Wetherbee Phelps, and Jennifer Clary-Lemon

Labored: The State(ment) and Future of Work in Composition edited by Randall McClure, Dayna V. Goldstein, and Michael A. Pemberton

A Critical Look at Institutional Mission: A Guide for Writing Program Administrators edited by Joseph Janangelo

Congratulations to These Recent Award Winners!

Antiracist Writing Assessment Ecologies: Teaching and Assessing Writing for a Socially Just Future by Asao Inoue, **Best Book Award, CCCC, Best Book, Council of Writing Program Administrators (2017)**

The WPA Outcomes Statement—A Decade Later
   Edited by Nicholas N. Behm, Gregory R. Glau, Deborah H. Holdstein, Duane Roen, and Edward M. White, **Best Book Award, Council of Writing Program Adminstrators (July, 2015)**

www.parlorpress.com

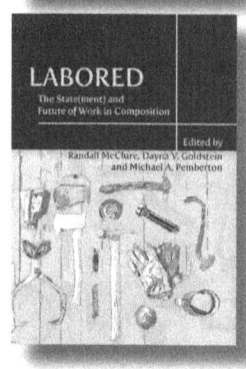

www.ingramcontent.com/pod-product-compliance
Lightning Source LLC
Chambersburg PA
CBHW031319160426
43196CB00007B/590